MAKE
WORLDS

Chris Steed

The Red Stain of Cain

Theological antibodies and the virus of violence

Violence is a public health issue. All too often it is legitimated by religion. This novelesque theory of violence shows why religious support for violence is a terrifying contradiction. Where are the antibodies against it?

Within Christianity, what is needed is a better theology of systemic power and violence.

An article summarising this book appeared 'Unio Cum Christo: the international Journal of Reformed Theology and Life Vol 7 no 1 April 2021'

© 2021 **Europe Books** | London
www.europebooks.co.uk – info@europebooks.co.uk

ISBN 979-12-201-0764-8
First edition: June 2021

Distribution for the United Kingdom: **Vine House Distribution ltd**

Printed for Italy by Rotomail Italia
Finito di stampare nel mese di giugno 2021
presso Rotomail Italia S.p.A. - Vignate (MI)

The Red Stain of Cain

To my students and the amazing staff of the London School of Theology

FOREWORD

In this book the Revd Dr Christopher Steed brings together insights from social sciences to illuminate the doctrine of atonement. The doctrine has been the focus of considerable debate in recent years and therefore this contribution is both timely and welcome. The London School of Theology hosted a symposium on the subject of the atonement in July 2005 (in fact during the terrorist attacks in London) and from that occasion a number of papers were published.[1] These papers offered a discussion of penal substitution as well as the subject of contemporary culture and symbolic exchange. In a sense, Dr Steed is following along the path of this debate, but he is also adding his own unique perspective. It is one that was written by him as he watched the trial of the perpetrators of the Manchester bombing of 2017. So, once again, a discussion of the atonement is considered against the backdrop of terrorism in the UK. The continuity of the historical events should not be lost on the readers of this book.

Dr Steed considers the nature of violence as a public health issue and within Christianity he links it to the question of power. Of course, we all know that violence is an expression of power. The divesting of power for the sake of the powerless is a theme well known in theology and it is exemplified in the cross of Christ. In fact, in a shocking

---

1   Derek Tidball, David Hilborn & Justin Thacker (eds.), *The Atonement Debate: Papers from the London Symposium on the Theology of the Atonement* (Grand Rapids: Zondervan, 2008).

9

manner, Christ embraces such violence for the sake of the salvation of the world. This very event stands at the heart of the biblical narrative and without it the overarching story simply does not make sense. But with this act also comes an exchange: life for death, sinlessness for sinfulness, justice for injustice. There is a great mystery here, that the incarnate Son of God should hang on a cross for the salvation of the world.

In this book, Dr Steed takes us on a journey that uses the atonement as appreciated through the idea of symbolic exchange. On the journey, he reflects on the value of human beings and the nature of violence today. For example, he discusses human trafficking, violence against women, war against Islam, masculinity, racism and the Covid crisis. He interprets these features in terms of denigration, de-personalisation, desecration, de-humanisation and demonisation. In the middle of these issues is the matter of human responsibility and identity. Using psychological theory, Dr Steed unpacks these concepts and mobilises them to address violence. This is followed by a theological reflection based on the atonement and the therapeutic dimensions that emerge from the discussion. In this way, the material connects the different metaphors of the forensic and the therapeutic in a creative manner.

There is much in this book that will provoke reflection. It pushes us back to the doctrine of the atonement with greater sensitivity. It ignites our imagination to consider different lenses through which to view this pivotal event in the history of the world and the church. It moves us to prayer, as we consider the rampant use of violence in our own day. And its causes us to bow the knee and worship the triune God: Father, Son and Holy Spirit with hope in our hearts because we know that the cross was not the end of God's dealing with humanity. The cross must always be set against the resurrection of our Lord Jesus Christ; and so we have hope for the new creation that is to come.

The Revd Professor Mark J. Cartledge, PhD, FRSA

Principal and Professor of Practical Theology

London School of Theology

RATIONALE

The red stain of Cain, the restless wanderer, haunts the world. The heart of the violence he inflicted is 'desecration': desecration of the sacred value of Abel. Personhood is valuable; whether human personhood or the ultimate personhood, God.

As I write this, the trial is taking place of those involved in the 2017 Manchester bombings, when Islamic terrorism ripped up lives and futures like so many bits of paper to be shred.

This book emphasises the need for theological de-construction in the mind of those whose thinking has been taken over, whereby they become perpetrators. The main focus though is that, using the lens of violence, the scene is set for a highly original exploration of what is at the heart of Christian faith: the cross of Christ. Violence is central to this rather than being a cruel accomplice only. Where were the theological antibodies to prevent it?

The pandemic has brought people together, but it has also exposed divisions in society that lead to a sense of simmering injustice. Yet so often, defenders of the atonement are found on the wrong side of the argument. The culprit is a limited understanding of how violence erupts from a system, from a culture. We are thereby de-sensitised from even thinking about an invisible enemy that takes over the body politic. The mind is hijacked, so that we are not aware that disturbing prejudice reflects how we were taught to think.

Christianity has never fully confronted its violent past. To take one powerful example with huge contemporary resonance, dominant forms of White evangelicalism were shaped in response to slavery, often to defend it biblically. Black skin was regarded as the accursed mark of Cain. The religion of 'the lost cause' led to Jim Crow laws. At the same time, a pre-millennial theology led to focus not on systemic problems, but on individualistic salvation associated with an unassailable sense of religious identity. Racist bias that is invisible, systemic and endemic urgently requires this to be re-visited. The real mark of Cain lies in the anguished questions of God – 'where is your brother?' 'What have you done?' How on earth has all this happened amongst the very people who especially espouse a high view of the cross and the substitutionary atonement expressed in terms of 'Jesus died for me'? Does Christianity have anything to say to the violence of our times? This book is not a historical study so much as calling for theological antibodies. It approaches the interface between atonement and violence through two innovative ways:

It picks up on the theme of atonement through the notion of 'valuable personhood', as I believe it to be key to the conundrum of how the death of Christ affects personal and societal transformations. As per my doctoral thesis at Exeter University, it is clear that violence sets up an intense transaction and a form of symbolic exchange in which the value of victims is scraped from their faces by perpetrators. This is 'violence as desecration'; a degree of human devaluation steep in intensity. As one of us, Jesus is identified both with devalued humanity and a God dishonoured. The worthy for the unworthy, Jesus exchanges status and love, paying for our sins. This is utterly central to a theory of violence and atonement with which it is intrinsically linked.

The potential for violence in the present situation is enormous- not least domestic violence. Will Covid-19 erode escalating political and cultural polarization we were trapped in and help change course toward greater solidarity and the naked power of love? Will we revert? What if we saw violence as a public health issue? Can we break its transmission?

Islam makes its own response with regard to dismantling terrorist mindsets. Within the Christianity I know best, theological antibodies which can prevent hijack by violence arise from the cross itself and the way Jesus provides redemption by being a victim of violence. Historically, although the church has had as much experience of domination as any other group in society, you will be hard put to find a theology of power amidst the categories used in its teaching. As a result, it cannot see the blindspots in social relationships where power lines become the means of transmitting cruelty.

We are trapped between two Enlightenment visions and versions of human society and nature. Covid brought out the best of times and the worst of times. There was the approach of Hobbes, who said that civilisation is just a veneer. Life is nasty, brutish and short; hence Government (Leviathian) is needed to control us (for example regulate panic-buying). Or we go with Rousseau, who said that society is the one corrupting us, and that natural goodness can shine. It is a toss-up between natural goodness and original sin!

DEVELOPMENT

What has haunted me in writing this book is two-fold. Firstly, it comes from talking with my Islamic or Jewish friends about how violence hijacks religion and often legitimises it. Secondly, the terrifying contradiction that those who stand most strongly for the powerful idea that Jesus shed his blood for us and instead of us are so often deaf and blind to the violence endemic in their culture that they end up legitimating it. Advocates of substitutionary atonement will 'sing the praise of him who died' and proclaim that the blood of Christ speaks better things than the blood of Abel. So far, so biblical (Hebrews 12v24). But they have been remarkably absent when it comes to violence such as tribal collusion with genocide, antisemitism, racial violence, gendered, domestic violence or child abuse and slavery. Nationalism trumps the value of sacred life most days.

I wanted to explore why this is, because it really matters. The gap between doctrine and practice, between rhetoric and reality, is simply staggering. How is it that those who have a high devotional ideal and professed love for their Lord, for their Bible and for their church, can be so lacking in awareness that this is so often used a cover for violence and Cain's murderous hand?

The sheer scale of White violence in America, of attitudes to black skinned people in southern Africa or southern USA, of antisemitism in Christian history, of collusion with ethnic cleansing between the Catholic (or Orthodox) churches in the Balkans or in Africa - beggars belief. But it does more than that; it challenges belief, for these are often carried out by those who believe passionately that Jesus died for our sins. Invariably, whether of the evangelical or Catholic/orthodox variety, these are believers who would repudiate liberal attitudes as soft compromise.

The reason why this is obscene is that the cross does not legitimate violence. Quite the opposite. How could it, when the cross was an act of the most violent State savagery and Jesus was a victim?

If those who cheer on (or wave away) mob rule, lynch parties or tribal bloodbaths, excuse violence against women and girls or give succour to child abusers' hold to a high view of communion and the atonement- they do so in violent contradiction with what they believe about the cross of Christ.

To save us, Jesus experienced the most horrendous violence. This is central to the story. He was no spectator in the violence but a fully immersive participant; embedded in it. Violence is far from being incidental to redemption: it was the means by which it came about. The degree of savage violence exhibited on that Friday sharply accentuated what happened to Jesus. It made the act of redemption more acute, than if, for example, Jesus had died in his sleep. Though freely laid down, his life was taken from him. The reason why violence was central to that great act of atonement was:

- It was a sacrifice – sacrificial acts are almost always violent for those on its receiving end.
- It was an exchange – usually, in a sacrifice there is shedding of blood, but something is given in return, favour, a stay of execution, good will and so on. It is death for life. It was an exchange too, in the same way as much violence is an exchange.
- It was an injustice – the public execution of Jesus arose from a trumped-up charge.
- It was a payment – the need for recompense or retribution because of wrong-doing arises precisely because of the moral worth of the individual who has been wronged. "Those who are responsible will pay the price" – (The Lebanese Prime Minister following an explosion in August 2020 that devastated the Port [1])

We will show how theological ideas such as these resonate with the very nature of violence. Sociological perspectives help illuminate that violence involves a sort of exchange, a trade. That is surely what is going on with the cross. It involves a trade in which a symbolic exchange takes place.

Some contemporary critics argue that the problem lies in

the doctrine itself, not just in its misuse. The very idea of the Father, the God of love, suddenly deciding to vent his anger and wrath on his own Son seems a form of cosmic child abuse. A vengeful Father, punishing his Son for an offence he has not even committed (penal substitution), mandates violence of the most extreme kind. From such perspectives, substitutionary atonement is a theory rooted in retributive notions of justice.

These attacks are profoundly mistaken. Perpetrators of violence can find no ground cover in the idea that 'Jesus bore my sin'. Firstly, Jesus experienced enormous violence through the events of the crucifixion – he did not take a poison pill and die quietly. By definition, Jesus was therefore a victim of violence. He does not side with those who inflict it but with those who are on its receiving end.

Jesus experiencing a particularly violent form of death means that he is a full participant sufferer in the savagery, the cruelty and the jealousy which characterise the cross. Everything that comes to the victims of violence comes to him. Evangelical theology can stress the substitution of Jesus in our place, but this is not *just instead of us* because he too is fully immersed in it. Both substitution and participation work with the idea of identification – Jesus dying as one of us, one with us and one for us. How can there be any dichotomy between a death for us and a death as God with us? The mistake lies in seeming to punish an innocent person. But collectively, Jesus is *one of us,* one *with us*.

There is another reason why staunch advocates of the cross as an element at the heart of their faith are compelled by that very faith to be strongly against the violence that disfigures human beings. That is because the cross upholds the infinite value of the soul, the value and worth of humanity. As we will explore, violence is desecration. Personhood is valuable. At the heart of sin is dishonouring someone. Every act of violence involves some sort of trade, of exchange. Jesus becomes thoroughly desecrated and violated but, by absorbing all that with us, he is able to offer his status and worth in exchange. The Bible word for that is *justification*.

The problem does not therefore lie within the doctrine but in how it is understood. If substitutionary atonement is seen as a way to accomplish the death of Jesus divorced from the violence of the human situation, we will not be attuned to its cruel context. If we see the cross (and faith generally) as being private and individual, we will not have an eye to the most fundamental reality of systemic violence. We simply will not have the vocabulary that takes us out of an individualised faith. Consequently, we will not have theological anti-bodies against religiously mandated violence which continues to disfigure our lives and our times. We will only see violence as a series of individual decisions to act, rather than shaped in crucibles of behaviour that have infected church theology.

The culprit therefore is not Jesus dying in our place, but in seeing faith as an individual act; not something that challenges profoundly the systems that shape our social experience. Those on the side of lynch mobs or antisemitism or tribalistic genocide had no idea that they were thoroughly shaped by social forces. They were brainwashed one might say; their brains hijacked by the virus.

Valuable personhood is a major and often overlooked driver in human action and interaction. This is the theme running throughout the range of reputable author books in different domains – whether economics, social commentary, politics or management.

In the first part of the book, we tour through the landscape of violence, often in a searing way, to probe both the reality and the very nature of violence. Violence arises within a culture. Almost always, people are completely unaware that they are part of a system generating much violence. Rather than question the system, they adopt an individualist perspective that sees a few bad apples rather than a rotten tree. Such cultural blindness is powered by the need to maintain identity.

In the second part of the book we ask the question, 'What is the meaning of the cross for our times?' The meaning of the wretched violence inflicted on Jesus is examined in terms of participation (Jesus being in solidarity with pain and searing separation) but also substitution (Jesus becoming one for us and in our place). The idea of atonement by blood has gone out of fashion in the circles of most thinking contemporaries. It seems irrational and unjust; a form of theology past its sell-by-date.

The value and worth of human beings mean that, when they are under assault or have been breached, something happens that demands recompense, redress or payment of some form. Violence sets up a sort of transaction (a symbolic exchange) in which value changes hands in much the same way as when money is offered or taken. 'Paying the price for our sins' is utterly true to psychological reality.

The supreme value and worth of Jesus are traded as it were for human demerit. It only happens because Jesus is one of us, fully immersed into the human condition. The desecration of Christ comes through a complete identification with us. In that field of transaction comes forgiveness.

In so doing, it shows what a contrast there is between the rhetoric of believing in the Lord who dies in our place for our sins and the reality of on-going violence that shapes the experience of so many. How is that those who affirm salvation by placing faith in Christ can be so blind to social sins that condone violence and encourage it? Can we find some theological antibodies?

SETTING THE SCENE -
ON THE DAY THE SOLDIERS CAME

Lullay, lullay
My little tiny child
By-by, lullay, lullay
Oh, sisters two
How may we do
For to preserve this day?
This poor youngling
Of whom we do sing
By-by, lullay, lullay
Herod the King
In his raging
Charged he hath this day
His men of might
In his own sight
All children young to slay
Then woe is me
Poor child for thee
And ever mourn and say...
Lullay, lullay
My little tiny child
By-by, lullay, lullay

('The Coventry Carol', remembering the Massacre of the Innocents)

2

When Cain left the red stain on the appalled earth, there

was only him, the restless wanderer of the world. In time, the soldiers came with hard boots and hard bodies.

With terrifying regularity, the day the soldiers came and witnessed violence and hard wailing; grief from bodies now broken apart and souls now split asunder, bodies and souls bleeding into each other and refusing to be comforted.

Somewhere in history, a child was crying. It was not the tears of a baby exercising its lungs, or the hurt of a little boy or girl who has fallen over, a leg gashed. It was a young life torn apart, mutilated, ripped in two, or three, burnt or disfigured for life.

Do you hear the cry of the child haunting us down the centuries?

It was one amongst a million and a half victims of administrative mass murder of children, routine policy; 'chasing the children up the chimney' in the gas ovens. The child crying was an orphan, a horrified spectator of war, when it's father and mother had already been killed before him on the day the soldiers came; orphaned again and again when that terrible day was re--visited and recalled.

Or a child of the past, not perfect in shape, who cried too much or cried too little. What terrifying indictment of humanity, when uncomprehending infants were thrown into rivers, flung into dung--heaps or cess--pits, placed in jars to starve to death or exposed on hillsides as food for animals. Until the day before yesterday, disposable children were an accepted, everyday occurrence.

The cry of the children was the result of century after century of battered people growing up to batter their own children; whole epochs where discipline was savage and the time parents gave to their children was a minimal gift, quickly withheld.

The cry of the children came from a million even in a country like this, which had experienced neglect, maltreat-

21

ment or the ugly face of abuse, where 100,000 children ran away from home every year.

The cry of the children was from a boy or a girl, who would draw forever upon a legacy of life - long haunting. The cry of the children was from Chinese women who remembered the day their foot-binding began. Reducing the size of a women's feet created unnatural hobbling that aroused men. It was for institutional cruelty that generation after generation of girls were praised for putting up with extreme pain of broken bones for life, women and their families colluding in a cruel eroticism.

The world still destroyed the lives of its children. Over half the world was now a vulnerable child.

We are haunted by the global menace of child prostitution; ten million innocent lives deflowered in sex tourism , a million children in South--East Asia traded each year, a million and a half children forever contaminated by HIV or the pornographic images of children, 'delecta graviora', the gravest violation now recognised by the Vatican, having conspicuously failed to report and respond to abuse. The record of sexual abuse is another signpost to a region we wish wasn't there, for it is both past and present. The dreadful deeds that have taken place in religious establishments responsible for teaching, instructing or caring for children over the generations are wretched. Perpetrators hiding in churches have wreaked huge damage on countless numbers of children, physically, emotionally and morally. It is not just perpetrators that have stained institutions everywhere. There are any number of self-righteous, self-appointed judges who bind others with their traditions and their legalism and who cry foul when their grim-faced legacy is challenged. The freedom and fullness of divine grace has yet to liberate their souls.

The cry of the children is the nine children a day ripped

apart in suicide bombings in Afghanistan, the world's most lethal conflict. How the perpetrators imagine they will gain fast track to eternal bliss leaves us mired in baffled and beggared belief for those blinded by their cruel ideology. Only theological resources can walk with political peace-making to disentangle the enormity of crimes that blind.

But then be haunted by the pied-piper song of a chemical induced route to happiness amongst teenagers or the millions aborted in the West over 50 years. It was the cry of the children.

It was a frustrated lynch mob attempting to take a young man out of a Tulsa jail; God-fearing' folk who went on to stir a race riot and burn a city a hundred years ago. We were different then (or not).

The cry of the children arose from a paedophile ring with its covertly advertised Internet activities. Shout at such electronic prostitution, taking the sin in men's minds and projecting it like some instant virus spreading muck across the world. It was children being groomed and passed round in towns like Rotherham in the UK, where culture and religion were horrible twins taking girls to hell. So much for anti-Western racist abuse – "our girls are chaste; white girls are trash." Lesser human beings, 2nd class sluts, not worthy of respect, kaffir, other. *"As a victim I was told I was worthless."*2

What had we done to the children? Were we deaf to their cry? The preciousness of children is never more keenly felt than when something happens to one of them.

If it didn't destroy its children, it demonised them. Children, even in the West, were feral creatures, insensitive and cruel; especially to be feared in packs surely, weren't they?

The cry of the children comes from a boy who trod on a land--mine. There is a stump where his foot used to be. The cry of the children is from one of a 150 million orphaned street kids, glad to find any scrap of warmth in the sewers in winter or food from dog--scavenged rubbish. Or twice that number chained up in enslaved child labour.

The cry of the children was the ten million children under five who died one year from disease or lack of food. And the next. And the one after that.

It was the cry of spoilt, trampled childhood and lost innocence from teenagers strutting around with Kalashnikovs where the gun was the medium of exchange. It was the child soldiers who haunted Africa, joining civil wars that were blighting a continent, forced to join guerrilla armies and be transformed into killing machines.

Weep for the two million children who were victims of war or the four million disabled by war over the previous decade. Hear the cry of the kids targeted in the Rwandan genocide, whose massacre was ignited by an inflammatory radio broadcast. 'To kill big rats, you have to kill the little rats.'

The child crying was among the boys of Bethlehem, put to sword in the jealous rage of a king who feared a rival would eclipse him. 'A voice is heard in Ramah, of weeping and great mourning, Rachel weeping for her children, refusing to be comforted because they are no more'.

THE MOUNTAIN SPOKE

The mountain spoke. It yielded its secret with a sand-paper abruptness that jarred every nerve. "Your daughter is good for wife!" the mountain said.

An earthquake had been and gone. Fault-lines had opened up between communities who had lived side by side for peaceful centuries. Serbian soldiers had organised a rape factory in their Bosnia barracks. Women were reluctant to share stories of ultimate shame in Muslim society. If pregnant, they faced a miserable future of rejection by their families, raising a child conceived in hatred.

A woeful memory stands out; the memory of a young woman, scarcely older than a teenager, who had come to Britain in those days. A Serb army officer told her father, "your daughter is good for wife". They forced her father to watch as the Serbs threw her to the ground and ripped off every part of her clothing. Her neighbours didn't understand why she now woke up at night screaming. In her mind was etched the torture that contorted her father's face before she fell into his arms.

His face creased. What was it that Bosnian woman pleaded with him? "Tell someone that we are worth fighting for. We are people, not animals for the slaughter or dogs for their sport".

The mountain saw and heard. In mute testimony, it witnessed that terrible day in 1997 when eight thousand Muslims were forced into trucks, brought to the Drina and shot. Lying amongst the dead, a survivor recalled the soldiers talking. "That was a good hunt. There were a lot of rabbits here". [3] In this part massacre, part blood sport, humans were converted into animals.

It was always like this. Call someone a rabbit (or worse) and you can treat them worse than a rabbit. Rabbits can be dangerous. The Muslims of Srebenicia had become dangerous. Or good for a wife.

Cain had come to mountains.

4

The best-known victim of violence was born to it. Eve, the mother of all living, became the mother of all violence. Her son was murdered in hot blood. Quickly, the red stain of Cain soaked the earth, which opened its outraged mouth to receive it, and shout for recompense. Much later, another Mother witnessed her son torn apart through judicial execution and a trumped-up charge. The unjust savagery of the cross claimed another victim, not for retribution anymore, but world redemption.

Ways to assault; ways to assert.

Firing a bullet from a metal rod that is an extension of you; a bullet designed to rudely rip the complicated formation of tissue, brains and blood.

The clenched fist or hands that grip objects of desire to weaponise.

A bomb designed to dissolve, dissolve human.

A knife to puncture or nails that enter wrists with savage penetration to pin someone to the wood.

But a clenched fist was also a hand; a hand at the end of an arm put around the distressed; the hand of friendship to the friendless.

And putting the boot in was also a foot that could run to someone's aid.

The thick darkness of human violence persisted despite all the efforts. It warped individuals, distorted relations between people and communities and shaped the destiny of nations. The red Stain of Cain was too deep dyed for it to be otherwise. Peace in our time has been postponed. There is only redemption. It cries from the ground, from heaven and the heaven of heavens and all stations between. But why? And crucially, how?

We are to probe how the violence that marks humankind interfaces with the horrific act of State-sponsored violence that took place one far-off Friday. Cain left his mark upon the red ground. The earth was disfigured, and this eldest son of the old Adam humanity was condemned to wander in social ostracism until going on to found cities and cultures built on violence (most are). Jealousy was his downfall, and with it, that selfishness and that greed which are ugly concomitan Being children of its times ts of ugly violence.

The blood of his victim, his unsuspecting brother Abel, struck down in cruel naivety, cried out for something to be done so the vicious primal act would not soak into the ground unanswered. Abel's blood, emblematic of the life soul and body of the man, demanded action; it demanded justice; it demanded recompense. The earth had absorbed and indeed drunk it, but at that point, like imbibing something that stirred restlessly within the stomach, vomited the scene in disclosure that would not be hidden. As Hebrews has it within the Newer Testament, the blood of another and final representative of the Adam humanity speaks to it but speaks better things. The divinely infused soul of Christ was subject to the violence of humankind and of State punishment renowned for brutality.

Mostly, the founders of major world religions died peacefully, with one very notable exception.

How does the wretched crucifixion become the means of human redemption? Like Socrates, could Jesus have drunk hemlock, or was violence endemic to the scene and the whole drama of reconciliation? Beyond personal forgiveness and restoration of the soul, this central act and fact, in which violence is central, speaks better things to the violence of the earth, which is daily stained with blood and the legacy of Cain's act? Does weeping atonement have anything to say to the sources for reconciliation and forgiveness this world badly needs to overcome the virus of violence?

Being children of their times, religious histories are as much complicit in this as anyone. We know why we have value, and from whence arises the indignant protest when that is trampled on and discarded. We are desperate to have our value upheld and feel both the psychological and social necessity to live in our world. With our value, we flourish; without it, we wither. Few of us – even mocking atheists or aggressive scientists – will be inwardly silent in the face of indifference (neither seen nor heard). Few of us will be comfortable with being diminished, cut down to size, or being meted out unequal treatment. Few of us will not react in the presence of indignity. Our value cries out in the night.

It is not good enough that, in an honour culture, people defend family honour to the extent of dishonouring and rubbishing the lives of those who have infringed or think they must avenge God. God can defend his own honour. God's name being dishonoured is a real issue. But not like this. Divine worth must be affirmed. It can no longer be aloof from upholding the value of personhood or the worth of the world. Hence the death of Christ that confronts this and the many roots and shoots of restless Cain: hence immersive atonement with its vast resource for transformative action, the power of love, forgiveness, participation and divine-human exchange. The capacity to restore rupture speaks to cultures of violence and narratives that sustain them so new stories can be told.

Individual transformation is the personal story that is told in the wake of another blood that soaked the earth. Christ in our place, one of us, one for us – this has enduring power. So too does Christ with us, ripped apart by crowds baying for his blood, showing love is stronger than death every day and speaking out of shredded humanity into a humanity. It was public. It was brutal. It was political.

Oceans of ink have been written to try to understand how the far-off Friday becomes a pivotal means of salvation and stream of love for generations yet unborn. Who; how does it affect? And why? We will confront the violence that was both central to the act; for it is also central to the red stain that old Cain left everywhere. His devaluing, degrading litany is the stuff of life; the independent autonomy his father had bequeathed him comes now to maturity. The dishonouring pathway – whether of God or humankind – is walked by both urban and rural dwellers of our time.

CHAPTER ONE
2020 VISION

"One night, he heard screams!"- the daughter of a former German diplomat who tried to explain why her father, once very pro-communist, radically changed his mind about Stalinism.[4]

"This war is not the end but the beginning of violence. It is the forge with which the world will be hammered into new borders and new communities. New moulds want to be filled with blood, and power will be wielded with a hard fist"- Ernst Junger. *Der Kampf als Inneres Erlebnis* (1928)[5]

The Red Stain of Cain does not possess its own story. There is no history of violence, only the history of humanity.

Just before the Pandemic struck, the USA was impeaching its President – but didn't. A deeply polarised society would remain. Everyone seemed to agree that such intensity of partisan emotion was not good for democracy. Either being 'on my side or against me' or 'if you can be keen on candidate x, you cannot be in favour of candidate y' was not a way to organise a political community. But who had the courage to step out of it? And what values should leading figures espouse to provide rallying flags? As political parties were faced with choosing new leaders, who would be the party of change? We had lost the art of listening and seeking to understand those who think differently. How we relate to one another must be an education for the third decade.

A recognition of complexity would help. The reality is that the issues are deep and complex. And the pace and scale of world transformations is beyond analytical capabilities of journalists or historians. In the twentieth century, people used the same industrial technology to build very different kinds of societies: fascist dictatorships, communist regimes, liberal democracies. The same will happen in the twenty-first century. AI and biotech will transform the world, but can we use them to create very different kinds of societies? Meanwhile, the environmental crisis is threatening all kinds of societies.

All our existential challenges are global problems that demand global solutions. But to do something effective, we need global cooperation. It is therefore of deep concern that just when global cooperation is more needed than ever before, many leaders who ride the wave of populism tell us that there is an inherent contradiction between nationalism and globalism. Fortunately, loving your country is not about hating foreigners. Nationalism is about loving your compatriots. And in the twenty-first century, in order to protect the future of your compatriots, you must cooperate with those outside the house. Our house is bigger than my house.

The Enlightenment had stressed ideals that led in a straight line to racial equality, a shared vision of justice and a model of citizenship based on common values rather than tribal ethnicity. That old heritage seemed ill-fitting for twenty first century minds and was being widely spurned. The idea of an open exchange of goods and services, of people and opinions, which had gone hand in hand with the notion of the State being the people's servant rather than their master, was becoming embattled.

We are now at a time when war kills fewer people than suicide, and gunpowder is less dangerous to your life than sugar. Most countries do not think about conquering and annexing their neighbours. They can afford to spend about two percent of their GDP on defence and far more on education and healthcare. Despite many international tensions, we are enjoying most prosperous and most peaceful era in human history. Peace now means the implausibility of war. France and Germany are highly unlikely to ever go to war again though wars rage in some parts of the world.

In his book 'The Better Angels of our Nature', Steven Pinker argues that, despite what the news tells us, violence of all kinds has been decreasing. [6] This is problematic. To attempt to measure a decrease in the suffering of violence entails that there is a common standard by which suffering of torture victims or wars can be quantified as it were and compared. Graphs in social science or history were not at all common before the 19th century so the urge to quantify and make such experiences the subject of statistics are part of the very story that optimists about progress seek to tell. Whatever its validity, this is, as has been observed, 'comfort history' in order to cheer us up. In this first chapter, we take a sweep through those violences which haunt our human landscapes today. Religiously inspired violence is a phenomenon we are all too familiar with, as is the spectre of political violence in places like Syria when nation States go to war or turn thuggish with their own people. It may be dipping now but, from the horrific experience of the Second World War to about 1980, violent crime had rocketed five times in a generation. Work - place wars were common; under provocation from long hours, worry about cut-backs and intense competition. Abusive shock--jocks filled the airwaves. On the roads, drivers scream at each other in road rage. 1 in 3 of us have experienced road rage since 2005. 1 in 3 nurses have experienced aggression and violence. Hate crimes are on the rise and social media allows for vicious verbal abuse.

EXCURSION – THE WAY WE WERE

A hundred years ago, the world began to recover from its drawn-out catastrophe of the Great War. That is at least the story. And like so many narratives, it is wrong – or at least true only in Western Europe. Elsewhere, the war to end war did not end war and certainly not the conflict that is politics by other means. The Great War was most definitely not followed by a period of peace until Europe imploded in a Second World War. That is the usual narrative and it is only the Western experience. Especially in the defeated lands of Eastern and southern Europe, there was no peace. Only a continuous arc of post-war violence prevailed, in which peace was an illusion. Stability it was not.[7]

The wrongly named 'Spanish flu' was wreaking havoc on the world, slaying its millions. It almost certainly hastened the end of Western European war in 1918, influenced the Versailles Peace negotiations through Woodrow Wilson becoming dangerously ill and led to rapid social change. The pandemic continued. In the US in 1919, 185,000 would die in its 3rd wave. Loss would be seared into the emotional world of millions. In the British dominions, the toll of wounded was over two million.

RELATIVITY RULES

In May of 1919, Arthur Eddington had confirmed that Einstein's theory of relativity was correct. The deflection of light by Mercury during a solar eclipse proved it. This was a new map of the world. Eddington had only eight minutes to operate, but the proof was clear. Weird things were possible. Light could bend. The old rules had changed. From that time on, Einstein turned into a superstar. Nothing seemed certain anymore. There was no longer any absolute, but this applied not only to time and space, but to good and evil too. Relativity merged imperceptibly into relativism. Einstein's work helped form the framework for the 20th century mind, coming as it did at the same time as the public reception of Freud's writings, mainstream at that point. Modernism sprang suddenly into life. A revolution in culture, with Einstein and Freud as markers, began to make itself felt. The world looked different. The broad dimension of what was going on a century ago was monumental, ranging from the flawed attempt to forge a peace to the relativity that characterised a whole era of upheaval of former certainties.

Only a hopeful spirit was constant. Only the violence was constant. The last hundred years have been a century of revolutions, evolutions and retributions; the politics, the protests and dizzying social transformations.

Far reaching social change was happening all around the survivors and acting upon them. Women had just got the vote. Far more were in work. The US Senate passed its female suffrage bill. The first non-stop flight across the Atlantic took place. A month later, the airship R34 made the same journey. The first US passenger service was set up. In Glasgow, the Army was called in to quell rent riots. The Police went on strike. Returning servicemen were promised their old job back. The Edwardian world of progress and power could not be regained. Nancy Astor became the first woman MP. Barriers to women entering legal professions were removed. Richmal Crompton's 'Just William' was introduced to British readers. KLM was born. The Austrian parliament approved an 8-hour working day.

Trying to hold the line, Pope Benedict published the response of the Catholic Church to current political issues. As Middle-class women became better off, they enjoyed greater social freedom - they wore make-up, shorter skirts and smoked in public. Above all, the automobile industry grew rapidly, courtesy of Henry Ford. With the cars pouring off production lines, there was a need for more rubber to make tyres, glass for windscreens and leather for seats. Social transformations were sweeping.

In 1933 a difficult experiment with democracy, a form of Government Germany had never known, came to an end. Someone Henry Ford admired, Adolf Hitler, came to power on a toxic mix of economic distress and mass unemployment. That combined with the strong imperative to redress a wrong. The public narrative fed off mass resentment and spectacular blame-shifting by a shifty military. Why was Germany being singled out for penalties at Versailles? Those who had started the war were not blamed. It was those who signed the peace - 'the November criminals' - as Hitler styled them in unrighteous indignation. After the devastation of the Great War, the world began the slow march to an even greater conflict. Promising to erase the humiliation, Hitler sought expansion in Eastern Europe, despite Poland insisting on territorial integrity. Left to its fate, Poland's anguish led to even greater bloodletting on a scale not seen since violence and Cain's Red Stain was invented.

How did entire nations handle what it was like to reel from a devastating psychological impact? In 1919 the survivors looked out on a world that had changed.

Scenes of devastation greeted the survivors across Europe. In June 1919, the Cenotaph, designed by Edwin Lutyens to commemorate the dead of the Great War, was unveiled in London. How does a nation come to terms with the scale of slaughter it had experienced? The impact was profound. There were far more women of a certain age than men. Peace teas flourished to celebrate the end of a sickening war (Armistice had taken everyone unaware). De-mobbed soldiers were unemployed

DRAWING A NEW MAP

The tribes descending on Versailles in early 1919 needed to draw a fresh map of the world. How do you go about that? Who were the main actors? What was driving them? Ireland and the Sinn Fein members declared an independent Irish State. The first shots were fired. In Scapa Flow, Germany scuttled her fleet as Admiral von Reuter carried out the last orders of the Kaiser. Victory parades across Britain celebrated the end of World War I. Versailles, signed in June, may have guaranteed twenty years of peace, but stoked up resentment and created a climate which will eventually pave the way for the 2nd World War. Keynes saw it would be disastrous. He was not alone. *"I can predict with absolute certainty that within another generation there will be another world war if the nations of the world do not concert the method by which to prevent it"*.[8] Kemal Ataturk embarked on his political career to create a new secular Turkey from Ottoman ashes. New nationalisms of largely Austro-Hungarian Empire territory were born through national self-determination. South West Africa (Namibia) came under South African administration, portentous for future conflict.

THE EVIL TWIN

In Germany, the mix was shaping up as conflict between the Far Right and the Communists, inspired by events in Russia. The Spartacus uprising in Germany was crushed. The crucible of devastating war shaped evil twins that began to emerge. Civil War in Russia rent the country apart and the new Bolshevik Government of Lenin fought furiously to cope. The war didn't stop in 1918. Royal Navy ships were lost by mines, aiding Estonia against the Communists. British troops came and went from Archangel. In Italy, a militant nationalist group led by Annunzio began to organise. Mussolini formed the Italian Fascist party. In September, Corporal Adolf Hitler is was ordered to investigate a small political party in Munich...

WILSON'S TRAVAILS

Americans were eager for peace, but security was another matter. President Woodrow Wilson sought to win the peace, but his own citizens felt he had gone too far. He suffered a breakdown in his health from which he never recovered. US Senate rejected (55-39) both the Treaty of Versailles and League of Nations. Wilson was a broken man. Communists became the subjects of a 'Red scare' thirty years before the McCarthy era as John Reed formed the American Communist Labour Party in Chicago. In one of his first acts as FBI Director, Edgar Hoover deported the anarchist/ feminist Emma Goldman to Russia. Race riots unsettled the country. 83 African Americans were lynched. The Klu Klux Klan was at its height. Jazz took off in Chicago. But the 18th Amendment was passed; Prohibition had arrived. (It was not just the US. Norway was about to follow suit). The anti-cigarette smoking league also started organising. There was another huge reality, the economic boom. The war had not directly damaged America; it had led to increased demand for American goods. Rapid growth of industry and farming ensued. The economy grew even faster when the war ended. Business made huge profits.

INFAMY IN AMRITSAR

1919 saw a Third Anglo-Afghan war as Great Britain occupied Afghanistan. It also saw infamy in Amritsar. British and Gurkha troops killed 379 Sikhs and injured more than 1200. The Jallianwala Bagh massacre, which took place in April 1919, is a stain on the British Government as it was carried out by the Army during the British Empire's occupation of India. A crowd of local unarmed people were protesting in the area during a period of martial law. General

Reginald Dyer from the British army saw those protests as defiance, so he ordered his troops to close all the exits of the park. With no warning to disperse, he led a group of 50 soldiers into the park and then proceeded to open fire at the crowd, including women and children. The soldiers kept firing until they ran out of ammunition. You can still see the bullet holes in the walls; the wall where the bodies were extracted from. What did that all mean - for Indian nationalism and for the Raj? It shaped the reactions during the following twenty years as Gandhi launched his first Satyagraha campaign. His movement had already taken form through offering health care in the devastating pandemic. As Churchill said, "this is an extraordinary event, a monstrous event, an event which stands in singular and sinister isolation."[9]

DOCTOR DEMOCRACY

The May 4th Movement of 1919 is the ideological origin of modern Chinese history, smarting under the unequal treaties imposed on China after the First World War. Out of strong patriotism, students protesting against the Treaty of Versailles initiated a movement, developing into a national protest movement of people from all walks of life. The May Fourth Movement was part cultural revolution, part social movement. In the intellectual ferment, answers were sought for the questions why and how China had lagged behind the West. Traditional morality, the clan system and Confucianism were seen as the main causes. China could only be cured by 'Two Doctors' who sought to make Chinese culture more accessible. Social aspects of May Fourth attempted to emancipate Chinese woman, although often limited to movements to bring foot-binding to a halt. The cruel eroticism left millions of hobbling. Various new ideologies sprang up, among which the spread of Marxism-Leninism was portentous. Out of this grew the demi-urge that was Mao, who lives again a hundred years later, (much like Cain still wanders the world).

History is back. A hundred years later, the new Millennium is now two decades old. The economy throwing a terrifying teenage tantrum, planes flying into skyscrapers, terrorists versus Governments, war in the Middle East, dark clouds of human-doing warming and shrouding the planet in a hot burden of eco-concern - this was not how things were meant to be!

It was not mere terrorism that mobilised national states. Acts of violence had been a feature of life since restless Cain wandered the earth. Revolutionary politics first began to be used to change society towards the end of the eighteenth century. But what now galvanised Governments was terrorism with a religious face - terrorism that was fervent, relentless and which reflected the dynamism of beliefs strongly held and a politics of grievance. Muslims had felt devalued and humiliated, going down to defeat again and again at the hands of a West they saw as corrupt and globally dominant, that thought the life of an African or an Iraqi was worth less than that of a Westerner.

But whether in Sri Lanka, Iraq or Afghanistan, when a suicide bomber blew himself apart and intentionally killed large numbers of people at the same time, he was treating the victims of violence as being of no value, as being worthless. The act of violence was shouting at the victims that they were ripe only to be desecrated or destroyed. Violence generated by the unique fire of religion scraped the face off a victim and relegated him or her to an object, a non-person.

Many battles for equality had been fought and won. But there was a large battle still to be fought against divisions and conflict which came from the negative way religion was exploited to dehumanise opponents. Conservative religion everywhere, strengthening the identity of the faithful, was suspicious of those outside the faith. Writing off those people who were not of your persuasion was the seed of violence.

STOP THE TRAFFIC!

More people were caught in a form of slavery at the time than the number of Africans sold in America all those years ago. Slaves were people's property, to be bought or sold. Slaves were spoils of war. People could become slave property through selling themselves to meet a debt. Or selling their children.

Slave societies were once common. But you did not make slaves of your own people. You found people ripe to be converted into property. Like Africans. It was Europe's sweet tooth that began the most notorious traffic in human beings' history. Two slaves out of three ended up in the sugar colonies, all to feed the growing demand. Betrayed by their fellow Africans, inland people living out their days had been caught, caught in a net like you would catch a butterfly. Except you would treat a butterfly with more respect. People were herded, herded as if they were cattle, herded as if they were devoid of feelings, and if they were, it was irrelevant. The one depended on the other. First construct people as animals, only semi-people. Then herd them. It was ok to convert them into property, people into animals, into properties. That was the alchemy.

Eleven million humans were shipped across the Atlantic, from cattle to sardines. But these were only the survivors. One third died and had to be tossed overboard to join the other sardines. Survivors were sold in the slave markets like property. When no longer useful, the slave was sold on, or abandoned to die. Now the former property and erstwhile sardines and cattle were like an old car not worth keeping going.

Stopping the traffic was the first salvo in the struggle for human dignity. It took a terrible war to stop slavery amongst the cotton plantations of the Deep South, where it was part of a way of life. In the founding of the American Republic, slaves had been included in the population count (5/8ths of a person was the rule of thumb, though to be fair that was more than a thumb).

But men and women, boys and girls, continued to be sold as property. There were as many slaves at that time as ever shipped across the Middle Passage in those inhumane centuries that never quite ended. Eight million children were trapped in forms of slavery - to pay a debt, to be child soldiers, involved in pornography, prostitution. Forced labour or sexual exploitation still claimed its millions; boys for forced labour - women and girls to be exploited for sexual services. Physical or emotional abuse awaited them. So did threats against their families, rape and death. Every year, ¾ million people were traded across international borders. Even in Britain, which had first stopped the traffic, people trading remained the most profitable activity for criminals - after drugs and weapons. One in three parents in West Africa said that they could not earn enough to feed their families. So, they were prepared to hand over their children to human traffickers.

WAR ON WOMEN

We take up a lament for the violence that continued to be perpetrated on the female spirit and female body. Since in some countries women were allowed to vote a hundred years ago, attitudes towards women were improving – mostly. Was feminism outdated?

For too long, we have been saying we can recognise the value of humans, but we haven't valued half the world.

In the West, women weren't prepared to see themselves as victims or go second class. We should celebrate diversity rather than go for equality; being ourselves. Struggles there though were on a very different level to what women in the developing world have to endure. Often, women were completely subservient and inferior to men. Defined by tradition and religion, they worked long hours in the fields in back-breaking labour. A hundred years to change? It was all too slow.

The experience or threat of violence affected the lives of women everywhere, cutting across boundaries of wealth, race and culture. In home and community, in times of war and peace, women are beaten, raped, mutilated, and killed with impunity. The World Health Organisation estimated that one woman in five will be a victim of rape or attempted rape in her lifetime. Raping women was a weapon of war as Yugoslavia disintegrated; a deadly virus in men's minds broke out again. Pornography reduced women to the level of objects and things. Women did not exist as humans but were merely there to satisfy a man's desire.

In the civilised West, one woman in four had experienced violence at home. Many studies in different countries said that between 20 and 50% of women had experienced domestic violence. It was a major cause of death and disability for a woman between the age of sixteen and forty four as she embarked upon a career of being a woman and a mother In the United States, land of the free, a woman was raped every six minutes. Every fifteen seconds, a woman was battered.

The spectre of domestic violence involved deadly magic that transformed a person into an object, an object who was then ripe for being battered. In traditional societies, husbands could do what they wanted with their wives; merely a different recipe for the domestic violence brewed elsewhere. In a globalised world, trafficking of women became a worldwide phenomenon where victims were sexually exploited, forced into labour and subjected to abuse. Murders of women in Guatemala, Russia, India, and Pakistan often went un-investigated and unpunished. In Pakistan, the Human Rights Commission said most rapists and killers go free because of poor policing and the victim's fear of speaking out. Gang rape and honour killings of women remain common in a country where feudal and tribal systems still too often hold sway.

Across Asia, when it came to marriage, divorce and custody of children, everyone else was in charge of the other half of humanity. Forced marriages still pressed women into unwelcome relationships. Then they were at the mercy of a bridegroom who could quickly become tired of them or aggrieved at the lack of dowry. Then they turned violent. In India, the dowry system could lead to tragic results. Every year, six thousand brides were murdered by their husbands, furious that they received no money along with their brides.

In Iran, women working for equality wore gags to show that they could not speak out without serious risk. Intimidation and imprisonment awaited the ungagged. In Iran, a woman is only worth 50%. Any evidence she gives in court counts for half of a man. Compensation for injury or death is only 50% of what a man gets. Many women are no longer willing to be repressed. There is a Campaign for Equality under way but it's highly dangerous. Get involved and risk serious intimidation. Keep a bag packed!

Female circumcision, a traditional custom in many African countries, sought to ensure that women should restrict sexual pleasure. Each year, more than two million girls in thirty countries had to undergo this mutilation because the community prized chastity in a girl until she married. The alternative was no husband and no economic security.

From infancy, girls often received less food, less medical

care and less education than their brothers. From being girls to adults, women continue to be at risk. Each year, thousands of women and girls were trafficked into forced prostitution.

Prejudice against girls started early. The lifecycle of violence starts with sex-selective abortion and infanticide in countries where girls are valued less than boys or considered an economic burden. Boys were future breadwinners who would look after parents in old age. Girls were a financial burden. In India, 10 million female foetuses were aborted over the last 20 years. In China, Government birth-control policy had restricted families to a single child; so 30 millions girls were missing.

What is there to say?

ON KAZANSKY RAILWAY STATION[10]

Two cups of coffee later, I paced up and down the platform. The train was late. I read a plaque on the wall. When the station began in 1913, peace and prosperity had dawned. There would be a flowering of the arts, of the sciences. Artists, writers, philosophers and everyone were filled with exciting possibilities. Relativity, psychology, sociology and Marxism were radical theories that went hand in glove with a future filled with planes, cars, wireless and electricity. Science and reason were driving the progress train, fuelled by noble optimism about our capacity to achieve a better world. Anything was possible. The world was conquered, the Titanic unsinkable. The Tsar still ruled Russia in those days. Then the First World War slaughtered its millions. And into the vacuum strode wild-eyed Bolsheviks with fire in their minds. They had been waiting for this that moment.

In Ulyanovsk, the Volga stretches far into the horizon of the far bank. A boy was raised. That was before Vladimir Ulayanov became Lenin and animus of bitter hatred stirred his soul to its depths.

In the darkness of the night, shadows arose. The dreamers of Communism hoped that people would be good, and power would not be abused. It was about regaining paradise regained, a hopeful place where landowners and factory owners would be swept away, a place in the sun where equality had arrived. But instead, a chasm of darkness opened up. A flawed dream completely ignored the possibilities of evil. And so few people were now standing round to see this big picture in the political exhibition. They had moved on to smaller pictures and smaller dreams. But at what cost! Both Communism and Fascism, its evil twin, generated a tragic waste of life. Now, Lenin's body lays embalmed in Red Square. It had passed into history, the death of an ideal, a golden age that was no golden age, a dream fatally flawed. It was a symphony of hope through social conflict, but only nostalgic revolutionaries were listening at that point.

It left the running of the perfect society in the hands of imperfect men. Like the Kims of North Korea, who had kept their country in abject poverty, its ideology a smoke screen for a sordid, failed state. Like Mao, a warlord totally indifferent to the death of millions, radically contemptuous of life, or of enemies of the people. There were so many people, China could afford to lose some of them. Like Pol Pot, a sad little man who had turned Cambodia into a killing field. Professional people of any sort - teachers, doctors, and intellectuals - all had to be exterminated for society to be rebuilt. A nightmare experiment in social engineering led to genocide and the death of two million of his own people. Even Mao did not kill a quarter of the population. Lenin had little love for his people either.

The songs of humanity have been many since those days; songs mighty in their influence, modern versions of reality, big symphonies, but with large gaps in the music. All such songs seemed to have been incomplete; baffled by the radical evil people do. They were powerful, compelling dreams.

For at the point, the Communist dream had been virtually driven out of business, a hopeful story that tried to paint the whole picture but failed so starkly. In the 1980's and 1990's, cynical passive spectators rose up with one voice and quickly swept it all away. The song failed, shown up at last in its incompleteness; a song blind and naive to the evil that men do; a song grey and drab because it did not sing to our createdness or take account of a Zhivago in love, an individual against the system. Apparently, people don't function well unless they feel their little lives count. Someone should have told Marx. It was meant to be utopia by the next train. Speaking of which, where was that train??

The end of the experiment had come upon humanity. For decades, the story had been told and the assumptions made. The only hindrances were external and destructive patterns, or so it was said. But despite countless manifestos, why were we not more at peace and more content? What was holding up the train? It had to arrive soon! The far side of hope was dark; very dark. It was hardly the beginning of the demonization of humans. But it was the end of dreams.

CHAPTER TWO
UNDERSTANDING THE TRANSMISSION

"Words of condemnation about sectarian violence are not enough. Young people who are now spewing sectarian hate have learned it from adults and the adults must now take responsibility to put a stop to it". Sean Farren, MP for North Antrim after a 15-year-old Catholic boy was chased by a gang in a Protestant town, cornered in an alleyway and hit over the head with a baseball bat before being stamped on his head. [11]

The use of the N-word and of anti-Semitic slurs was just part of the way it was. It was background. [12]

THE KEY OF IDENTITY

Jesus is the sacrifice that cleanses violent, sinful humanity. The red stain of Cain is more than matched by the red stain of Christ, wrought from savagery and systemic violence. How and why? What if we saw violence as a public health issue? Can we break the transmission? Theologically, can there be lockdowns? Maybe we can never be free of the violence. We will have to cut back on breeding grounds. It requires a different attitude to the past and opening the door to a different future. In particular, the collusion between religion and violence needs to be radically cleansed. Some might dismiss this as being a problem, particular to Islam or Hindu nationalists. It can therefore be waved away as pertaining to extremists. That though is false comfort. The collusion between the Christian church and violence is both terrifying and on-going. To leave it at the exit gates of history is debarred to us. An angel with a sword of fire blocks our way.

Violence is an overflow of the cognitive dissonance, the warped thinking of the human soul. The heart needs to be changed. Personal transformation is one thing. Violence does not just take place because it stands at the portal of a single human heart and overwhelms it, like Cain's dog waiting to pounce on one individual who was in danger of personal jealousy consuming him. Yes, that often happens, and we are all susceptible to the door pushed open by a prowler who gets over the threshold once and jumps on the furniture as if he owns the place.

We can grasp that more easily as it applies to an individual being sucked into violence. Cultures of violence qualify (or undermine) any idea that individuals are morally autonomous. The way violence and injustice are built into the walls is harder to grasp. If it is in the culture, in the system, it is harder to pin down to answer 'who is responsible?' In sociological terms, it is the age-old question of personal agency and social structure. For instance, moving from personal, moral explanations of unemployment to economic and structural causes is one of the main features of social analysis in the 20th century. Disentangling these factors is extremely complex. Cultures of violence reinforce dominance and power, or, as is it the case with Islamic radicalism, seek to win power.

The same is true for identity. Those espousing the Confederate Flag in the South of USA are being shaped by social forces in their history that make them want to defend an identity under attack. White supremacists strongly believe their way of life and who they are is at grave risk. It is surely because of the native strength of identity that white evangelicals adopt an individualist lens. There are no broad patterns or malign social systems: brutality is about some individuals being violent.

Society is experiencing a profound culture shift in our political ideas from wanting economic goods towards wanting identity and respect. The quest for equal and inner dignity and the human desire for recognition and respect have become hugely important, especially for those that had felt marginalised. White voters who used to support the left of politics felt they had lost ground and pushed back as the former tribes of the dispossessed moved inexorably towards centres of power.

Politics and its tribes used to be based on economics and the power to maintain people's hold over resources. Now, in landscapes that are re-shaped, they are more likely to be based on culture and identity. The politics of identity rooted in nationalism and hostility to immigration is are a strong driver on the contemporary scene. The UK Demos Think

Tank has identified nostalgia as a cultural and political force which is driving populist policies across Europe.[13] Life was better than when we were growing up? Or was it? Our sense of belonging, of tradition is a powerful driver, appealing as it does to tribal identity. As I write this, there is strong criticism of Turkey for restricting Hagia Sophia in Istanbul to Islamic worship as befits a Mosque. President Erdogan proclaimed Turkey to be a Muslim nation. In the same week, India's Prime Minister Narendra Modi laid the foundations of a the Ayodhya Temple to mark the birthplace of Ram. These political projects are about the revival of a new golden age; a cultural and spiritual repudiation of secularism and return to how things used to be. 'This is who we really are', these acts were proclaiming. It is about identity.

February 1979. The Ayatollah Khomeini landed in Tehran. The Shah had fled. The revolution Khomeini helped to bring about was partly an appeal to populism amidst a country where rich elites lived on a very different level to the ordinary people. It was partly an appeal to assert a new identity, an Islamic identity in a country which either felt itself devalued by the Western powers or could be made to feel that it had been a backyard where Western powers could play the game. The 'resistance' inspired by Islamic resurgence heeded Ayatolloh Kohmeini's call to replace the 'colonised brain' with the independent brain'. [14] It has been about Islamic identity rather than Islam per se. A result of three decades rule by the Mullahs is that Iran became the least religious major nation in the Middle East.[15] These were themes that played thirty years on. A supporter of the erstwhile Iranian President Ahmedinajad explained it like this. *"He helps the poor people and makes us proud to be Iranian, standing up to the West"*[16]

Radical Islam has been confronting the twenty first century anew with the spectre of violence in the name of God.

A wave of suicide bombings across the world has combined with movements such as Al Queda, Boko Haram in Nigeria and ISIS to produce terrorist networks and horrific acts of carnage.

The ideology that infects the minds of mostly young people drawn into terrorism is one that persuades people that violence is the right way to go – indeed the only way. Nothing else will create such a theatre of the deed, as anarchist revolutionaries used to say. Idealism is channelled into maiming and killing. God wants it. Apart from bringing the full force of the State to deal with it when terrorism raises its ugly head, the route to dealing with the infection is to disrupt it theologically. The equivalent of soap in this context is to de-construct the warped thinking whereby violence seems acceptable. Theological de-construction has to be the way to fight the disease. After all, in Islam, humanity is supposed to be the vice-regent of God just as in Christianity; we are a mirror image.

The problem with this is that the mind-set that sees terrorist violence as acceptable is not an isolated thought: it is a part of a narrative. A story is told about what is going on and why joining a violent cause is the remedy – much as people are persuaded to join up to fight in wartime.

It is an urgent task to talk to those who carried out violence thinking they were doing God a favour, those who instilled in communities of the faithful the lie that a people bomber was a martyr to be celebrated. As I write, the longest life-sentence ever handed down by a British Court has been served on Hashem Abedi, accomplice and brother of the Manchester Arena bomber in 2017.

"Who deceived you?" We want to shout. "Who told you that God requires this, acts that rip human flesh apart along with families and their tattered dreams? Who gave you the instruction in God's name that the cause they have instilled into you with hot collective indignation necessitates this act? Can a sacred cause you were recruited for depend on the desecration of that which is also sacred?"

Religious groups routinely disrespected each other, not seeing each other as people in their own right, but as enemies who must be opposed to protect God's interests; foes who lost the colour of blood and became cardboard cut-outs; not real people.

When radical clerics sought to stir young men and women into radical action, leaving them heavy with a sense of obligation; when the logic of that action pointed inexorably towards violence being acceptable and then mandatory; when suicide bombers were dispatched on their mission to fulfil such a logic, where were the antibodies that asked why they thought Al'lah had demanded such a chilling disregard for human life? It was surely blasphemous, As Muhammad had said, he who kills one man kills all humanity.

Sacrifice and martyrdom were part of many cultures. There was a reason. Often, resistance seemed all they had, and violence was the language of those who would be unheard no longer.

But the terrible deceivers, the recruiters of the grim task, the staff officers of the lethal mission to detonate yourself and pull a hundred people limb from limb. And when a crowd gathered to help the victims, showing far more humanity than the bombers, they instructed another poor fool to hurl himself into blood spattered oblivion along with the crowd. And Al'lah would calmly smile on the bomber, now promoted to the rank of honoured martyr! They had better to be right, those recruiters and staff officers! They are not praying, but instead preying – on those for whom identity matters.

Yet, though the terrorists claimed the nervous headlines, the good news went largely unreported. Like the countless

Muslims everywhere who patiently endured the frustration of being tarred with the same brush as the exploiters of religion. Like the Islamic scholars who wanted to dialogue with Christian scholars. Or the Fatwa on terrorism from the Conference at Deobandi against this "inhuman crime". 70,000 Mullahs of all sects had agreed to be bound by it. It was the greatest assembly of beards seen in India for a long time.[17]

It was not mere terrorism that mobilised national states. Acts of violence had been a feature of life since revolutionary politics first began to be used to change society towards the end of the eighteenth century. But what galvanised Governments then was terrorism with a religious face - terrorism that was fervent, relentless and that reflected the dynamism of beliefs strongly held, and a politics of grievance. Muslims had felt devalued and humiliated, going down to defeat again and again at the hands of a West they saw as corrupt and globally dominant.

But whether in Sri Lanka, Iraq or Afghanistan, when a suicide bomber blew himself apart and intentionally killed large numbers of people at the same time, he was treating the victims of violence as being of no value, as being worthless. The act of violence was shouting at the victims that they were ripe only to be desecrated or destroyed. Violence generated by the unique fire of religion scraped the face off a victim and relegated him or her to an object, a non-person.

CHRISTIAN HISTORY HAS A PROBLEM TOO

Christian history has no less a problem with violence in its history. War on the whole Islamic world is a prime example; hence strong reactions in Muslim cultures against the very word 'crusade' if used by western politicians. So too is the war on women (witchcraft and domestic violence legitimated by the church). What stands high in public consciousness at the time of writing is growing awareness that the whole black experience across the centuries has been one of violence, injustice and untold oppression. The original sin of racism constitutes war on the skin; absurd, if it was not so tragic.

Recognition that we haven't moved very far from racism is not about increasing diversity and then say, 'we have ticked that box, can we move on now please?' The cross takes us to something much deeper, for it defines the pattern of life. It weighs very heavily on anyone who experiences oppression.

Christian backing for this stems from particular ways of thinking about God, Jesus and the cross that constitute criminal theological evasion. White theologians rarely speak of race or culture as a theological category. Sin is about what bad people do as individuals. It is inescapable though that faith played a huge role in authorising the violence endemic in the system.

Take the case of the good Rev Dr Hudgins, Pastor of First Baptist Church in Jackson Mississippi from 1946 to 1969. His big focus was to keep white supremacy intact and he did this by ensuring that you did not question the system. Christian faith was about personal and individual salvation. The Jackson Daily News extolled that *'few among our theological leadership equal his power in exposition and amplification of the gospel'*.[18] The cross of violence had no implications for the social and racial upheavals going on outside the church in the Civil Rights movement of the 1960's. Racial integration equated to a threat to purity. Doctrines were shaped to preserve power and control by the status quo; hence justifying White supremacy.

"The commitment amongst white supremacist States to a brutal pigmentocracy was matched only by a fervent belief in Jesus Christ and the fear of change (rendered 'impurity') strained this fragile dialectic towards an inescapable apoth-

eosis of violence. " Charles Marsh documents how the former Imperial Wizard of the Klu Klux Klan, Sam Bowyers, thought it was his Christian duty to kill heretics and bomb churches in the name of the Lord.[19] Augustine Tanner, an Anglican Ordinand, relates how his grandfather in the Deep South witnessed Klu Klux Klan gatherings around the lynching tree, against which there was a banner saying 'Jesus saves'.[20]

At the heart of such obscenity were narratives, vicious narratives, that reflected and sustained ways of seeing. Narrative imagination and the use of stories is key to developing reflexive learning to provoke awareness by people about their own violence and the violence of others. Stories are powerful, encoding meanings. We dream in stories, think in stories and so often structure our understanding of the world around narratives. One only has to observe the way young people find adverts memorable to realize that narrative has enormous potential for encoding knowledge and meaning. How much when it comes to cultures? Cultures are sustained by rude, crude generalizations.

Incidents of collective violence arise initially out of common occurrences or shared experiences, such as a drunken brawl, the theft of an idol in India that led to communal violence, the rape of a girl or such occurrences as terrorism. Some remain localized, while others fit into broader frameworks of meaning for that culture, supplied by dominant ideologies. This is a question of identity. Continuing talk of violence contributes to its persistence rather than its reduction. Communal identity is sustained by myths, legends, stories of 'this is who we are and this is how we do things'.

Experiencing and re-experiencing the past is a matter of collective memory. White attitudes to black people or things like retaliation or the desire for extending the conflict depends upon a continually re-lived past which merges with the present and constrains the future. The cycle of hatred draws on and is fuelled by the dangerous combination of myth and history. It is as if the past, with all its saga of action and counteraction, is before the participants to evoke a crowd psychology, a collective memory. Rehearsing the past with a prejudicial perspective becomes more and more reinforced with successive acts of violence or perceived injustice. This led to Jim Crow in the southern United States featuring cruel pushback against liberation of the slaves after 1865. Such emancipation could not be tolerated. Somehow, violence and memories of violence become grafted on to successive generations and embedded in their thinking. Cultures of violence are substantiated by the memory of who is good out there and who is bad in a way that conflates myth and history. In this representation of violence, the story of what happened is repeated. It is re-cycled. The message that is acted out in the next generation is held in its collective memory. Narratives become entrenched.

The texts of violence operate through cultures, through systems. As tempting as it may be though to see violent acts as the aberrations of a few rotten apples, there is much evidence to suggest that violence is not just about those who inflict it, but the situations that foster it. The Stanford Prison Experiment carried out by Philip Zimbardo in 1971 showed that 'situational thinking' influences violent social behaviour more than 'dispositional thinking' (character 'will out'). Playing the game of 'prisoners and guards' demonstrated how 'guards' could become sadistic bullies within 48 hours, while prisoners were cowed into impotent submission. Applying this to social and political scenarios facing the next generation, Zimbardo argued that a bad system produces bad situations in which people act badly.[21]

In short, human beings find themselves in collective contexts in which something else kicks in. It's called 'culture', or sub-cultures, in which personal agency can hardly be disentangled from social pressures which have shaped their thinking at an invisible level.

Violence erupts when certain conditions are 'fulfilled'. Its breeding grounds are cultures and environments that cultivate it. Once it takes hold, like all cultures, it is sustained by custom, by practice and narratives – both told and untold – about 'this is how we do things round here.' For culture is a layered concept. It refers to the social, to the practice, both large and small, which is learned and becomes familiar. It also refers to the biological, to the horticultural: cultures which can be grown.

Among the ultra-poor in rural Bangladesh is a region of the world where three out of every four women are abused by a romantic partner at some point of their life, and half were abused last year (Bangladesh Bureau of Statistics, 2013). Physical and/or sexual violence from hands of an intimate partner are rampant throughout the entire country, with 54% of the women experiencing either form of violence during their lifetime. In Bangladesh, violence against the women is exacerbated by traditional gender norms that prescribe the man's role as the breadwinner, limiting the woman's economic independence. Child marriage, female seclusion and high acceptance of wife beating represent just some of the prevalent norms that dampen Bangladeshi women's wellbeing.[22]

We need a theology of culture. Otherwise our thinking is cramped. We see an individual lashing out. Is it only individuals who act? Two cultures from different parts of the world illuminate the question.

RUSSIA

"If he hits you, that means he loves you," quotes Diana her mother's saying, the old-fashioned Slavic belief, a reason why domestic violence in Russia is still widely underre-

ported — as well as most forms of physical assault-, making it a "norm" rather than a crime. [23] This is a zero-sum game. Competition means there is only so much significance to go round. A threat to masculinity needs to be countered with force. The social responsibility of males to provide for their females is not only materialistic in the former Soviet Union, but more alike paternal duty, where a woman is looked after by someone responsible for her, because it's his moral obligation and delight. Rape is something that "happens", and is accepted as a fact of life, not a social problem. For Russian men cheating on their girlfriends is not just normal, it is expected and a matter of honour. A man who never cheated on his other half is looked at with disdain, including his wife (is he not man enough?)

A generation before, Dostoyevsky addressed the reality of a brutalised and largely docile society, dreaming of a society where everyone, including the hopelessly marginalised, could live whole lives. That was for the future. For now, Russian society had scant respect for the human subject. [24]

Within such a climate of human devaluation, life in Russian peasant villages before the Revolution was characterised by enormous brutality, especially for dissident behaviour. Adulterous wives could be dragged naked through the village tied to a horse and cart. Maxim Gorky in the essay *"On the Russian Peasantry"* asked if the Revolution had not simply brought out the cruelty of the Russian people. Such cruelty was sustained by the violence they were used to, in the humiliations ordered by the Land Captains, very public and very violent. [25] A practising physician, Chekhov protested that corporal punishment: *"coarsens and brutalises not only the offenders but also those who execute punishments and those who are present at it."*

Is there a link with the present? Disturbing pictures of the violence that was routine within military training has often scandalised Russia. The Russian Army has been characterised by brutality towards conscripts.[26] Post-communist Russia is not a kind place. Ruthlessness and police thuggery are regular features on the landscape.[27] Brutalisation is a phenomenon that seems a normal way of doing things in that culture; normal in that respectful communication seems out of place; no less disturbing for being accepted in many ways of life. Cultures of violence are reproduced from one generation to the next. The black crime rate, both black-on-black and black-on-white, is increasing.

They are sustained by rude, crude narratives, bidden or unbidden, taught and sometimes spoken. Traumatic roots of violence lie in harm visited upon us, resulting in an injured psyche that looks for redress. A wounded soul gathers justification from other wounded souls, an eye for an eye.

NORTH AMERICA

Violence is written into the order of things. Its sinister muscle is to do with searching for redress.

In the United States, violence against indigenous women has reached unprecedented levels on tribal lands and in Alaska Native villages. More than four in five American Indian and Alaska Native women have experienced violence, and more than one in two have experienced sexual violence. Alaska Native women continue to suffer the highest rate of forcible sexual assault and have reported rates of domestic violence up to 10 times higher than in the rest of the United States. American Indians and Alaska Natives are 2.5 times as likely to experience violent crimes and at least twice as likely to experience rape or sexual assault crimes compared to all other races.[28] American Indian women living on Indian reservations experience unique challenges that intensify the epidemic of violence against them. On some reservations, indigenous women are murdered at more than ten times the national average.[29] Native children exposed to violence suffer rates of post-traumatic stress disorder three times higher than the rest of the general population. Until recently, discrimination in law has meant that Indian nations were unable to prosecute non-Indians, who reportedly commit the vast majority (96%) of sexual violence against Native women.[30] The history of the treatment of tribes is replete with examples of violence, displacement, and forced assimilation, all of which have contributed to historical trauma for many individuals. The historical trauma of being disconnected from their tribal roots has contributed to the mental health, substance abuse, and domestic violence issues of concern among many American Indian communities.[31] This is cumulative emotional trauma spanning generations of American Indian and Alaskan Natives.

What do we say about this? The Red Stain of Cain has spilled over into the north of North America. Violence is how we do things. Its sickening legacy is a sick soul, mental ill-health, disease of mind.

It is both tragedy and travesty that Christian history has a dark past that has not yet had its day. Its callous disregard for people's lives shows a chasm between doctrine and practice that reaches to heaven. The USA, known for its religious and social conservatism, has witnessed enormous violence at the junction where religiosity and slavery met. This shapes attitudes today. Underpinned by religious faith, a racial caste system defined its existence until the Civil War. It found its aftermath in the gruesome story of national domestic violence in the form of lynch mobs, an ugly episode in its history. The most unsettling reality of this lynching is the degree to which White evangelical Americans embraced it, not as an uncomfortable necessity or a way of maintaining order, but as a joyous moment and a family day out: *'Girls giggled as the flies fed on the blood that dripped from the Negro's nose,'* as one newspaper reported in 1930. [32] As W.E.B. Du Bois warned at the beginning of the twentieth century, long-term impact on a child growing up in places of endemic violence would be devastating. Conditions in White supremacy States perpetuated a violent cycle that would spin far into the future.

IT'S THE SYSTEM

Entrenched attitudes form within a collective memory. 'This is who we are' becomes a subculture. White responses to any demand for sharing political power, for justice, were shaped by a theology of individual and personal salvation. In this way, the system doesn't need to be questioned. This goes far beyond individuals failing to do something about excesses. Personal acts are not a sufficient reason for bringing how we do things into scrutiny. People come together as the basis for collective action. It is not that people talk together and now decide on a course of action. Their minds were infected.

Take the manhunt for Broadus Miller in 1927, a black man wrongly convicted for the rape of a white woman in South Carolina. A seventeen-year-old boy, John Alex Mull, was walking home from church *"when a car came tearing around the corner at the courthouse, screeched to a halt, and several men jumped out with guns. They opened the back door of the car and dragged a man out by his feet, which were wrapped in bloody rags."* It was Broadus Miller. Nearly half a century later, Mull still marvelled at the fervour of the "angry mob" who had wanted to desecrate a corpse. *"It makes me wonder just how thick our veneer of civilization really is"*.[33] An onlooker was disgusted. "Some people are such good Christians. They go to church every Sunday—twice every Sunday, and Wednesday they go to prayer meeting," a local black man told a researcher. "But they've got so much hate. Now, how could you hate somebody and be a Christian?"[34]

And all this was scarcely challenged by evangelical or other churches through to the 1950s.

The church colluded with any form of so-called 'justice' in that situation, and in dark episodes such as the Rwandan genocide more recently. Wretchedly, the blind spot in the history of such violence is that theology and psychology mix with social dynamics. All three must combine in order to unravel terrifying cultures of violence that disfigure the sacred cause or social dream they seem to serve.

BOYS WILL BE BOYS

In case this book is perceived to be aimed at White guilt, let's take a very different example.

It was a crime that captured national attention. In the idyllic suburb of Glen Ridge, New Jersey, four of the town's most popular high school athletes were accused of raping a retarded young woman while nine of their teammates watched. What went wrong in this perfect American town?

"The Glen Ridge Rape and the Secret Life of the Perfect Suburb" is a case study of boys in a New Jersey community who were regarded as 'jocks', adored by the community because they were 'our guys', products of a national and local culture that reminded them constantly that, because they were white, straight, privileged and especially athletes, they could get away with anything. These were, after all, their guys.[35]

Glen Ridge was a community always on the verge of violence, whether against girls, women, blacks or non-athletic boys - anyone who was not quite as privileged as themselves. The hyper-masculinised toughness was exhibited by what were known as 'jocks'- white middle-class athletic lads. For these high school boys, *"the essence of jockdom was a practiced show of contempt for kids and teachers alike. They tried to humiliate any wimpy guy who got in their way, but they reserved their best shots for girls who ignored them or dared stand up to them"* (p 111).

The Jocks didn't invent the idea of mistreating young women. The ruling clique of teenagers adhered to a code of behavior that mimicked, distorted and exaggerated the values of the adult world around them. These values extolled 'winners' and denigrated 'losers'. Glen Ridge placed the elite kids - the kids with masculine good looks, the kids who stood out on the playing field - on a pedestal. It was teenage culture where girls were frequently abused and humiliated at destructive, sybaritic parties. It was a town that carried on embracing its celebrity athletes despite the havoc they created. These were "our guys."

How do you sustain this particular way of speaking (discourse)? Numerous girls and other young women showed uncritical support for the four boys eventually indicted for the rape (ranging from current girlfriends to a 28 year old jurist who wept when a Defense attorney described how unfortunate and distressing all this was for the boys). The primary way of upholding the narrative was, however, the culture of high school sport with all its emphasis on competition, winning and achievement. Lefkowitz shows how this discourse is a common thread in sex crimes in the West:

"In the community where they grew up and which celebrated their athletic achievements; in their isolation from women and their evolving attitude towards girls; in their fascination with voyeurism and pornography and in their actual treatment of young women; and finally in their choice of victim - in all these

respects, the Glen Ridge Jocks resembled the contemporary profile of other privileged and popular male groups, accused of committing sexual assaults of women" (p248-49).

This broad social context of misogyny and male privilege with its hyper-masculinised style was *"a heavy burden for a kid to carry through adolescence"* It blocked the boys from growing their own masculine identity, "forcing them to develop their own grotesque version of manhood" (p114). The community ensured compliance in this type of domineering masculinity. Only White Anglo Saxons (wasps) owned homes. The community protected its athletes from any form of accountability. A litany of behaviors had been written off as boyish pranks - from public nudity and masturbation in school to destroying a young woman's home. The police, school and parents maintained things by disclaiming, 'boys will be boys'.

These are complex, many-layered matters. The noxious weeds of violence are tangled, interwoven things. They thrive in communities, be they unchosen communities of the family or neighbourhoods.

Violence is often seen as essentially an individual phenomenon rather than moulded by social processes that have shaped the experience of those involved with cultures of violence. Do we have a theology of systemic violence, created in rough conditions where rough ways are normal? The breeding grounds that normalise violence will have to be decontaminated one day.

Our last example is class-based.

NOT SO TALL STORIES FROM THE FRONT-LINE

In Bellfield Junior School Birmingham, two thirds of the children are classed as disadvantaged. [36] Scores of children have special needs. Situated in the Northfield area and the well-known Bourneville estate, teaching is only a part of a school's role. Bellfield is beset by a crippling pastoral care burden.

Desperate parents begging for help for food or pay the electricity bill, children coming to school hungry, dirty or with no coat bruises, mothers with debt problems, fathers with drug addictions – children grow up tough round there. One in three Bellfield's children are on the vulnerable register. Gun gangs are just the start. A nearby head-teacher apologises for pungent smell of cannabis in the classroom. Because parents smoke so much at home, it gets on their clothes. With social services and children's services also decimated, schools are expected to backfill. Which school will tell a child who has just lost his mother he or she will have to wait 6 months to see a counsellor? The last OFSTED inspection took place when there were police on the roof because of a raid on a house over the road. Classroom doors that don't shut, teaching assistants the school can't afford- this is grim.

Yet it doesn't stop dedicated staff working with some very enthusiastic children. One young lady is being encouraged strongly to go and get some qualifications in order to make something of herself. She shrugs. 'Either that or I open my legs'. Someone has to keep telling these children they can fly'.

The children grow up tough. Or as a former resident related on social media, *"I was finally liberated two years ago when I moved to Halesowen – another town, but nothing on the scale of Northfields. We found ourselves separated from the mainstream as most of the houses were bought, but it didn't stop them cutting through from time to time to steal badges off cars and car stereo systems. It had to be the only street on Earth where nearly every car was missing a badge! On the opposite side of Bell Hill was the Ley Hill*

Estate – once proposed to be the 5th worst council estate in Europe."37

From the old drunks who sit on the bench outside the shopping centre, shouting abuse at poor folks who go about their daily routines, to the ACC (Anti-College-Crew), who dress up in tracksuits going around picking fights with anyone who happens to glance in their direction, this is grim. In days gone by, Victoria Common Park was where you play football and watch bowls. Now it is home to drunks and drug addicts who congregate in large numbers, leaving bottles, cans and needles lying about."[38]

And now comes an official Report by inspectorates that include UK education regulator OFSTED, the Care Quality Commission and HMI Constabulary. It showed that abused children lack protection. About 15-20% of girls and 7-8% of boys are estimated to be victims of abuse. Two thirds take place in the home. Young people who exhibit harmful behaviour themselves are too often treated only as perpetrators of abuse rather than being investigated to see if they have been victims themselves.[39]

The inescapable conclusion we draw from this assortment of circumstances in which people resort to violence is that violence is home-grown. It is shaped by the subculture of that group; be it a family system, a neighbourhood, a gang or a political movement. People don't generally wake up and decide to be violent. They are shaped and moulded such that agency and social structure combine.

There are seedbeds for cultures of violence. Violence takes place in a system or a micro-culture. That is not to excuse moral responsibility, but it does mean that it is not just about individuals lashing out. It is situational. To be sure violence draws on the destructive tendency that humans find in themselves when they pierce the darkness within themselves. Yet people deploy violence because it is their way of communicating. Like all communication, it is embedded in language and narrative. 'This is how we do things' goes the narrative. And like all narratives, it can be taught, learned and unlearned. A version of faith only in terms of a personal link with Jesus offers no theological resources for addressing this beyond seeing it as individual sin, selfishness or cruelty. Correcting that is part of the urgent task to develop anti-bodies that can react against the virus of violence.

CHAPTER THREE
UNDERSTANDING THE SEPARATENESS

"The Muslims have come to conquer Europe. I believe there will be civil war in three years time. We can either surrender and let them take over our country - rape our country - or prepare ourselves for resistance, that's what we are doing now".40

"My instructors told me that this is how I can serve God, by attacking Britain and America"- a young British Jihadist in Afghanistan".41

The globe is still shrouded with the curious but deadly face of racial violence.

Curious because only 10 genes of the 50,000 that make us distinctly human had anything to do with skin colour. Skin-colour was barely skin-deep. Race science had been exposed as a sham. Yet light was might. For centuries, light-skinned people thought they were superior with natural right to dominate and rule. Because of race, whole populations were systematically exploited and exterminated down the years.

What is vital now is for high quality social analysts to combine with activists and show how a new world becomes possible and what it looks like: one where every life really does matter. The basis of racism is different levels of value placed on different lives by society.

"Viruses of the Mind" was a term coined by Richard Dawkins. It opened up a new science of the meme. Now it takes on a terrifying, new significance as so many are saying that there is a virus of racism that was in people's minds. If that is so, antibodies are needed. Here's how.

A new significance? Hardly that, when considering racism has been around for as long as people dominated and enslaved each other. Pervasive concentrations of power seep through the very language we use about ethnicity, gender, age or intact bodies. White privilege and exceptionalism shapes standards and debates about what tone to use and what is correct.[42]

During the Pandemic, we have seen the spectre of America burning. The London and similar protests have been vibrant with a sense of that simmering sense of injustice boiling over with the revolting death of George Floyd. I remember well the sheer sense of rage that engulfed the American street after the assassination of one of Martin Luther King in April 1968. Current events have strong resonance with that – except now we have Smart camera phones to record and transmit images faster than Covid.

Inequality matters because it gets under the skin. It digs into the role that our sense of value or its absence plays in human action, generating psycho-social effects as well as lack of cash and poverty of power. But racism doesn't just get UNDER the skin, though it does that to be sure. Racism is an attitude of mind that shapes both perpetrators and victims. Steve Biko, the black South African leader who died under Apartheid-era, brutality diagnosed a submissive state of mind and lack of self-respect as illness. We collude with the definition of ourselves that others impose upon us.[43] Racism is inscribed ON the skin

It is a curiosity of history that white people in the time of Queen Elizabeth 1 used to prize their skin colour so much they would rub whiteness into it. Now a suntan is a mark of health and vitality. It is though a tragic curiosity that so much misery has been played out on the surface of human beings. A casual observer looks at this central phenomenon of history with complete astonishment. If the configuration of genitals and gender has evoked so much historical agitation, how come that, in addition it has been the colour of skin, and not just the colour of money that has so sharply divided the human consciousness? Who was responsible for this? If the answer is, 'we did it', then who are the 'we' who subjected our fellow men and women to such unimaginable cruelty and abuse? Why would we do it?

And who determined that skin should witness such mortal combat? Who set the pattern that the darker the skin, the greater the inferior status? Racism has been so deadly because it combines the sharp divides of history into a lethal challenge. This is all the more surprising since 'race' is a largely artificial construct as is 'religion', with which it is closely intertwined. Do either actually exist as the basis for pernicious cultural inequalities? Not really.

Martin Luther King's sad adage has been much quoted in recent days – 'in the final analysis, violence is the language of the unheard'. The sad reality is that, though overt racism and violence towards ethnic minorities is rare thankfully, different treatments and attitudes remain. Our minds have been infected. We didn't know we were carrying a virus. It is called implicit bias. But then again, so can antibodies become ingrained: part of the body politic.

The lens used by the evangelical Right that undergirds White supremacy in America is utterly smudged. All such people at present see are anarchists threatening our moral order. That reaction is no doubt due to the question of identity. 'Who we are, our way of life' is being threatened. But where is the lens that can see more deeply and more wisely to understand the outrage and the demand for justice? How are so many so blind? Just like Islamic radicalism requires theological de-construction, so does this – urgently! Implicit bias needs calling out.

Education has to be the great antidote to inequality everywhere. Wanted: an early warning system about devaluation of human life; especially of those who are different. Antibodies need to build up.

Those days were passing. A black President had been elected in the US. But the original sin remained. In the West, a significant minority of young people expressed dislike of other groups. Boys were more likely than girls to feel this way. Muslims, Asians and Iraqis were potential terrorists; refugees and asylum-seekers received preferential treatment; newly arrived communities were not entitled to live there. They should be in their own country. They don't obey the rules; they look down on white people. Black communities were part of the crime scene. Some black and minority ethnic young people thought white people were arrogant racists. Both were converted into objects.

Dislike or fear was still being mixed with pre-formed pictures in a deadly brew. It was startling how easily the people had learned prejudice, how easily they held opinions about others not based on the facts; an ideas suite about a group of people and how they behave, based on nothing more than their physical appearance. There were the in-groups and the out-groups, those at the centre and those kept at the margins, the valued and the devalued, the valuers and those who could not name their fate. Racism reduced people to an object, less than a person, devaluing and demonising those who were different. Antisemitism or white supremacy was a virulent plague that still erupted. The alien group was cast in the role of enemy: not just object but evil object.

It had been mainly the light skinned people who had taken on themselves the right to rule. White and light is might and right! But it was not just light, white people doing this. The Mundrucu tribe of Brazil divided the world into themselves and "Pariwat"- all the rest, who were seen both as fair game and animals. Fear and mistrust must be aroused. Scapegoats gave a group cohesion. Aggressive feelings were deflected on to dummy enemies in a way that strengthened the group through fear. Racism and xenophobia were exacerbated by insecurity about national identity. The KKK thrived on maintaining the purity of the race and white supremacy.

2

Violence is an act of violation, a desecration of what is sacred, the citadel of the soul. A spiral is set up; a human tornado that feeds off desecration and in turn engenders further violation. *"I feel crap"* is often part of the inner psychological environment that sets people up to doing things to compensate for the deficit, to relieve the pain. Brian Keenan's five-year captivity in the Lebanon drew powerful insights about the inter-play of such desecration that violence represents in presenting a devalued self. *"Cruelty and fear are man-made, and men who perpetrate them are ruled by them. Such men are only half-made things. They live out their unresolved lives by attempting to destroy anything that challenges the void in themselves"*.[44]

Miroslav Volf articulates the powerful, contagious and destructive evil he labels 'exclusion'. This is paradigmatic, driving communities apart. It is something the church colludes with if it does not distance us from our own culture, and hence echoes reigning opinions and mimic its practices.[45] The original sin of exclusion entails cutting the bonds and separating from the other, who does not emerge in the pattern of interdependence but as an enemy, an inferior being who must either be assimilated or subjugated. Beginning with exclusion from a situated self, it leads to exclusion from communities with its terrible culmination in washing away the filth of the ethnic body, the cleansing that pollutes the ethnic space. The result is a world without the other.[46]

Ethnic cleansing and genocide may be denounced strongly as barbaric defacing the diving in the human, but in their western equivalents of segregation, holocaust and apartheid, the church has been complicit (as Volf argues, because polarised distance has not been overcome yet).

Multiculturalism had thrown up any amount of power struggles or collective negotiations of cultural, ethnic and racial differences. To add to this on-going experiment in social engineering, throw in asylum seekers and casting Islam as the enemy.

Such tribalism has constantly evoked the unleashing of the primeval murder of Cain.

Matthew 23v35 reads like an A-Z of murder.

From the blood of righteous Abel to the blood of a man called Zechariah, innocent lives were shed in a holy cause. The first martyr to the last (as recorded in the Old Testament in 2 Chronicles 24v21) fell victim to a descent into violence. It is true that there were mixed motives in these two accounts. The blood of Zechariah was shed through stoning because the people were living in an age of apostasy and couldn't cope with the challenge he brought to return to God's ways. This son of Jehoida the priest (the name 'Barachiah' in Matthew 23 is almost certainly a copyist error) was stoned to death through faithful witness to the covenant God. Even as he lay dying, his blood was crying out for vengeance (a rough word that rasps our sensitivities, though it speaks of come-back on the perpetrators that they must not be allowed to escape the consequences). How very different to the stoning of Stephen, the first of a long line of Christian martyrs that continues into our day. That day the stoners had blood on their hands as well as rocks. Their violence was reflected back in his love. "Lord, lay not this sin to their charge' (Acts 7v58).

The story of Cain and Abel is a deeply instructive paradigm of a descent into violence.

It does not start as many flare ups do in our world, where people have been trapped in a cycle of violence, an eye for an eye with blinding repetition. This is not Cain dealing death and murder in the only language Abel will understand. Cain is both originator and perpetrator. How do we understand this primal act, so potent in consequences? Cain's name in Hebrew means 'to create' or "to acquire". This speaks of possession, of consuming, taking. It is a stance that causes separation. Sex, religion, land, property, money – all are seized with a definite root desire, the desire to possess. Abel's name means vapour, vanity, nothingness, a comment on the murder that negates him and lack of offspring that ensued. But perhaps he can also represent a balance to the poison of possessiveness, an ability to give freely, to let go, to simply be or not be.

Born the son of a Mafia hitman, Leorco Chindamo seemed destined for a life of violence. His mother Paquita split from her husband Massimo after he threw her out of a window, breaking both her legs. His father was later jailed for 15 years for throwing acid in someone's face. The terrified mother brought her three sons to North London where Chindamo was soon making a name for himself in the only way he knew. By the age of 12, known at school as a cry baby, he was arming himself with a knuckle-duster. By 14, he had moved on to baseball bat and knife and followed his older brother into a gang named Venom. As an initiation, new recruits were brutally attacked by older members. The gang, which included Filipinos, Colombians and West Indians, modelled itself on the Chinese Triads. It began terrorising and robbing other children. Chindamo stabbed a London Headteacher, Philip Lawrence, to death as he tried to stop the gang attacking a 13-year-old with a metal pole. The gang was later responsible for the merciless rape of an Austrian tourist, left for dead on a canal towpath.[47] Charco was trying to act big in the only world he knew. Cultures of violence produce imitative behavior. Aggressive modelling bred aggression: here is *"seed-corn for intergenerational violence"*[48]

Commenting some years later on the murder of her husband, Frances Lawrence said, *"it's the separation of human beings from each other, we don't value one another in the way we used to perhaps. Everyone needs to be valued. Chin-*

damo needs to be valued as much as my son".49

Cain had become separate from Abel. When God spoke to him directly after the deed had been done, Cain didn't acknowledge he had responsibility for his brother. Abel had still been his brother, but something had happened that led to fratricide. Something had happened that led to disconnection, to being separate from Abel. Abel had become foreign to him to the extent that his own kid brother had to die. How had it come to that? Mutuality had already died. From having been the little chap he played with and protected, Abel was at that point 'the other'; an 'other' whose life had to be extinguished.

The narrative is sparse when it comes to how the antecedents shaped Cain's attitude to Abel. Cain was the first born. Along came a baby brother. We can only go as far as the narrative will allow, but it is going too far to ponder that there was a displacement going on. Maybe Cain felt usurped by this little kid brother. There is perhaps a clue to the emotional tangle when God said to Cain, 'if you do well, will you not be accepted?' (Genesis 4v7) We read that with respect to the offering Cain made that somehow fell short, but what does it say about the way he was looking for acceptance that also fell short? Acceptance is the cry of the human heart and Cain did not feel in any way that his offering was accepted. Maybe that is because he did not feel acceptable in himself.

Yahweh re-assures Cain that to be accepted, he too could DO well. Perhaps the problem is not one of DOING but BEING. Cain was very likely walking the same road that many would follow. Actions take place, words are spoken and those on the receiving end feel suddenly that it is not what they are doing that is on the line. At stake is who they are. The boss, a partner holding the reins of power, a teacher, a policeman in a racialised society can say things that point out deficiencies in what we are doing or not doing. Within seconds the scene has shifted. It is not merely an action that is on trial, but the person who is hearing that message. Doing has become translated into being. You yourself are under sharp question. Being and doing have swapped places.

Whether anything of this familiar pattern is going on, Cain is on the line. The only way he can extinguish this threat to his being is to rid himself of the cause of that threat. He thinks it is solely about him but about something he has done, or not done. Anger brews. Cain is very angry (4v5).

'Sin lies in wait', Cain is warned. A commentator on Genesis observes that *"the comparison of sin with a beast of prey lying before the door is strange as is the purely figurative use of 'door' as in 'door of the heart'... it is only a very short distance from the inner emotion to the act".*50 Sin is an objective power, a beast growling at the door waiting eagerly to take possession of Cain though he can curb it.

Some ancient scrolls have the words 'let us go out to the fields' in v8 as, deaf both to God and the menacing beast, Cain lures Abel to his doom. As with the first sin, God is on the spot immediately, but not to ask, 'where are you?' Instead God asks, 'where is your brother?' (4v9)

Cain expelled Abel. It is the first act of sibling rivalry. It is in such ways that 'the other' becomes a threat that cannot be tolerated. Writ large, this sibling rivalry is the story of racial violence.

For the theologian - sociologist Rene Girard, the innocent victim whose murder is crucial for society has its progenitor in Abel, the first victim, murdered by Cain, who then founds the first culture. The basis of this culture is sacrifice - the violence that expels violence. Everyone else joins together.51

It is deeply instructive that Cain did not at first sacrifice anything. The offering of blood was made by sheep-rearing (and shearing) Abel, not farmer Cain. Then it was that Cain made an offering – Abel! His own brother was sacrificed on the altar: the altar of brooding, the altar of jealousy.

What was it that tipped Cain over the edge from surly brooding into third degree savagery?

"You too can be accepted!" The longing for acceptance was an ontological misreading. He could have done some things, and all would be well. But Cain felt he himself did not measure up and was below the radar of acceptance. It was not just that what Cain brought was a one dollar offering compared with that of munificent Abel, Cain himself had become second grade.

3

This goes to the heart of the theory of violence and atonement developed here– an exchange of value. To recover his own worth and acceptance from the perils of demerit, Abel the scapegoat, the focus of Cain's misfortune and repository of greater value and acceptability must be sacrificed. Only then can compensation be made, and a transfer of status effected.

It has strong resonance with contemporary violence. Christianity has never fully confronted its violent past. To take one powerful example with huge echoes, the voice of the black guy George Floyd, focus of the storm of civil rights protest in the lockdown America of 2020, is hoarse from asking if anyone hears. It is salutary to remember that the dominant forms of white evangelicalism were shaped in response to slavery, often to defend it biblically. Black skin was regarded as the accursed mark of Cain. The religion of 'the lost cause' led to Jim Crow laws. At the same time, a pre-millennial theology led to a focus on individualistic salvation associated with an unassailable sense of religious purity. Racist bias that is invisible, systemic and endemic urgently requires this to be re-visited, despite the lament of large segments of white society more concerned about tranquillity and the status quo than about justice, equality, and humanity. Violence is about hatred; it is about fear.

This leads to the anguished questions of God.

The real mark of Cain lies not in black skin, but in those anguished questions – 'Where is your brother?' 'What have you done?' We have, in the words of James Cone, failed to "hear the cry of black blood." We have failed one of the first and most basic demands of scripture – to be our brother's and sister's keeper (Genesis 4:9-10).

The differences and dissonances associated with Cain's sin have come to this deafness. He has made himself the centre and now everything is permitted. He is not being sarcastic. Apparent truculence is in fact ignorance. Cain has either never appreciated the importance of human solidarity – or maybe he had, and the bond that united him with his brother had eventually been overridden and torn asunder.

In some contemporary Jewish Midrash, Rabbi Jay Asher Levine makes the point that the text does not reveal what Cain said to Abel. Given the biblical context, we can assume that jealousy is at play. The plain sense of the story seems to be that Cain, confused, hurt, and angry about God's preference for Abel's offering, lured his brother into the field – a location associated with vulnerable isolation elsewhere in the Torah– and rendered Abel incapable of ever offering anything again.[52]

Understanding the separateness requires us human beings to grasp how they come to see another as 'other', someone with whom they have severed mutuality and responsibility. For centuries, people have depersonalised or depreciated the other because of race, class, gender, disability, sexuality and age. These set up a power imbalance often based upon grotesque inequality in access to wealth and ability to change our situation. The disability movement has followed a similar trajectory to other disadvantaged groups. Disability is now widely seen as shaping social experience. The main solution is to remove discriminatory treatment and prejudiced thinking. This is not going to equalise the situation for people in a post-industrial society. Social attitudes are not the only reality, however. People are disabled not only by the way they are treated, but also by barriers to being part of society which prevent their being able to fit in by dint of their health impairment. The health problems generate limitations but so too is the way that disability generates health problems.[53]

Similarly, mental illness is often misunderstood and gives rise to differing scales of how people fit in. Those affected are devalued; routinely shrouded in prejudice and fear.[54] Dementia, the mental plague of our time, can be a de-personalising condition in which its sufferers, usually the elderly, are lost before their time. Dignity can creep away along with rationality. Observers can write them off.

Ageism too demonstrates a social ill rooted in de-personalisation. The old are shunted off. The fear conceals hatred, something we would rather push away outside the boundaries of self and of society for it is the fear of death.[55] Even Freud remarked that at 50 one is too old for psychoanalysis![56]

4

According to the ethical philosopher Levinas, whenever a human face calls out to me, I can only respond with the words, "Here I am ..." We might wonder, "Why should I feel responsible in the presence of another person's face?" But that is precisely why Cain asked of God, "Am I my brother's keeper?" He was a man who had yet to learn. He had small conception of what it meant to be responsible for another human being.[57]

Was his response sincere? It is not so much that he lacked a conscience: his remorse will see to that. Cain was out of touch with his own humanity. He didn't understand that the human face is special because it bears a trace of God in each person. Yet, God held Cain accountable—not because of any verbal commandments instructing how not to behave toward his brother. Emmanuel Levinas puts "the face of the Other" at the centre of his ethical philosophy.[58] *"Encounter with the other consists in the fact that, despite the extent of my domination and his slavery, I do not possess him."* "The face is present in its refusal to be contained." It "overflows." It is infinite. "To be in relation with the other face to face is to be unable to kill." The Other is precisely what makes us uniquely human. Through this, speech and discourse are possible and, with it, religion, politics, and philosophy.[59]

"The epiphany of the face is ethical," writes Levinas in an extended meditation on "Thou shalt not kill," which Levinas does not see as a command emanating from a God in the clouds, but as an invocation radiating from the human face, that makes possible humanity and freedom."[60]

Levinas had re-presented Sartre's argument that the ego is born of self-knowledge, triggered by the gaze of the Other in a way that assaults the self and provokes resistance. Not so, Levinas asserts. The self is born as we stretch ourselves towards the Other. *"To be human means to live as if one were not a being among beings...It is I who support the Other and am responsible for him"*. The sociologist Zygmunt Bauman quotes Levinas with approval about Cain's response to God in Genesis (the primitive act of violence) *"Ontologically, each one of us is separate from any other... something must happen to bring us together, into a kind of relationship in which the question, 'where is your brother?' Will sound nat-*

ural... Inter-subjective relation is non-symmetrical relation. In this sense I am responsible for the 'Other' without waiting for reciprocity, were I to die for it. Reciprocity is his affair. "The Other is not a force but a face ... postmodern ethics re-admits Other as neighbor."[61]

For Levinas, it is not the alien quality that allows us to treat others in such ways. It is the desire to destroy the difference that makes torture and murder possible. Destroying the face of the Other, we destroy our own face—torture and murder are just as self-annihilating as any bomb could ever be.

Researchers have come to realize just how much human beings matter to each other. Trauma is a disturbingly sudden cessation of human interaction. The link between our capacity to be violent and our need for each other is intriguing and important.[62] A cycle of rejection is set up in peer interactions and with teachers. With increased rejection, a child develops a sense of self or other people as 'bad'. This leads to violence. The rubbished become rubbisher. At some point, people see others as vulnerable and fit to be trashed. The cycle goes round and round. Can you get off?

CHAPTER FOUR
THE LONGEST HATRED AND THE DESCENT INTO DARKNESS

"WHO ARE YOU?
A NUMBER.
YOUR NAME?
GONE. BLOWN AWAY. INTO THE SKY. LOOK
UP THERE. THE SKY IS BLACK, BLACK WITH
NAMES"[63]

"Remember only that I was innocent and, just like you, mortal on that day. I too had a face marked by rage, by pity and joy, by quite simply. a human face."- Benjamin Fondana, murdered at Auschwitz August 1944[64].

"I do not know what a Jew is. I only know what a human being is" – Pastor Andre Trocme, a French pastor who helped hide Jewish people in his village in 1942).[65]

The Covid-crisis was a signpost to a profound crisis in our civilisation which the devastation to health and economic contraction was a marker of. Antisemitism and all de-humanising attitudes like racism were an epidemic as pernicious as Covid. Viruses like these requires strong social antibodies.

Staying with Protestantism, the record of antisemitism baffles observers from a different time. Somehow, Martin Luther managed to combine total allegiance to Jesus with an implacable hostility to the Jewish people which Jesus emerged from. His treatise of 1543 runs to 65,000 words. 'On the Jews and their lies' describes Jews as *"base, whoring people, that is no people of God, and their boast of lineage, circumcision and law must be accounted filth."*[66] In shocking texts that featured in the infamous Nuremberg rallies, Luther urged that Jewish schools and houses should be burned, religious writings should be confiscated and that Jewish people should be required to work as rural slaves. It was nearly twenty years since he had urged similar treatment be meted out against the peasants who revolted in 1524. The fact is that those who were outside of Christian society had little value, but this was also true of those who were at the bottom rung of the ladder of social hierarchy.

But our other examplar of the tragic gulf between rhetoric and reality is the well-trodden attitude which has made the Catholic Church especially open to attack. We leave on one side the on-going controversy about the role of Pope Pius XII regarding the Holocaust. The church's role in setting up schools and hospitals has been notable (though many schools have since been sharply critiqued as being vehicles for abuse). Catholic social teaching has remained as a lofty statement of ideals, a rich treasury of wisdom about building a just society. The dignity of the human person has also been a key theme of the Catholic worker movements. It became the starting point of the way the Worker's Catholic Action denounced the capitalist system as inhumane. This body of teaching is grounded in the notion that humans have an immense value. The example of Abbe Pierre is but one of many. Founder of the Emmaus Movement in Paris in 1949, in the war he had smuggled Jews to Switzerland and went on to launch a labour movement that focussed on the plight of the poor and their need for housing. A loan company and home-buying co-operatives grew out of this, as did an institute for action against world hunger. All Abbe Pierre's work stemmed from wanting to be the voice of the voiceless and to enable human dignity in a world where 'poverty is dumb, and power is blind'.[67]

The totality of this tradition is expressed in Papal, Conciliar, and Episcopal documents. In summary, there are strong themes at the heart of the Catholic social tradition. In 'The Life and Dignity of the Human Person' - [68] the Catholic Church proclaims that human life is sacred and that the dignity of the human person is the foundation of a moral vision for society. This belief is the foundation of all the principles of its social teaching. Yet it is a matter of historical record that there has been another reality.

As I write these words, his successor but one has just announced the beatification of Pope John Paul 11nd, whose superstar reign spanned 27 years at the end of the twentieth century. In a previous beatification fifteen years earlier, Pope John Paul 11 declared that Archbishop Stepinac of Zagreb was one of the outstanding figures of the Catholic Church.

The Vatican's role in maintaining the independence of Croatia in the 1990's echoed the role that Ante Pavelic had 50 years earlier as fascist leader of the Utashi terrorist movement and then leader of the Independent State of Croatia, the ISC. When Pavelic took office, he said "within Croatia, there can be no compromise between the Croatian people and others who are not pure Croats; Utashi must extinguish all trace of such people". Archbishop Stepinac recommended that the Holy See immediately recognise the Utashi regime. Pope Pius XII appointed him military chaplain, received Pavelic in May 1941 and the Vatican continued to maintain close ties with the Utashi. A million or more people were killed; at least 350,000 non-Catholics and 250,000 were forcibly converted to Catholicism. The Croatian Minister of Education and Culture, Mile Budak, declared that *"the basis for the Utashi movement is religion. For minorities such as the Serbs, Jews and Gypsies, we have three million bullets. We will kill a part of the Serbs. Others we will deport and the rest we will force to accept the Roman Catholic Religion. Thus, the new Croatia will be rid of all Serbs in order to be 100% Catholic within ten years."*[69]

The Franciscan Friar Dionizije was head of the regime's Religious Department. He said *"In those regions beyond, I arranged for everything to be cleared away, everything from a chicken to an old man... it is not sinful nowadays to kill even a seven year-old child, if it is standing in the way of our Utashi order"*. A Catholic priest was appointed to serve with every Utashi military unit. Stepinac never restrained the priests and friars who were actively involved, e.g. when a member of the Franciscan order, Friar Filopovic, was appointed commander of a camp at Jasenovac and admitted killing about a hundred inmates in this camp personally.[70] Stepinac was put on trial after the war and found guilty. Astonishingly, Pius XII made him a cardinal and excommunicated all those who had taken part in the trial. This was the man whose beatification was proclaimed in 1998.

The 1948 United Nations Declaration of Human Rights had been seen as smacking too much of liberal individualism. It took 15 years for "Pacem in Terris" to be issued by John 23rd. Similar Declarations such as "Dignitatis Humanae" and "Guadium et Spes" committed the church to reject the status quo and the abuse of power that brought. "Gaudium et Spes" (The Church in the Modern World) focussed on a concept of dignity as underlying human rights. The church should embrace the poor, be on their side in the quest for freedom, peace and justice and stand up for the UN Declaration. Similarly, Nostra Aetate demonstrated that the church was determined to free itself from its historical stance.

Historically the church had opposed revolutions. There followed Christian involvement in revolutionary movements in Nicaragua, El Salvador and Guatemala, taking sides on political movements aimed at power in order to carry out revolutionary programmes. The objectives have been economic transformation and democracy through violence as a means. The church had to ask itself if it should make an option not just 'for the poor', but 'on behalf of the poor' too. As Archbishop Romero said, 'There is no possible neutrality. We either serve the life of Salvadorans or we are accomplices in their death.'[71] The French philosopher Emmanuel Levinas attacked the powerful self-assertion implied in the modern subjectivity of the person. Human beings become real humans when they are converted from their subjective assertion and their will to power to accept the face of the Other. The theme of the face of the Other developed by Levinas was accepted implicitly by the Catholic Bishops at Puebla. What is missing, he said, is not the private acknowledgement of the voiceless but their public acknowledgement, entering into public awareness. The cause of the voiceless was taken up at Puebla and Medellin.

This reflected a new sense of solidarity with the Latin American reality. *"We recognise that we Christians, for want of fidelity to the gospel, have contributed to the present unjust situation through our words and attitudes, our silence and our inaction,"* said Bishops in the closing statement of the 36th Peruvian Episcopal Conference in 1969.

"Pacem in Terris" contained a list of human rights virtually identical with the UN Declaration, with one important exception. Certain duties corresponded to certain rights. Addressing the UN General Assembly in October 1979, Pope John Paul 11nd spoke on the subject of human rights and the fundamental importance of that 1948 Declaration. The death camps he had recently visited in Poland were a 'warning sign on the path of humanity today, in order that every kind of concentration camp everywhere may once and for all be done away with.' The Pope condemned the modern continuation of 'the various kinds of torture and oppression'. Throughout his papacy, he continued preaching a powerful message about human rights.

The reality was far more ambiguous. John Paul 11nd fully agreed that the church should defend human dignity. It was a strong theme. But the reality was continually compromised by the Catholic Church's accommodation with the ruling juntas that suited the Bishops well. As Romero pointed out, *"They believe in the security that gives them privileges, or that renders them apparent respect."* Romero's valiant but fruitless attempts to recruit John Paul 11 as an ally were dented by the latter's highly ambivalent attitude towards him, seeing him as manipulated by the left-wing.

The political influence of the Catholic Church in Latin America is well documented. The Vatican for instance supported Pinochet as a devout Roman Catholic. The attitude of Pius XII towards the holocaust remains deeply ambiguous but is also ground well trodden. The virus of antisemitism during the war was deeply held, for example by the saint Maximilian Kolbe, whose virulent antisemitism was of a piece with the way that Catholic clergy frequently proclaimed antisemitism, including someone like Josef

Kruszynski, who wrote in 1920, 'if the world is to be rid of the Jewish scourge, it will be necessary to exterminate them, down to the last one'.[72]

The role of the Catholic Church in the Rwandan genocide is less well known. As Robert Calderisi observes, its sins were often sins of omission, rather than commission, but they were grievous nevertheless. "We can't all be martyrs" one cleric pleaded. Some were far more ambiguous in colluding with the brutal suppression of the Tutu tribal peoples.[73] John Paul II made consistent pleas for killing to stop and to respect humanity but in, Rwanda, for example, his pleas were ignored. In a country that was 2/3rds Catholic, bishops, priests and nuns were perpetrators and ignored the Pope enjoying the Church's support. Within a year, the Pope denied any responsibility of the Church.

Although there has been so much progress in all peoples having equal dignity and worth and that such evils as bullying and racial discrimination (or any other kind) should be outlawed, there is so much to fight for. At this rate, it will take a hundred years to achieve gender parity. Violence in the home scars our world and indeed worsened significantly during the Emergency. We had some temporary respite from State-sponsored cruelty in such places as Syria, but the sickening spectacle of indiscriminate radical terrorism had little let-up. For sheer devilry, nothing can match the slaughter of Mums and massacre of the innocent new-borns in Kabul in May 2020. What kind of cause did that serve, or warped satisfaction did that bring? The imagination can only shudder, numbly.

The rejection of racism itself is both vital and rising. Vital because, unless the root of superior attitudes is exposed, lesser value will continue to be placed on some countless lives; rising because increasing numbers of people are seeing racism as a major problem in their societies. De-radicalising warped minds that have no sense of the sanctity of life, despite it being divine mandate, will take a bold mix of psychology and theology. It will take a theory of horror that can generate antibodies against the collusion of churches with nationalisms or tribal identity, or in Islam, against hijackers.

2

"Throw your dice and move your smiling Aryan piece around the board. Then start rounding up the Jewish pieces. They are easily recognisable. You can't miss them. They are the nasty, grisly counters that can be found on various squares where they linger. When you have found six such pieces, take them to the collection point and maybe you will be the winner!"

This was a board game for the entire family to enjoy. It was produced in 1938 and forms a collection of Nazi artefacts, books and cuttings that are now part of the Wiener Library in London, the institution that began documenting the Nazis in the 1920's. It was all part of the cultural products that acclimatised the most enlightened nation on earth to be instrumental in mass murder. How could the country at the epicentre of European civilisation and philosophy go down this dark path?

Did it start when Jewish people waited in lines after the train pulled in to Auschwitz, shuffling forward to where SS guards divided them into groups marked for destruction or (temporary) survival? Did it start one stage earlier when those facing deportation were herded on to those trains, often used for transporting cattle, crammed into suffocating, in-sanitary conditions that degraded them - human beings reduced to the level of cattle, stripped of humanity, completely de-humanised?

Did it start earlier when Jewish people were stripped of

their status as citizens of Nazi Germany by the infamous Nuremberg laws in 1935? Or when racial prejudice against the Jewish people (antisemitism) raised its ugly head in Germany, to find urgent expression in the politics of Adolf Hitler?

The root of the mass murder of Jewish people in the Second World War is as a reaction to the sense of betrayal and humiliation felt by the Germans after the First World War. The sense of de-valuation and relegation led them to see themselves as victims. In turn, this led to complete devaluation of the Jewish people and denial of their human status. Feelings of anger by many Germans after the First World War became directed against those who were not to blame for their anxieties, the Jewish people. The scapegoats were blamed for the source of their troubles, perceived as national defeat. That was combined with Nazi ideas of racial superiority of Aryan people. Other races were inferior.

Perpetrators in Nazi Germany lived in a society in which they were bombarded with antisemitic propaganda that encouraged them to de-humanise Jews. It was a few short steps from crossing the road to avoid Jewish people to begin violent campaigns against them. Ordinary Germans became de-sensitised from their actions. Jewish people were seen as a public health menace, as vermin. In a bizarre twist, the mocking Joker in the pack, public health solutions were combined with industrial death in such a way that enabled officials to maintain a distance from their actions.[74]

Jewish people were killed not for what they were, but simply for <u>being</u>. The Holocaust was a holy war to annihilate Germany's mortal enemy. In Nazi ideology, the Jews were the primal adversary, the biological archenemy of the German people, whose physical presence seemed to threaten the very existence of the Aryan race. No other people, nation, or race held that status. Slavs were subhuman (Untermenschen). German racists assigned to the Slavs the lowest rank of human life. The Jews did not even feature. But no plan to murder the Slavs was ever hatched, though treated like slaves. No other group was earmarked for total extinction. Murder of the six million stands apart from the deaths of the others that perished, not because of any distinctive fate that the individual victims endured, but because of the intent of the murderers and the unique effect of the murders.[75]

"God, are the doors really being shut now? Yes, they are. Shut on the herded, densely packed mass of people inside. Through small openings at the top, we can see hands, hands that will wave to us later when the train leaves... the train gives a piercing whistle and 1020 Jews leave Holland".[76]

It was a project of de-humanisation on a monstrous scale. The horror of the death camps extended far down the railroad tracks that carried Jews to their deaths. Jammed on to train cars, Jewish deportees faced long journeys in conditions so unbearable that many people were dead on arrival. Nazi medical officers immediately divided the living into those who were fit to work and those who marked out to die. The latter were marched straight off to the gas chambers. Families would never see each other again.

Once de-humanised, housing and sanitation for those not immediately sent to their deaths were abominable. Beatings, hangings and shootings occurred at the slightest provocation or with none at all. Medical experiments were performed on human guinea pigs, sexual abuse, disease, torture and constant fear. A special vocabulary of understatement was used to mask murder. In Dachau, "Chasing the Children up the chimney" meant only one thing.

At Auschwitz, slavery was brought to its perverse perfection. Inmates were considered a consumable raw material to be discarded in the process of manufacture and recycled into the Nazi war economy. Jewish slaves were worked to death or reduced to a condition that rendered them incapable of work, then selected for death. Even body parts were then recycled into the Nazi war economy - gold, teeth, hair and body fat."[77] Genocides were not new. But recycling human beings was evil incarnate.

The Holocaust was the ultimate act of de-humanisation, stripping human status from people, reducing them to less than people. Rudolph Hoss, the commandant of the Auschwitz concentration camp, reportedly remarked to a visitor that the inmates, "are not like you and me. You saw them yourself: they are different. They look different. They do not behave like human beings". It had never occurred to Hoss that he had created the conditions that reduced the prisoners to the level of rats scraping and fighting for every crumb of bread. Beset by malnutrition and disease, how could they have looked average, when the camp was devised to reduce people to the animal state?[78]

3

Amongst the source of screams on the contemporary landscape, antisemitism continues to disfigure our world. Hate crimes of all types are on the march; hatred of Jewish people shows up in the actions of societies that see themselves as anti racist. Patterns of prejudice singled out an ethnic and religious group here in a way that is both terrifying and baffling. What was it about Germany, epitome of civilisation at the time, that could provide such a seedbed? How do we go from neighbours living side by side to one group seeing the other as mad, bad and dangerous to know?

Where were the antibodies in German civilisation that could immediately react against this?

The everyday world of moral experience shows how easy

it is for 'lines to be crossed'. Under pressure of what we label 'temptation', defences fall, and barriers are eroded, usually by stealth and usually because of the disruption that has occurred to the normal order of things. New thoughts take hold and susceptibility wins. Actions and behaviour previously ruled out become a new normal. An adjustment to a new morality has been reached; previously alien norms have been internalised.

There is a considerable difference between these erosions of limits and what we are considering here. With extreme politics, terrorist use of Jihad or genocide, actions and behaviour get darker and darker. This is not an individual yielding to moral compromise. This is a climate that has been created in a culture or people group that leads from personal abuse to prejudice and writing others off through violence which is now routine, de-humanisation by States and those holding the levers of power who no longer consider Jews or other groups as fellow-human beings. Then we hit rock bottom with genocide and ethnic cleansing.

The longest hatred had been developing for centuries. For centuries, European Christian society had subjected Jewish people to discrimination and pogrom. Amongst all social groups, attitudes that portrayed Jewish people as inferior were widespread. Massive figure though he was, Luther wrote a treatise in 1543 entitled 'On the Jews and Their Lies', in which he repeatedly attacked the Jews. The consequences of this treatise were far reaching, even extending into the present day, as his writings continue to be deployed by neo-Nazi and anti-Semitic groups. His writings were circulated during the most horrifying event of the 20th century: The Holocaust. "In Mein Kampf", Hitler named Luther as one of history's greatest reformers. Certainly, antisemitism and such perversions as 'Protocols of the Elders of Zion' found ready acceptance in many countries where people believed it to be true.

The continuing question is a quest. How was it humanly possible? Could it ever happen again? That is said about the Shoah and attempt to exterminate the Jewish people. Yet genocides have happened since 1945. The need to understand what happened and what were the steps by which an entire people had to be wiped out – this is urgent and imperative.

So how do we understand the process? How do you go from a history of antisemitism in Germany to the Holocaust? It must be by a series of small steps. It must be able to affect a whole population. And how do we understand the mindset of radicalised terrorism that rejoices in mums and newborns coming apart at the seams? Warped theology needs de-constructing to be sure, and that has to be a key component of de-radicalisation. But a psycho-social lens is critical to any kind of understanding of how difference generates such horror that disfigures our humanity so profoundly.

Here is a way of understanding how trashing people is humanly possible. It is an early-warning system, as a sort of Likert scale on which we can plot descending levels of devaluing the human and increasingly oppressive ways people experience it. Most emphatically, this is at the level of how people experience what it means to be disvalued, not that perpetrators at one level go down:

- Denigration
- De-personalisation
- Desecration
- Dehumanisation
- Demonisation

It is at each of these different levels that antibodies need to kick in and fight against the devaluation.

Once a way of speaking and practice becomes thinkable, the mind is prepared to go down to that next level which can be acceptable. You don't have to of course, and you certainly don't start with genocide (the ultimate depths of horror). But the descent into darkness consists of a series of steps. This descent is not only within time (affecting increasingly moral complexity by the same people and community), but it also takes place within history, over time, as attitudes change significantly and ingrained perceptions of one generation can become toe curling de-sensitised reactions of another.

LEVEL 1 - DENIGRATION (A KINDER WORLD)

"Be kind, for everyone you meet is fighting a hard battle"
- Plato
Eliza: "You see, really and truly, apart from the things one can pick up, (the dressing and the proper way of speaking, and so on), the difference between a lady and a flower girl is not how she behaves but how she is treated. I shall always be a flower girl to Professor Higgins, because he treats me as a flower girl, and always will, but I know I can be a lady to you, because you always treat me as a lady and you always will"- Pygmalion, George Bernard Shaw.

Experiences of human devaluation occur frequently - in the inter- personal sphere, in the field of economics, in the way that difference is sustained, in the exchanges of human violence, in the public square and in the kind of extreme politics that assault the sanctity of life. This constitutes a sliding scale of experiences of being disvalued. Disvaluing the human is experienced across the human landscapes with gathering intensity as the light grows dim and the skies darken over.

It doesn't start with State violence or genocide. It starts with the suspicion in everyday life, a neighbour on your doorstep who puts you down and belittles you. This is the sphere of inter-personal life, the politics of assault; treated with indifference, sarcasm, or belittling that evoke some sort of reaction against being devalued. Once the put downs take place, there has already been a changed atmosphere. On an individual level, people are already seeing certain others as those who at best must be tolerated. As the Nazi grip on Germany tightened, people turned away from Jewish friends. School students were shunned, abused, discriminated against and isolated. *"Their friends turned away either shamefully or with hostility"*.[79] A barrier was breached. Conditions are in place to go down a level.

Empathic understanding is trying genuinely to see the world from the perspective of the person in pain in front of us.[80] Denigration immediately clouds that.

It seems we are compelled to live as if we had value. Here is the actress Kate Winslett. *"I've always been very, very aware of wanting to be understood as being the person that I really am"*, she said, not wanting to be dismissed as an arrogant young actor which would be devaluing.[81]

Here is a disgruntled sailor when the Imperial German Navy was ordered to sea for one final battle at the close of the First World War? *"I would have fought hard if I had been treated like a human being all these years instead of an animal!"* [82] A former soldier leaving the British Army with a serious injury is incredibly frustrated with the lack of attention from either the public or the State. *"We're not getting listened to. It's not being noticed after all we've done, not getting the respect we deserve."*[83] There is a discontent that arises from unbearable possibility of being greeted by a yawn.

Immanuel Kant wrote about the disgraceful punishments that dishonour humanity, punishments more painful than loss of possessions and life to one who loves honour (who claims the respect of others as everyone must).[84] We are faced with humanity's hungering to be noted, to be recognised as having value, to be heard against the mocking indifference with which life can greet us. People require respect. It is vital to human flourishing that we feel respected and worthwhile. Dignity and respect are central to the search for idealised life. For lack of being worthwhile, we wither, self-esteem plummets and we end up regarding ourselves as a waste of space and time. Stronger in some than others, diminished in many lives, there is an impetus within the human psyche towards being a valuable person doing worthwhile labour. Conduct that enables us to hold our head up high and respect ourselves is, paradoxically, conduct that evokes the respect of others. It is salutary to note experiences people report of being put down, treated with indifference, sarcasm, or belit-tling that evoke some sort of reaction of "I count, I matter!" - or "I want to be heard!"

Having free and equal social relations that are respectful is not something that can be achieved by Government diktat though relationship education and effective programmes of civics to build the decent society. Where this issue is impor-tant is when it comes to the workplace.

Disgruntled employees often report being written off or not heard. But often, bullying will be an issue also or there will be abuse from customers which will not be tolerated. The gap between rhetoric and reality yawns insistently. Part of the issue that received wide exposure at the failure of the Royal Bank of Scotland in 2008-9, which marked the downturn at the financial crash (when taken into govern-ment ownership), was a culture of bullying. Authority must not be challenged.[85]

Workplace bullying is a fact of life in the corporate jun-gle. Bullying is too widespread to be the result of a few pathological individuals. Most harassment is carried out by employers who in all other respects are similar to those employees they try to control. It arises from the quality of relationships in the workplace.[86] The essence of trying to address it can be summed up in the internet advertisement, *"Bully in the Workplace driving you nuts? Gain the respect you deserve."*[87] It is about respect.

Anti-bullying has entered Codes of Practice, but attitudes remain. Detoxing the mind will be much harder. It is often the case that children who have been subject to family cultures where casual denigration and put-downs are the norm will learn that behaviour. Attitudes to others, especially those who are different, are shaped in such cultures. This is very far from the respectful relationships that will be the breeding ground of positive attitudes that characterise the good society. The Frankfurt School theorist Theodor Adorno tried to plot a straight line between negative, over-strict regimes many German children experienced at home and 'authoritarian personality'.[88] It led to what became known as the 'F' scale of Fascism.

Those who have experienced kindness and respectful relationships are less likely to embark on trashing others. There is a real case to be made that schools teach relationship, not just sex education. Those relationship practices that breed mutuality rather than domination will spill over.

LEVEL 2 - DE-PERSONALISATION

At this level, social pressures apply. In a cauldron of prejudice or abuse come experiences of being denied, a name or face, treated by impersonal economic or organisational forces as on a production line or being written down as being part of a social group which is neither highly prized nor standard-issue. Society values or devalues groups on the basis of gender, class, ethnicity, disability, sexuality, age or religion. It is the arena of struggle for inclusion on equal terms rooted in people claiming equal value to those who set the agenda. The Holocaust is a continuing and terrifying warning against de-valuing human life. As Primo Levi, the Italian writer who survived Auschwitz, said, "My name is 174517. We will carry the tattoos on our left arm until we die."[89] But de-personalisation had taken place long before. The racial identity laws of the Third Reich had designated Jews as outside the new society the Nazis wanted to recreate very soon after they had come to power. A boycott of Jewish businesses organised by the Nazi Party began in April 1933 and was followed by anti-Jewish legislation aimed at removing Jewish people from public life. The Nuremberg Laws of September 1935 defined Jews as members of a separate race who could not be members of the German State. Spontaneously, ordinary citizens in all walks of life began to avoid contact with Jewish neighbours.

In Nazi Germany, an increasing number of Jewish people got lumped together as a pestilence, a threat. People would cross over the road to avoid them. Fuelled by power-driven emotion, ultimately such attitudes permitted the moral bankruptcy to blank out a whole people group. De-personalisation is where people are not seen as free and equal human beings with their own possibilities. Instead they are stripped of their name and their face; made invisible or converted into objects.

Racism is an attitude of mind that shapes both perpetrator and victim. Steve Biko, the black South African leader who died under Apartheid-era brutality, diagnosed a submissive state of mind and lack of self-respect as illness. We collude with the definition of ourselves that others impose upon us.[90]

It is salutary that the social distancing that shaped so much of life for half the world was nothing less than the everyday racism experienced by millions. Being distanced by others has been their lifelong normal, not a new normal: that goes only for a white–majority culture. Black people have experienced the glances to check if their house or car was locked or being stared at before someone crosses the road. Muslim women wearing the niqab encounter the same thing.

Before race was a concept, it was an experience of the black man as a different sort of human.[91] Being 'white' can seem to be colourless, neutral. Yet it is a building site of enormous labour in power-laden assumptions about superiority. White is as much a colour as non-white. *"I was taught to see racism only in individual acts of meanness, not in invisible systems conferring dominance on my group,"* observes Peggy McIntosh, describing assumptions in everyday life by white folk. Inequality persists in education, health and police.[92]

"We don't want much, only to be treated as equals", protested two gipsy immigrants from Romania, who had come to live in Italy six years before. *"We had to come. We couldn't afford to feed the children back home."93* Devaluation has been virulent in attitudes towards migrant workers. In 20th century Britain, the whites used to feel they were superior to the blacks and the Irish. As later waves of immigration brought competition for jobs and housing, older migrants became suspicious of Polish workers, asylum seekers or refugees. Refugees attract strong suspicion today. *"So, I have a new name – refugee. Strange that a name should take away from me my past, my personality and hope. Strange refuge this. So many seem to share this name- Yet we share so many differences" (14-year-old refugee from Zimbabwe)94*

Value and disvalue shape inner and outer worlds. Words like oppression, injustice and discrimination capture the reality of social evils. The value of humanity is a barometer of society and a political system. De-personalisation is a common element in class, gender, ethnicity as well as discrimination based on ageism, homophobia and disability. The question is whether the rich world or the poor world can find the political and economic will to create a fair society. Think of the advantages experienced by high-value people. These lucky ones have the right education, ethnic background or gender that enables them to get on in the world. An unreachable luck and privilege seem to follow them about.

The classic formulations of how the world is divided up have to do with class, ethnicity (as 'race' is usually termed now) and gender. These social realities overlap and intersect each other in complicated ways. Other forms of differentiation have become important. Attitudes are also moulded by such factors as age, sexual orientation and religion. These are not just ways of organising the world but constitute forms of prejudice and deliver discrimination for millions of people. The common thread is that they are all forms of disvaluing and writing off human beings.

LEVEL 3 – DESECRATION

"The more physical, emotional and verbal abuse he received, the more he expected it, eventually believing what they were telling him: that he was useless & worthless, stupid: a fear he keeps in a dark place "- Billy Connally[95]

It is a short step from here to violence. Germans crossed over the road to avoid meeting Jews face to face in the streets. It hadn't started with violence but then it came; random acts of violence, shops being stoned, and Jewish people being beaten up by thuggery. One terrifying November night in 1938, the "Kristallnacht" saw violent attacks and destruction of synagogues and property.[96] Violence forcibly creates labels, constructing identity. It's like someone hangs a label around your neck or pins it to you. Violence has many strands. Acting in violent ways, people are saying different things, transmitting differing messages. There are many instances in which respect or honour are in deficit and need to be extracted, forcibly, from the face of another. Though it wears many faces, the essence is the same. Violence is violation, desecration. Killing someone is a sacred act.

In Nazi Germany, once the line had been crossed and Jewish people were denied the respectful relations that come from being seen as people in their own right, then came the stone through the window. Gradually that led to Kristallnacht in November 1938 when many acts of random violence took place and synagogues burnt. It was the next stage in the descent into darkness. The line of acceptability had been crossed. Desecration had occurred, not just of synagogues but human beings.

In the Covid emergency, the violence of domestic abuse was a major concern. Calls to a domestic abuse helpline rose by a half at one point as (mainly) women were trapped with tormenters.

Child involvement in violent gangs and knife crime is growing. Mutual protection, the need to act big and be clever, boredom, a mind-set of retaliation and instant recourse to violence play their part as does the need to belong. It is now clear that disrespect is also key to these kinds of processes. *"Everyone carried a knife- some of us for protection, others for status... I don't dislike the police. I have had officers disrespect me and I had other officers who have treated me with respect."*[97]

The notion that violence can be understood as a bid for respect is argued by James Gilligan.[98] He suggests that the mechanism by which unemployment and economic inequality stimulate violence depends on the fact that they trigger feelings of shame, of inferiority. Some violent acts may be a reaction against perceived humiliation or loss of status. In acts of violence, its actors feel lack of respect - 'he disrespected me'. Forms of disrespect might lie in a perceived look, a verbal insult or a territorial claim. Violence is an assertion of self-respect. Could we build a society without such gangs?

The American psychologist Rollo May saw violence as a bid for significance by the powerless; *"an explosion into violence may be the only way individuals or groups can get release from unbearable tension and achieve a sense of significance."*[99]

Violence is a forcible exchange of value, recovering someone's value through dehumanizing the other. The essence of the many faces of violence is violation or desecration. Violence is often the language of the unheard. Killing someone becomes a sacred act. Once that line has been crossed, you can go further down and collude in killing on a bigger scale. Joan Smith shows how domestic violence can turn young men especially into terrorists.[100] Misogyny or abuse often comes before the action, for example of those London gang members who joined ISIS. They practised in private first.

LEVEL 4 - DE-HUMANISATION

De-humanisation is the assault on the value and dignity of persons through the indignity of human rights abuse, human trafficking, extreme politics and war. Here the focus is on the sanctity of life itself, not just loss of face and name or of property. Political processes either give value to the human or deny it. *"The Nazis had become convinced that all the so-called 'dregs of humanity', first and foremost the Jews, but also Poles, Gypsies, gays and disabled, had to be eliminated or at least their influence on culture and human development significantly curtailed"*[101] Do Governments care about human life? This level is not about individuals being violent: this is where the State turns thuggish and demonstrates no concern, no regard for the life of people.

For the most part, everyday racism flourishes on that 2nd moral level. It is de-personalisation, treating people as if the colour of their skins gave them the cloak of invisibility. And then it crosses the line down into violence. Sometimes that takes place through the authorities. In the midst of the pandemic, Minneapolis burned. Late May 2020 saw riots protesting the death of George Floyd, a 46-year-old black man who died after pleading for help as a police officer pinned him to the ground with a knee on his neck. Racism is, declared the Mayor, a virus in the US worse than Covid-19. It sparked off an extraordinary wave of global heart-searching and a civil rights movement.[102]

It is time for that virus to be eradicated from the social body by building antibodies of hope. But that will not happen without concerted education to flush this poison out. Churches have a major role to play in a country which says it is Christian. Understanding descent into darkness is a theological issue.

We might have thought nationalism had gone away but

when the crisis came, it was national States that had to take action. Covid might have exposed populism as such governments did not handle the pandemic so well, depending on whether they took expert advice seriously or not. But it's about having a State that people trust, and which can get things done. There is no substitute for an effective State.

Most governments would say that they care about the lives of their people. Yet, what position do nation States and the Church come to take on 'the sanctity of life'? Do we believe it? President Assad of Syria made a historic blunder in 2011 when his troops fired on peaceful protesters in Deraa. The only lens that the regime had which to view this challenge through was to brand them as 'terrorists". Label people terrorists and you can get away with murder. Five years later, according to the Syria Network for Human Rights, the regime and its backers were responsible for 188,000 deaths – 92% of the total.[103] ISIS could not hold a candle to this industrial scale murder.

State sponsored execution (call it by its name- murder) dehumanises as it is lethal. De-humanisation is the assault on the value and dignity of people through the indignity of human rights abuse, human trafficking, extreme politics and war. Here the focus is on the sanctity of life itself not just loss of face and name; on political processes that either give value to the human or deny it. Dehumanisation was Nazi Germany herding Jewish people like cattle into railways trucks even before the mass murder.

Take the Chinese treatment of the Uighur people. In Xinjiang Province there is a sharp divide between the Han Chinese and the Uighurs. The divide is cultural, of language and geographical. It is also historical. 2009 saw a violent ethnic clash, sparked by the killing of two Uighur factory workers. The clash made the Han Chinese more suspicious of Uighurs. They were definitely 'the other'. In 2016, the authorities began building a gulag to incarcerate a million people – mainly Uighurs. Despite being designated official vocational training centres, all the evidence is that these camps are brainwashing Uighurs, so they are less attached to their Muslim/Turkic background. Even without such camps to force people away from Islamic culture, there is definite apartheid in Xinjiang. Han Chinese interact very little with Uighurs and have their own newspapers, hospitals and media.

Take persecution of Christians. The number of Christians facing intense or high persecution is rising sharply. According to World Wide Watch, every day eight Christians are killed for their faith; 23 are raped or sexually harassed. Artificial intelligence and biometric surveillance using cameras with face-recognition technology are being installed in churches so that congregations have to queue before a service to keep watch on who is coming. There are fears that this will happen in India.[104]

LEVEL 5 – DEMONISATION

"They [the prisoners] began rushing towards us, in a big crowd. They were weeping, embracing us and kissing us. I felt a grievance on behalf of mankind that these fascists had made such a mockery of us. It roused me and all the soldiers to go and quickly destroy them and send them to hell."

"We ran up to them and they gave us hugs, cookies and chocolate. Being so alone, a hug meant more to me than anybody could imagine because that replaced the human worth we were starving for. We were not only starved for food but we were starved for human kindness. And the Soviet Army did provide some of that."[105]

There surely needs to be a wholesale reform movement

within Islam in order to purge the political violence and Jihad promising the instant admission to paradise that fuels suicide bombers. It is human desecration. Deradicalising a toxic mind will take theology and psychology. Muslim radicalism continues to agitate our world. Is that genocide? Probably not, if you mean ripping the unbelievers apart in random acts of terrorism and treating them as a class of people ripe for wholesale extermination. But the treatment by ISIS of the Druze peoples of Syria surely counts.

A clearer case of genocide is to be found in Myanmar where, during the crisis, in May 2020, it the government was accused by the humanitarian organisation Refugees International of the crime of genocide against the Rohingya peoples. They do not deserve to live. They must go. What would the UN make of this?

As I write this, it has been announced that Félicien Kabuga, one of the most wanted suspects in the Rwandan genocide, has been arrested near Paris. Kabuga was detained by gendarmes in Asnières-sur-Seine, where he had been living under a false identity. The International Criminal Tribunal for Rwanda has charged the 84-year-old with genocide and crimes against humanity. He is alleged to have been the main financier of the ethnic Hutu extremists who slaughtered 800,000 people in 1994. They were targeting members of the minority Tutsi community, as well as their political opponents. Kabuga was indicted in 1997 on seven counts of genocide, complicity in genocide, direct and public incitement to commit genocide, attempt to commit genocide, conspiracy to commit genocide, persecution and extermination. After a plane carrying then-President Juvenal Habyarimana - a Hutu - was shot down, killing all on board, Hutu extremists blamed the Tutsi rebel group, the Rwandan Patriotic Front (RPF) - an accusation it denied. In a campaign of slaughter, militias were given hit lists of Tutsi victims.

Many were killed with machetes in acts of appalling brutality. The ruling party's youth wing, the Interahamwe, which set up roadblocks to find Tutsis, incited hatred via radio broadcasts and carried out house-to-house searches. Kabuga also founded and funded the notorious "Radio Télévision Libre des Mille Collines" (RTLM), a Rwandan broadcaster which actively encouraged people to search out and kill anyone who was from the Tutsi ethnic group.

In a strategy of demonization, animal metaphors abound. *'It's time to stomp these cockroaches!'*[106]

There is a tribal loyalty which is positive and about place. But genocide is the ultimate form of trashing human lives. It is where the descent into darkness takes you, where xenophobic forms of nationalism take you. It is the logical destination of habits of heart and mind that exhibit a virulent animus towards other social groups – be they Jews, black people or members of another tribe.

Grasping the importance of "every life matters", not just the wealthy and the privileged, is a project in moral and theological education and is an urgent task. Synchronicity of Covid and the wretched virus of racism ought to challenge us profoundly. To break the transmission, children need to be taught how minds can be infected as well as bodies, that power and control colour and warp human action.

There is a long history of black people being compared to dark-coloured animals. At the global level, cooperation has also been conspicuously absent.

WHY THE SLIDE?

In a speech in 1923, Hitler said, *"The Jews are undoubtedly a race, but not human. They cannot be human in the sense of being an image of God, the Eternal. The Jews are the image of the devil."107* Twenty years later, after the Wannsee conference when the Final Solution was planned, Hitler said to his table companions: *"The discovery of the Jewish virus is one of the greatest revolutions undertaken in the world. The struggle we are waging is of the same kind as, in the past century, of Pasteur and Koch. How many diseases can be traced back to the Jewish virus?"*

Such a descending scale is a project in moral education. It shows the need to put in place strategies to help prevent society going 'down a level', the calibration for a kind of early warning system regarding the unique value of a life amidst cultures of violence. Attention needs to be paid to level one or we risk degenerating to level two. Once lines have been crossed, and human groups are de-personalised, it becomes acceptable next to subject them to random acts of violence, subsequent de-humanisation and ultimately acts of ethnic cleansing. Through such a scale, history warns us.

This is not to say that the same people necessarily go from stage to stage down this sliding scale. Rather a climate has been created in which the next level down becomes THINKEABLE. The climate is one of moral acceptability. Lines are crossed. This is happening at the level of society, not a particular person. Social processes have been conditioned so much so that what was previously out of the question starts to become possible. 'We would never do THAT!' is a gradual process downhill.

Why though do they do this? How is the holocaust or ethnic cleansing humanly possible, such that decent or civilised people can be de-sensitised?

What accounts for the moral slide, the gradualism in the disruption to what has been normal but is now moving in a dark and dangerous direction?

It is a many-stranded rope. One strand is the way that beliefs are formed. How we see, the world is drawn from many fields of vision, many perceptions. Many in Germany and

Nazi sympathisers elsewhere were prone to a way of looking at Jewish people in different terms to those of others. Misrecognition of the status of people- not classing them as equivalent and normal – is a belief, a pattern of the mind. It is also a pattern of minds (plural). Antisemitism is a shared belief, a sad, social phenomenon that goes beyond individual perceptions, to a collective view held by many.

Is this the same process that leads to defending slavery, which *"often meant regarding enslaved people as lesser human beings and thus not to be treated in the same manner as free individuals"*. Slaves were described as animals, though not to be treated so harshly as to threaten their life or their productivity.[108] They were not seen as being people too with the same value as their masters.

The decision to use African slaves was not about profit. Colonists in America could not imagine using European labour in this way. Africans were different. It was acceptable to enslave them. Africans were not fully human but, if human, clearly inferior to whites in mental and spiritual faculties.[109] Once slaves were de-humanised, treated as objects and not people like us, the slave trade helped build a mindset of racism that became deeply embedded in attitudes to black people later. *"Basic food and shelter were provided, at least as long as the slave was of value to the master. Procreation was encouraged to produce additional slaves - additional capital assets. Medical care, horrible and inadequate as it was, was provided so long as the slave was useful. When no longer useful, the slave was sold to someone less fortunate, or abandoned to die, much as we might treat an old car that is either repaired until repairs are too costly and is then traded, or, when beyond all utility, junked.*[110]

The politics of grievance is another strand to the rope. Knowledge is not just located in rationality – to deploy the contrast between 'head and heart' that Westerners like to use. Emotional cognition has to be entered into the equation. We think with emotions as well as by logic reasoning. Extreme politics seems bewildering, a Wild-West where irrationality defies the normal rules. It was not rational in the sense of being reasonable that Hutu people rose in Rwanda to slaughter their Tutsi neighbours with machete. The Nazi party traded on resentment by many Germans at seeing their once proud nation experience the humiliation of Versailles peace treaties. They were aggrieved!

On a wider canvas, slavery was practiced in the no-man's land of the Putumayo region of Colombia into the twentieth century. The rubber barons ran an Empire of unbelievable brutality. Native Indians had hands and limbs cut-off if quotas were not met. To ensure the labour needed for rubber plantations continued to be extracted, children were executed and whole villages were murdered.[111]

The anthropologist Michael Taussig made the point that, amidst shocking de-humanisation, some humanity in the tortured is part of the bond between them and their torturers. *"In their human or human-like form, the wild Indians could all the better reflect back to the colonists the vast baroque projections of human wildness that the colonists needed to establish their reality as civilised people. And it was only because the wild Indians were human that they were able to serve as labour- and as subjects of torture. For it is not the victim as animal that gratifies the torturer but the fact that the victim is human, thus enabling the torturer to become the savage."*[112]

To de-subjectivise people, they must first be seen as subjects. Subjectivities exchange places and the tortured can become an object. It is only humans that can be enslaved-whether on the Putumayo or elsewhere. It is only a living thing that can be murdered. The Nazi's did not mis-identify their victims; it is only humans that can be treated as sub-human. Mengele knew exactly what he was doing.

CHAPTER FIVE
BETWEEN RHETORIC AND REALITY: DENIAL AND HUMAN RESPONSIBILITY

"It was relatively harmless and left no conspicuous scars on my body. And yet, twenty-two years after it occurred, on the basis of an experience that in no way probed the entire range of possibilities, I dare to assert that torture is the most horrible event a human being can retain within himself." [113]

THE ROOTS OF REFUSAL

Across the world, the way society has been organised is to value some groups of people and devalue others. Instead of seeing different types of people as being on the same level as us, people have seen others in layers; superior and inferior, fully human and deserving equal treatment, or less than human. Access to power is both unequal and destructive.

'Where is your brother?' Cain dodges. Evasively, the gap between rhetoric and reality is wide and getting wider. The violence that desecrates is always easier to name when committed by someone else. Is he the first person in history to engage in truculent blame shifting? Emphatically not. *"The woman whom you gave to be with me, she gave me fruit from the tree and I ate"* (Genesis 3v12). The first chapters of Genesis are an extended sermon on moral responsibility and sin's evasiveness.

As I write these words, they are pouring 8,372 cups of coffee at Srebenica (July 11th 2020). Cups of commemorative coffee do, we suppose, taste the same as the ordinary kind. Yet the massacre at Srebenica remains dreadfully disputed. Amongst the leaders from across the world, who sent videos of solidarity rather than drink Balkan coffee, some were conspicuous by refusal to drink the moral cup. The local Mayor ignored the event. Mladen Grujicic denied that a massacre ever took place despite some 7,000 being identified and then given a proper burial.

Even with pandemic restrictions, Bosnian Muslims marked the 25th anniversary of the Srebrenica massacre, the worst atrocity on European soil since World War II. Thousands of mainly Muslim men and boys brutally murdered in the July 1995 massacre during the Balkan wars, in what the United Nations calls the "the worst atrocity crime on European soil since the Second World War". Bosnian Serb troops led by Ratko Mladic (routinely defended and given folk-hero status) entered the Srebrenica enclave before systematically massacring Bosnian men and adolescents. *"The husbands of my four sisters were killed,"* said Ifeta Hasanovic, 48, whose husband Hasib was one of the nine victims whose remains have been identified since July 2019. *"My brother was killed, so was his son. My mother-in-law lost another son as well as her husband."*[114] The nine victims were buried in the cemetery of the Genocide Memorial in nearby Potocari where the UN protection force was located.

Srebrenica could have been saved. But, appallingly, with help of the UN Peacekeepers, men and boys were separated from women. Mothers dressed their teenage sons as girls so they would not be taken to their deaths. Daughters spoke of waving goodbye to their fathers as they ran into the woods to join the Trail of Tears, turning around to blow them a kiss. They next saw their fathers when they were pulled out of mass graves many years later. Most of those men were hunted down on the Trail of Tears and died like animals. Some had their throats slit. Others were shot before falling into graves they themselves had been forced to dig.

Bosnia is one of the world's darkest shames, a wound we will never heal, and an example of all that has gone wrong with wars that might have been halted. The UN Security Council declared Srebrenica a "safe area" in the spring of 1993. But troops led by Gen Ratko Mladic, who was later found guilty of war crimes, crimes against humanity and genocide, overran the UN zone. Ratko Mladic was sentenced to life in prison by a UN court in 2017 over war crimes, including the Srebrenica genocide. He awaits the decision on his appeal. He is still revered as a hero by many Serbs.

The Srebrenica massacre is the only episode of the Bosnian conflict to be described as genocide by the international community. Yet, while for Bosnian Muslims recognising the scale of the atrocity is a necessity for lasting peace, for most Serbs -- leaders and laypeople in both Bosnia and Serbia -- the use of the word genocide remains unacceptable. In the run-up to the anniversary, Serbian President Aleksandar Vucic described Srebrenica as *"something that we should not and cannot be proud of"*, but he has never publicly uttered the word "genocide". Glorification of war criminals like Mladic is widespread. There has even been a revisionist history. In 2019, Peter Handke, an Austrian writer who has cast doubt on the Srebrenica massacre, was awarded the Nobel Prize for Literature. Despite the weight of evidence, this is extraordinary. The Centre for Missing Persons was set up in Sarajevo in 1996 at the initiative of former US President Bill Clinton. The mandate was to locate the bones to try to identify bodies so families could bury them at the memorial in Potocari, outside Srebrenica. But many still do not have their loved ones' remains. Many people have yet to be identified.

American academics such as global terrorism expert Jessica Stern, wrote My War Criminal about her fascination with Radovan Karadzic, leader of the Bosnian Serbs and the architect of the destruction of Sarajevo. Between October 2014 and November 2016, Jessica Stern held a series of conversations in a prison cell in The Hague with Karadzic, who had been indicted for genocide and other war crimes during the Bosnian War and who became an inspiration for white nationalists. Though Stern was used to interviewing terrorists in the field in an effort to understand their hidden motives, the conversations she had with Karadzic would profoundly alter her understanding of the mechanics of fear, the motivations of violence, and the psychology of those who perpetrate mass atrocities and intentionally target non-combatants, in violation of ethical norms and international law. It makes for chilling reading. How do leaders persuade ordinary people to kill their neighbours? What is the "ecosystem" that creates and nurtures genocidal leaders? Could anything about their personal histories, personalities, or exposure to historical trauma shed light on the formation of a war criminal's identity in opposition to the Other who is targeted?[115]

It is an important question to understand. How and to what degree are we responsible for our characters, our lives, our misfortunes, our relationships and our children? This question is at the heart of moral responsibility, the accusations and denials for particular acts, responsibility for character, and the role of luck and fate in ethics. Moral responsibility as the grounds for a theory of punishment because of retribution is closely tied in with questions of forgiveness, parental responsibility, and responsibility before God.[116]

On the day of the 2020 commemoration, the town's Serbian mayor Mladen Grujicic - who was elected in 2016 after a campaign based on genocide denial - said that *"there is new evidence every day that denies the current presentation of everything that has happened"*. Bosnian Serb political leader Milorad Dodik has also described the massacre as a "myth". This stood in sharp moral contrast with the Muslim member of Bosnia's joint presidency, Sefik Dzaferovic, said: *"We will fight against those who deny the genocide and glorify its perpetrators."* He was supported by Bosnia's grand mufti Husein Kavazovic. *"Despite all that has happened, life is reborn in Srebrenica".* [117] Life is re-born. That is visible in Muslims and Serbs jostling together now in the dailiness of life. How do people get to be re-born, how do communities get to be re-born unless they accept what has happened and accept some responsibility for it? Tragically, Srebenica is not the only case in point.

HISTORY IS COMPLICATED

History is a complicated enterprise. The crimes of nationalism are justified by an appeal to history but history itself is a blur between fact and fiction. That is as true of larger controversial events as it is of personal life. The tangled roots are nearly always to do with identity and threat to 'who we are'.

Accounts of historical events are massaged to whip up public support or downplay horrors. With it, people trade in two important commodities – power and prestige.

Accounts of notorious markers such as 'the back hole of Calcutta', the cramming of British people into a suffocatingly small cell in 1757, are contested now but in its day, whatever the exact number of those who perished, the story served to underline the horrors of Indian native rulers and the moral cause of imperial rule (there is nothing so potent as a moral cause). Representation and remembrance are entwined. It makes those who hold the reins of power (or those who contest it) feel good about themselves. Myth serves a cause that is not moral: the task of building self-image. The pure nation (or pure person) can thus be justified and no one needs to hang heads in shame.

This might help explain crimes that nationalism has to answer for. Bosnian Serb leaders regard what happened in Srebenica as 'fabricated myth' not because they contest factually the events, for which there is more minute-by-minute evidence than any war crime in history, but because self-serving narratives avoid what must be avoided at all costs – shame. There is nothing so potent as unsullied identity. It is for this that stories are re-told and 'spun'. It is for this that traditions are re-invented.

Perhaps it is the case that in the Balkans everyone wants to be seen as victim rather than perpetrator. We could incorporate into our narratives a sense of the way fate or things outside our control affect what we are, but this is not really about free will. It cuts deep in our whole ethical self-image and our existential predicament. Moral responsibility is bound up with what it is to blame someone, to hold someone responsible. The inter-connections between shame and blame are many and tangled. In his *'Responsibility and the Moral Sentiments'*, R J Wallace shows that the fairness of holding people responsible depends on their rational competence: the power to grasp moral reasons.[118] Maybe freedom is not necessary for responsibility and that we can be held accountable even though strong forces are compelling us to act in certain ways. In another take on things, Bernard Williams in his *'Shame and Necessity'* argues that free will is an illusion. Those who live in sin-based cultures have just as much a necessity to act as they do, as people who live in shame-based societies do. Williams disputes that the ancient Greeks had primitive ideas of the self, of responsibility, freedom, and shame, and that humanity has advanced from these to a more refined moral consciousness. In our rejection of slavery, we work with a similar circle of ideas.[119]

Collusion has often been indulged in by the church. The Patriarch in Belgrade publicly congratulated the Serbian President Milosovic for 'following the hard road of Christ'! The Orthodox Church welcomed his violent nationalist land grab in the collapsing Yugoslavia. Most senior bishops travelled in the war zones of Croatia and Bosnia, blessing Serbian forces shelling towns like Sarajevo. So often focus of church criticism was not that the Government committed atrocities in trying to create a new Serbian empire, but that it was unsuccessful. *"We blame Milosevic not for not trying to defend the nation, but for failing,"* said Bishop Atanasije. Despite statements about Kosovo, Bishop Atanasije said the church was not rethinking the support that many of its senior priests, including the Patriarch himself, gave in blessing Bosnian Serbian forces, whose leaders have now been indicted for war crimes. One priest, Father Filaret Micovic, photographed in Bosnia on a tank while brandishing a Kalashnikov rifle, was promoted to bishop.[120] In principle, these complex motivations are no different from First World War era clergy egging their countries forward or American Civil War ministers having no doubt that God is was on their side – and so it goes on. Serbia is perhaps the most egregious example in recent times, though we could have looked at shameful complicity in Rwanda in much the same time by church leaders who failed to speak out or gave tacit support to genocide.

The church has played for nearly seven centuries a pivotal role in gestating and defending the idea of what it means to be a Serb. *''Being a Serb and being Orthodox mean the same thing... our church itself has generated nationalism.''* argued Mirko Djordjevic, author of a book about the church and its ties to Milosevic. In realizing the church's long-held dream that all Serbs should live in the same state, the rise of Milosevic in the late 1980's was the best news the Serbian Orthodox Church had heard for decades, Djordjevic suggested. *''The church believed Milosevic was the Messiah who had come to smile on all Serbs''.*[121]

After decades of Tito's Communism, during which the church was repressed and controlled by the Government and some of its vast properties were confiscated, Milosevic allowed the church to reclaim its role in Serbian society. Priests appeared on state-controlled television. He pledged to allow religious education in schools and to return church property, promises later broken.

As Yugoslavia unravelled and wars began in the early 1990's, Serbian paramilitary leaders -- many of them responsible for atrocities and wholesale campaigns of theft in Croatia and Bosnia -- invoked the church as their inspiration for defending Serbs. The warlord Zeljko Raznjatovic, known as Arkan, indicted as a war criminal, said publicly that his ''supreme commander'' was Patriarch Pavle. Before Arkan's indictment by the war crimes tribunal in The Hague, but after worldwide publicity about the brutality and greed of his paramilitary fighters, Orthodox priests officiated at his lavish and very public wedding in Belgrade. Djordjevic, regarded as a leading expert on the Serbian Church, said that Patriarch Pavle was ''shocked'' by the evidence of atrocities that he saw in Kosovo since the 11-week war with NATO ended. That shock resulted in what Djordjevic described as a new direction for the Serbian Church, with the Patriarch and Bishop Artemije, the most senior representative of the church in Kosovo, speaking openly of ''evil'' by Serbs against Albanians. Where were the antibodies?

The historic gulf between rhetoric and reality has been huge and damaging. Algerian writer Fritz Fanon laments that the church in the colonies is *"the foreigner's church... she does not call the native to God's ways but to the ways of the white man, of the master, of the oppressor"*.[122] Subtly, the church has been able to turn the Word of God to serve political ideologies and support for nation.

This is not a religious story per se. Turkish refusal to name the Armenian genocide of 1915 is another case in point. This is not a story about religion but self-serving cultural blindness and refusal to places the sanctity of life above violence. There are numerous examples of secular ideals being seriously compromised. Russian support of the Syrian horror is a recent example. This is obscene but it is because human life should not be trashed that it is obscene. The record countries have against their own professed ideals on the value of life exposes yawning gulf between rhetoric and reality and unconditional support for 'our people'. A culture of denial lays the groundwork for future genocides.

THE SANCTITY OF LIFE? – WHO ACTUALLY BELIEVES IT...

4th June 2019. Chinese authorities surround Tiannamen Square with tight controls on the anniversary of the massacre there. Thirty years have passed since heads were crushed by tanks, that day in June. It took a fortnight for the authorities to find soldiers prepared to fire on the students. The students were the victims of China's infighting. One leader went to talk to the students. Then he was deposed. Intriguingly, his aide went on to become the Premier of China at the time of the twentieth anniversary. The number of deaths is not known but at least a thousand protesters perished.[123] *"That is why we want democracy"* said one present day activist. *"A democracy would not have ordered the troops to fire on the people."124*

On the eve of the 20th anniversary of the massacre, China released a 54-page document promising to improve civil and political rights for its citizens. Fair trials and the rights of citizens to participate in Govt were provided for, abuses of detainees proscribed and the rights of women, children, the elderly and minorities were protected.[125] One eighth of the world's population were under a regime that was still contemptuous of human life. To be sure, China had moved on a great deal from its hard-line Maoist days. Its leader won plaudits for responding to disasters by the power of presence and issuing apologies for a baby milk scandal- in short behaving more like a Western politician.[126]

Mao had no love for the peasantry of China. *"A revolution is not a dinner party"*, he exclaimed, as early as 1927.[127] Yet in contrast to the father of the Chinese revolution of 1911, Sun Yat-Sen, who initially placed little emphasis on appeal to peasants, Mao Tse-Tung was clear. *"Whoever wins the supports of the peasants will win China; whoever solves the land question will win the peasants."*[128]

The grievances of the peasants were real. Injustice was real. It was to change things that Mao and his cohorts went into political business. This was the vision of the Chinese Communist before it became corrupted. The political activity of the Party was originally a vehicle to mobilise the anger and grievances of the peasants. Mao's high ideals about bridging the gap between rich and poor still played in the new China, despite an apparent philosophy the new capitalism of 'everyone for themselves'.[129] By October 1st 2019, China had been transformed. The 73-million strong Communist Party still dominates its economic and political life.[130] 70 years before, Mao proclaimed the birth of a new China. A tragedy was about to unfold. Utopia became dystopia. In the Great Leap Forward and in the Cultural Revolution, between twenty to thirty million people lost their lives. Mao, who believed they were enemies of the people, was unconcerned. [131] He saw himself as a philosopher. As Jung Chang pondered, are there any other philosophers whose ideas led to the death of so many?

In Mao's China, humiliation was the main tool of the Cultural Revolution, whether this was parading through the streets with degrading slogans on placards worn round their necks, being made to wear dunce's caps, having an iron ring through your nose[132] or be daubed as clowns[133]. In her book *'Wild Swans'*, Jung Chang describes the distress of her grandmother in response to such humiliation.[134] *'Mercy to the enemy is cruelty to the people,'* she heard a seventeen year boy say, quoting the Chairman as he beat up a kneeling and bloodstained woman. By getting them to hate each other, Mao turned the people into the ultimate weapon of dictatorship. *"In bringing out and nourishing the worst in people, Mao had created a moral wasteland and a land of hatred"*[135]

Some political systems give value to humans, others have no regard for the sanctity of life. Life is cheap. People are of no value; their lives don't matter. It is a growing consensus in the West that good government should be about reinforcing human dignity. Yet historically, even the sanctity of life was slow in coming to the West. The foundation of the Red Cross by Henry Dunant in the 19th century and the basis behind caring for the wounded in war was the moral sense of the value of each life.[136] Political systems that respect life will usually be those that respect the rule of law.

There is a direct association between these ideas. *"We have to persuade the local inhabitants that Government people won't harm them"*, declared a NATO General endeavouring to win hearts and minds in the Afghan struggle.[137] Arguably, that is the security of a tradition that respects a law-based system and ensures civilian control of the military. Government people won't harm or hurt them, turn thuggish, lock up its opponents, sponsor cultures of violence or subject others to arbitrary arrest. Nationalistic authoritarian regimes of any colour or persuasion display scant regard for valuing the human. There is a capacity for an outrage that is a litmus test for humanity. The moral test of a political system is how far it allows the weak and unproductive to stay on the radar.

Attitudes towards the value of people and of life continue to be beset by xenophobic nationalism and pride. The Kremlin of Vladimir Putin has massively re-written history, approving textbooks that rehabilitate Stalin as "an effective manager"[138]. The value of individuals - so obviously trashed under Stalin or ultra-nationalists - takes a back seat. Russia seemed determined to whitewash its darker past. If the intellectuals in Chekhov's plays could have guessed what was looming, *"all the heroes would have gone off to insane asylums. Yet, not only Chekhov, but what normal Russian at the beginning of the century... could have believed, would have tolerated, such a slander against the bright future?"*[139] The daughter of a former German diplomat tried to explain why her father, once very pro-communist, radically changed his mind about Stalinism. *"One night, he heard screams!"*[140] With these five words, she wrote, he saw through and swept away the myths of the 20th century. Screams that rip through the myths of the twentieth century articulate lessons for the Twenty First.

CHAPTER SIX
THE MANY FACES OF CAIN: A QUESTION OF DEFINITION

"Violence is a slippery concept- non-linear, productive, destructive, and reproductive. Violence defies easy categorisation. It's in the eye of the beholder."141

Cain has many faces, many disguises.

Some would say that we cannot write 'a history of violence' but only many histories, each with their own impetus. Perhaps there are so many different manifestations and complicated causes that to speak of the phenomenon of violence is thoroughly misleading. What is violence after all? Terrorist violence surely cannot be domestic violence writ large. Is all violence the same in essence?

How we characterise violence matters when we try to understand whether violence is increasing or decreasing. It matters when we try to understand the contemporary face of Cain or the blood of Abel that cries for recompense. It matters when we fathom how the violence of scapegoating might be visited upon an innocent victim such that the he or she might bear the weight of the world. It is crucial for how we can give any account of global redemption through the Christ who transmutes violence into forgiveness and hatred into love. Otherwise we are left with Shylock – *"If you wrong us, shall we not revenge?"142*

This cannot be understood through assessing the degree of bloodshed as if acts of fearful bloodletting can be compared, violence's volume for volume. Cain's violence is multi-faceted, drawing on gender roles, sociological, historical, economic, familial, biological and psychological roots for its impetus and strength. Violence surfaces within inter-personal, in the home, in workplace wars, at school, in criminal acts, in communal and racially motivated violence, gangs, crowds becoming dangerous (hooliganism), politics genocide, revolution and mobilisation for a cause and war. A wide range of meanings are involved.

Three questions arise at the bloody gates of the twenty first century. Why are humans still violent? What makes some humans violent while others do not demonstrate lethal aggression? Could we all be violent in the right circumstances?

Why won't these questions go away? Perhaps violence is part of being human. Jealousy and rage surface in traditional societies with feuds over land, grazing, water or women. In some societies, such as the Tasaday Indians of the Philippines, there is not even a word for war.[143]. Yet for Yanamamo Indians of southern Venezuela, sex-biased infanticide is all but one way the cultivation of ferocity or nurture of aggression can affect an entire culture.[144] In Darwin's lens, we are of the earth; to the earth we return. The difference between humanity and animals is a difference only of degree. Darwin devoted an entire chapter to the topic of hatred and anger.[145] The anthropologist Konrad Lorenz spoke of a parliament of instincts - aggression is one drive amongst many.[146] Freud suggested that there was an aggressive instinct, a death wish in humanity, biological in origin.[147] The psychologist Anthony Storr concluded that *"there is so far no convincing evidence that the aggressive response is, at a physiological level, any less instinctive than the sexual response"148* Violence is about territoriality and ritual, much like animals and birds have to compete for survival. Hatred is about "paranoid hostility". The fact that in human societies anger can be transformed into hate, vindictiveness or permanent hostility, points to acts of violence as culturally, not biologically determined, rooted in fierce competition against all rivals.

Or take a recent approach, advocated by Randall Collins. His 'micro-sociological' theory argues that people turn violent when the social dynamics of a given situation take them beyond motive and morality. Social bonds are set aside.[149] But this fails to explain racially motivated violence or how the inter-play between social forces and personal agency arise with domestic or gendered violence.

There are at least ten forms of explanation as to why violence occurs. Each of these narratives represents a different type of map in popular debate and is situated in a different discipline. Researchers who deal with anti-social problems in children for instance employ different theories, concepts and terminology than those who focus attention on older adolescents and adults. [150] Different approaches are involved in addressing them.

Explanations of violence could be:

1. Biology- it's an instinct in the genes or exacerbated through hormones[151];
2. Temperament – 'it's someone's personality type'[152]
3. Parenting styles – 'it's the parenting style that has shaped you'[153]
4. Gender wars – arising from the different way genders are socialised[154]
5. Learned behaviour - 'it is the culture you have downloaded!'[155]
6. Socio-economic factors – a reaction to low income and unemployment[156]
7. Inter-group hostility - competition between social groups drives violence[157]
8. The availability of triggers - e.g. guns, knives, bombs, alcohol and drugs[158]
9. The media representation of violence – too much exposure to violence[159]
10. Political violence and the use of war to settle competitive goals[160]

Beyond these 'formal causes' of violence, there is an interpretive approach which has something to do with endeavouring to decode the meaning of violence - an attempt to read its ugly texts. What is playing under the surface when people are verbally or physically violent is laden with meaning. Violence is rarely random; context and sub-text are everything.

So, for example, a Rational Choice theory assumes that offenders rationally calculate the costs and benefits of committing a crime.[161] The 18th century Italian writer Cesare Beccaria suggested an original simple model of human choice:[162] crime is purposeful; the individual performs rational calculations of costs and benefits. The cardinal rule of rational choice theory is not to dismiss a criminal act as senseless, but to try to understand the purpose of the offender.[163] This approach is a limited view of human action, assuming that the difference between the 'on-switch' or the 'off-switch' to no violence is firmly under someone's control. The French sociologist Michel Foucault in his book *"Discipline and Punish"* discussed the meanings that criminals and deviants have for dominant social groups and the meaning of actions they take to control the troublesome.[164]

Though there has been an expansion of this type of approach,[165] and it raises a host of ethical and legal issues when researchers become participant observers in order to study those involved. Criminologists traditionally explained crime in terms of 'background variables' such as race, class, gender and social location. Some argue that it is much more important to try to understand the criminal in terms of 'foreground variables' - what it feels like to commit a crime[166]. One proposal is for five types of crime to be distinguished: passion murders, adolescent property crime, gang violence, persistent robbery and cold-blooded murder. In each case, a criminal is engaged in a project to achieve something. Hence, we must look under their skin and investigate the meaning violence has for its perpetrators. [167]

So, can a notion of human devaluation offer a fresh map of violence? Five messages it transmits might show how violence holds the inter-play of value and devaluation when competition tips over:

1. 'I might lose myself!'-or "don't touch me! -violence as desecration of identity.
2. 'I will take what you are!'- Violence as domination

and enjoying the domination.

3. "I want to be who you are"- Violence as imitation of highly prized people.

4. **"This is not all of me!"- Re-imaging the human landscape through Protest.**

5. 'You will pay for what you have done!'- Violence as retribution & exchange.

'I MIGHT LOSE MYSELF!'-OR "DON'T TOUCH ME! - VIOLENCE AS DESECRATION OF IDENTITY

The violent act out of their particular pathology that stems from much primal wounding. Their identity has been shaped by the devaluation. It has become them and given them a label they must struggle to remove. The violence creates internal deficit with little in the bank of personal worth. The desecrated, devalued self responds with fear and insecurity. The violent have developed an operating system that is unconsciously looking for compensation for their own primal wounding in order to make up that internal deficit. The devalued self wants to scrape the worth off the face of another. It turns them into the hunter, not just the hunted. Behind an abusive relationship is a story of the abuser and the abused. Face and name must be scraped off someone else now. "I have been desecrated. Now you must be!' We will return to this in the next chapter.

"I will take what you are"- Violence incorporates an aspect of exercising power 'over' someone and enjoying such domination as an addiction.

Thre French social philosopher Michael Foucault showed that power was a much more fluid concept than we had supposed. It was not just exercised in formal ways from the strong to the weak, from authority figures to the vulnerable. It flowed in many directions. People can exercise agency and make a bid for power even though they hold fewer cards. Power imbalance is inevitable simply because humans are never, and can never be, at the same starting point. Access to resources and capability is unequal and will be so until the end of time. Emphatically, that does not have to mean pernicious forms of domination. An uncomfortable feature of narratives of violence is the stark reality that some perpetrators want to be cruel. They enjoy the infliction of cruelty on their fellows and the heady domination of others. The Austrian Josef Fritzl dubbed the cellar where he locked his daughter and his three children by incest as "my kingdom."[168] His own father he described as a 'waster', a 'loser' who rejected him. After she kicked him out, it was his mother who taught her son discipline. The need to dominate his two families, one by marriage, the other by incest, stemmed from a need to be controlling and controlled. He placed a high value on respect, but it was respect for authority, not for his family. Adolf Hitler was given a rapturous reception in Fritzl's hometown of Amstetten when he visited it in 1938: Nazi ideals were formative in Fritzl's career. The pattern of brutalized children visiting brutality on others is well-established (as Hitler and his evil twin Stalin both attest). Investigation shows that violence is developed through a process of brutalisation, people undergoing coarse, cruel treatment at the hands of others that produces a lasting and dramatic impact on the course of their lives.

Violence reminds us of what is fundamental to the human condition, that we are hunters as well as hunted. We are, all of us perhaps, capable, under the right conditions, of becoming violent, of acting as devaluers and desecrators of others. Violence as power and domination is men needing to feel powerful, to keep the upper hand at all costs in case their wives should rise up a bit. It is whites controlling the blacks, masters their slaves. It is a bully needing to keep control in case they lose it. It is a woman disrupting a marriage so that she can have a man and then discard him. Look under the surface, behind the need to dominate and control, and there often emerges insecurity about being taken over, a threat being acted upon or a reaction against being abused or disrespected. A fundamental meaning of crime for the criminal is to escape control of others and impose control.[169]

But there is also an aspect present with domination that is terrifyingly addictive. Through myriad acts of violation that distort the human situation, it is clear that the violent may acquire a taste for blood. The feature of all addictions is that an object of desire produces 'a hit'; it registers in a way that may be disturbing but is nonetheless compelling and sought after. As in all addictive processes, perhaps violence fires neurons in a way its perpetrator wants, needs and cannot do without. Engaging in crime achieves moral dominance, generating a thrill that is experienced during the commission of the crime. The senseless act is converted to being sensual, seductive, magic, creative and deeply compelling. *"There's nowt to do"* was a lamentable reason given by the Edlington boys for their torture. It could be a sense of achievement against a threat of *ennui* by unemployed youth.

Or crowd violence that has addictive qualities by a thirst for action and a quest for repetition.

"I want to be who you are" - Violence creates disciples, apprenticed to role models perceived as having high value and worthy of emulation. Violence is mimesis, imitation of highly prized people.

Cultures of violence are types of schools, schools where teaching and learning is a routine. Narratives of violence are replete with educational experiences. Many violent protégées grew up in abusive households where they were conditioned to think that this is what you do to children or how you treat women. This is why early intervention is crucial in addressing potential offenders. Abusive households may reproduce themselves. In the case of two Edlington boys in the UK in February 2010, one only broke down and wept in the dock when his defending barrister pointed out that he had adopted his father's exact tone of voice when he acted cruelly. The brothers were said to experience 'a toxic childhood,' a phrase coined by an educationalist critiquing the complex web of factors disturbing the well-being of children.[170]

Feeling disadvantaged compared to others in the same society, the violent often develop lifestyles that allow them to become someone. They are trying to get their value back through the kind of people in their world that are highly prized and to whom they are apprenticed. Violent follow a sense of who is 'cool', the kind of people they value in their micro-culture, regardless of whether that role model is a hero to anyone else. Devaluation is sustained by all sorts of messages individuals and groups download about the kind of people that are valued and prized as against those that are written down. Especially in circumstances of low social approval, people make up the deficit by staking out ways in which they can be kings and queens on their own turf. They compensate by creating a micro-culture in which they will be dominant, based on the kind of people inhabiting their world they perceive as being 'cool', someone to aspire to. The role models offer deadly education.

Violent coaching assumes a set of learning experiences in which the subject is placed into the position of a novice. Usually an older person takes the role of a coach and teaches the proper course of action towards people who provoke them.[171]

Through violence, people are acting out what they have learnt from role models out of a desire to imitate. Rene Girard drew attention to the illusion of *"attaining autonomy as we imitate our models of power and prestige"*. This autonomy, however, is really nothing but a reflection of the illusions projected by our admiration for them. Girard locates this in mimetic desire, desire for what another had originated from a child desiring what its role models desired. This leads to conflict and violence if our desire to be like a model is strong enough. We imitate rivals even as we compete with them. *"The principal source of violence between human beings is mimetic rivalry, the rivalry resulting from imitation of a model who becomes a rival or of a rival who becomes a model."*[172] Mimesis is individuals and groups moving in the only social world they know, reproducing patterns that have become embedded within them. They have not consciously learnt ways of being and doing appropriate to the practice they are acting out. They are apprentices, imitating because they have absorbed a violent process, internalized to the point where they approve of it. They can see it works. You have to defend yourself in order to survive. From bullying, you graduate to more violence. Violence witnessed either at home or in the media is learned as a script to be stored and used. The script is encoded as a learning format, a way to behave.[173]

In his social learning model, Albert Bandura contested that people learn violent behaviour from observing aggressive role models.[174] Parents model aggressive behaviours not unlike those they are seeking to discourage. Recipients later adopt aggressive solutions in dealing with their problems.

Violence takes place in a system, a family system, or a micro-culture. Researchers have come to realize just how much human beings matter to each other. Trauma is a disturbingly sudden cessation of human interaction. The link between our capacity to be violent and our need for each other is intriguing and important.[175] A cycle of rejection is set up in peer interactions and with teachers.

After the Second World War, German people gradually faced up to the horror of the holocaust. By the 1960's, the generation that would be most shamed by the past was already passing. The terrifying events cast a long shadow. As I write these words, a 93-year-old former Nazi concentration camp guard has been spared jail after being found guilty of accessory to 5,230 murders. Bruno Dey was handed a two-year suspended sentence for his role in the killings when he was an SS tower guard at the Stutthof camp near what was then Danzig, now Gdansk, in Poland. This is likely to be the last such case involving surviving Nazi guards given that Dey was only 17 when he began his year-long service at the camp in August 1944 (the nine-month trial therefore being held in a young offenders' court). Dey refused to recognise his own guilt right until the end. *"You saw yourself as an observer,"* said the judge, clearly not a perpetrator. He was, he said, following orders in the tired explanation of moral retreat of which we have heard much. But apart from increasingly rare instances of this sort, open discussion of the past has long been possible in Germany and few have the emotional investment to defend it.

Domination is heady. When you feel powerful, you think you will command respect. It is saying, 'I want to be someone, I want to walk into a bar and be 9 foot tall!' Issues of value and disvaluing that arise amidst the tawdry tale of human violence come back to this - the need to restore relationships: relationships between individuals and within communities. It is when we become disconnected from each other that poverty and violence distort social bonds and spread like a virus. So, what overcomes the separation and help re-image the human landscape?

CHAPTER SEVEN
A QUESTION OF DESECRATION– VIOLENCE AS VIOLATION

Our theory of violence and atonement here is that violence is experienced as violation of sacred space. A similar idea is desecration. The Latin word 'violentia' means "vehemence" or "impetuosity" and emerges in our English language words 'violence' AND 'violation'. A violation is defined as *"to do violence to"* or, in a softer form, *"to fail to observe duty"*[176], but has connotations of abuse or being defiled. Violence so fundamentally structures our world that 'unviolated existence' is rare.[177]

Take the scourge of domestic violence, one of the biggest causes of social distress. It spiked by 80% in some instances during the pandemic for men as well as women as lockdown meant that they were being locked in with their accusers. As a social scourge of our time, it will also be the social scourge of the next because it has potential to be passed on from one generation to another. As it goes, this scourge destroys lives and families, bringing nothing but damage in its wake. Such domestic distress sharpens the sense of raw violation which many experience because this is intimate partner violence. Perpetrators becomes de-sensitised to the terror they bring, while those on the receiving end learn to cower and become a shadow. This turns into a perpetrator's paradise.

Whether domestic violence involves marital rape, it certainly inflicts immense harm in intimate settings because of coercive control. Despite being labeled a crime only recently, it causes immense harm. A controlling partner will try to cut you off from friends and family or spy (monitor) your activity throughout the day. They do this by wiring your house with cameras or recording devices, denying you freedom and autonomy. They will manipulate, lie, and gaslight to get their way and convince you that you're wrong. It is designed to exploit, control, create dependency and dominate. The victim's every day existence is micromanaged and his or her space for action as well as potential as a human being is limited and controlled by the abuser. Over time, coercively controlling behaviour erodes someone's sense of self, their confidence and self-esteem, agency and autonomy. An abuser creates an unreal world of contradiction, confusion and fear. This leaves a violated self, though more than half of victims do not even know that they are being abused, manipulated and controlled.

The fact that this pattern of behaviour is usually verbal rather than physical highlights an uncomfortable truth; violence does not need to be physical in order to qualify as such. Verbal abuse also qualifies.

"THIS IS NOT ALL OF ME!"

Violence forcibly labels victims but doesn't always need to constrain them. *"Victims need to be treated like human beings first and a piece of evidence after"*- a rape victim.[178] The effect of violence or aggression, verbal or physical, is that it forcibly shapes our identity. Such labels, either adopted or projected, are generated when violence occurs. Violence marks out labels and identities, bullies and bullied, criminals and victims, winners and losers. Those who experience violence or participate in it are shown as someone to whom violence happens, someone who inflicts violence (a macho type of persona), or someone who lives in a violent-prone part of the world. Human identity is shaped by the felt interior experience of the person that positions someone in a force field of relationship power.[179] For so many, the process of forming their identity is inseparable from their experience of violence, as the abuser or the abused, dominant or the weak.

An aggressor takes spray paint and paints a label on someone else marking them out as victim. It becomes part of their story. "I am a raped woman. I am a victim of violence." The terrifying use of rape as a weapon of war in the Democratic Republic of Congo creates new identities. *"My family refuses to eat from the same plate as me,"* says a 16-year old girl, rejected by rape.[180] The world is rudely divided into victims and perpetrators with far greater social taboo assigned to the former.

'Violence as violation' is helpful for three reasons. It underlines how violence is an unwelcome invasion of the sacred space of an individual or group. In achieving this, the act of violence can either be physical or verbal. Thirdly, emphasising violence as violation of sacred space shows there must be an intentionality to human violence. A 'violation' or desecration carries with it the idea of violence being unwelcome and intrusive. The assumption is that humans have a sacred space, a value, a dignity, which is being forcibly invaded and infiltrated. The definition of rape for instance creates a nightmare for the law: judges and juries have no idea where the boundary between rape and bad sex lies. Women can report having unwanted sex to please their partner or because their partner made them feel guilty. There is a post-modern way of defining rape. Rape is however one wishes to define it. The crucial factor though seems to be that a woman has been pressed, coerced, violated.[181]

Violence is an act of violation, a desecration of what is sacred, the citadel of the soul. A spiral is set up, a human tornado that feeds off desecration and in turn engenders further violation. *"I feel crap"* is often part of the inner psychological environment that sets people up to doing things to compensate for the deficit, to relieve the pain."

It may be that violence is the norm and therefore peace and harmony are not the usual state of affairs. Yet, it is surely blasphemy! Adopting a notion of violation of sacred space sees violence as a forcible and unwelcome intrusion into the human value of individuals or groups in a bid for respect or to extract value by devaluation of others. When this happens, there is protest. If this is correct, it raises more questions about religious justification for violence. Where does this fit in?

Much violence is about an exchange, compensating for being trashed or made to feel rubbished, by extracting it forcibly from someone else. Those who have a healthy sense of themselves rarely are the bullies. One young lady reported how she needed to re-create the experience of pain through rubbing soap hard into herself to blot out her overwhelming feelings of abuse. *"I'm worthless. If he had just been my stepfather, it might mean I had some value. But I was flesh and blood and he trashed me. He hurt me. So, all I have memories of is pain in my body's openings"*.

An abuser is often one who internalises both perpetrator and victim. Then he or she acts it out, maybe having witnessed domestic violence. They are trying to get their value back through the kind of people in their world that are highly prized and to whom they are apprenticed. 'It's payback time!' Violence is often reproduced by those who are bereft of any sense of worth through abusive experiences, then try to scrape it off the face of victims as compensation to recover their value or to protect their own value (honour). The victims of violence have experienced jagged reality that is all around, pervasive in militancy. With searing abrasiveness, they have encountered power: the power that is at the heart of the darkness and the dark powers. In its lashing, they come up against the wanton essence of sin; the primordial power that stands over against God. Gratuitous scraping the value off the face of another as a china plate can be marked - this is what sin does in violent, mocking disregard. As the assassin of John Lennon, Mark Chapman, confessed in an interview. 'I thought if I killed him, I would become him, I would acquire his fame".

Much violence in the world is driven by the motor of devaluation. Perpetrators will often have had experiences of being denigrated and de-personalised, becoming an It in the eyes of someone who is more powerful. It is by no means the case that everyone who has experienced assaults on their value will recycle this and become perpetrators themselves. But these experiences contribute strongly to violence – unless the power of forgiveness interposes.

The idea that violence equates to violation of sacredness is closely linked to what it means to dishonor someone. A dishonorable action is one that is harmful, base, shameless or discreditable. It is unworthy to the extent that it lacks any value.

Violation or being violated might involve a breach, infringement, or transgression, as of a law or a promise. We would speak of a parking violation which then calls forth a fine. *He was fined for a traffic violation. But there is also* 'desecration' or 'profanation', *the violation of a cemetery or* a sexual molestation, especially rape.

Torture is an extreme example of desecration of bodies and souls. *"It was relatively harmless and left no conspicuous scars on my body. And yet, twenty-two years after it occurred, on the basis of an experience that in no way probed the entire range of possibilities, I dare to assert that torture is the most horrible event a human being can retain within himself."* [182]

VIOLENCE AS A BID FOR SIGNIFICANCE

The American psychologist Rollo May saw violence as a bid for significance by the powerless; *"an explosion into violence may be the only way individuals or groups can get release from unbearable tension and achieve a sense of significance."* [183] It is the essence of violence that it engenders, statements of an intrinsic worth being assaulted. In narratives of violence, victims report feeling stripped of their worth and dignity. Progress comes when a client can say, *"this is part of me; it is not all of me!"*[184] Identities need to be de-constructed, the alien element removed. Forgiveness becomes a powerful approach that unfreezes the past. The Protest can then be liberated to emerge and re-value the wounded self. Latent or patent, bidden or unsolicited, the Protest is there, reacting against the mocking crudity of injustice, the shame of indignity, the shudder of contamination, the violation of rape or the presence of a burglar, a bully. It is vital to recovery that the victim can come to declare that they are worth more than what happened to them and that it was wrong.

Violence is often reproduced by those who are bereft of any sense of worth through abusive experiences, then try to scrape it off the face of victims as compensation to recover their value or to protect their own value (honour). The tortured landscape of human violence often discloses a significant reality. Where there has been a cost, there must be a payment. These are associated in degree though demand for payment and may or may not be proportionate. Familiar reactions crowd the stage, which may be more easily explained through some form of exchange system and relationship trade to make up the deficit. Losing name or status results in compensation being needed. Comfort eating may well be a human response to this loss. Or the individual may indulge in the blame game - 'I'll make them pay'. Unconsciously, the plan is how to act on it so as to stop feeling this way so the pain can be relieved. Authority figures such as police forces are often accused of attracting those who have an inferiority complex and who then need to compensate by throwing their weight around or by reacting unpredictably. This is a strategy for the restoration of their value.

The traumatic roots of violence lie in harm visited upon us, resulting in an injured psyche that looks for redress. A terrifying reality then confronts us. These strategies to re-value ourselves are transactions at the expense of another. It is a competitive marketplace in which my sense of worth can only be gained if yours is denied. The violent thus engage in a form of monetary calculation in which they assume there is only so much to go round. When it comes to intimate love, land and scarce resources, they may be right. Some sort of exchange is going on, whereby we are driven to seek compensation somewhere and from someone. Retribution will ensure that my depleted bank account of value is filled again at your expense. The impetus to make up the deficit is then relieved.

The warp drive to claw back a sense of worth or esteem is played out in many inter-personal dramas. It emerges in tragic narratives of traumatised women identifying with their own violent mothers and projecting dark feelings on to their child. It is most obvious in situations of gang culture and honour killings but also in racial violence in evidence at the time of writing.

Urban warfare between two gangs in Liverpool - the Croxteth crews and Strand Crew - terrorised the neighbourhood. Dressed in either balaclavas or hooded tops, the young people went about on quad bikes, BMX bicycles or even high-performance cars. Their weapons of choice were pistols, sawn-off rifles and sub-machine guns. While they dealt in cocaine and cannabis, the violence perpetrated by their mainly white members was no longer fuelled by drugs. Instead, they were prepared to wound and kill for power or just the simple respect of their peers. As one former member of the Croxteth Crew said, *"it's not about drugs anymore; all anyone wants is respect- that's what it' all about"*.[185]

The notion that violence can be understood as a bid for

respect is argued by James Gilligan.[186] He suggests that the mechanism by which unemployment and economic inequality stimulate violence depends on the fact that both trigger feelings of shame, of inferiority. Some violent acts may be a reaction against perceived humiliation or loss of status. In acts of violence, its actors feel a lack of respect - 'he disrespected me'. Forms of disrespect might lie in a perceived look, a verbal insult or a territorial claim. Violence is an assertion of self-respect. Violence is a forcible exchange of value, recovering someone's value through dehumanizing another. This also stands out in honour killings.

RACIAL VIOLENCE AS DISVALUE

Racism is not based on some empirical generalization; it is based rather on an ontological affirmation. It is not the assertion that certain people are behind culturally or otherwise because of environmental conditions. It is the affirmation that the very being of a people is inferior.

Coined by Eddie Glaude Jr., the value gap is understood as the general assumption that in America white people are valued more than black people. Because of society's inability to admit to any idea that society values white people over black people, he argues its vision of democracy is distorted. The value gap is formed by the "differences and dissonances" that exist between the moral, social, political and religious values of groups. The value gap is prevalent in many ways, specifically in the way in which white people speak to black people. The value gap is present in the difference between predominantly black and predominantly white neighbourhoods where there is a difference in the size of houses, how parks are maintained and how the sewage system works. There are more black children in poverty than white children and white children outnumber black children

3-to-1. Glaude suggests this increase in poverty may be a result of lack of access to networking opportunities required for so many jobs. Since a majority of networks consist of almost all white people, it is harder for blacks to find jobs. Such perspectives savage the idea of a post-racial society.[187]

That was written in 2017. Three years later it was a more urgent issue. Widespread protests in response to the death of George Floyd at the hands of police, and in response to the long and bloody history of racism and racial injustice in the US, are the backdrop to the painful reality of a value gap. In the 1960's and 70's, the writer James Baldwin had borne witness to the difficult truth of race in America today in the wake of the Civil Rights movement, when a similar attempt to compel a national confrontation with the truth was answered with the murders of Malcolm X and Martin Luther King. As witnessed in his publications in those years, spanning from the publication of *The Fire Next Time* in 1963 to that of *No Name in the Street* in 1972, Baldwin was transformed into a more overtly political writer. From those seminal times, Baldwin emerged with a more resolute sense of purpose to force America to face the lies it tells itself about race.[188]

Baldwin's most powerful polemic on racial violence as de-humanising is in his 'Another Country'.[189] The root, Baldwin was convinced, was rage. Not just white rage and hatred but black rage. "There is no Negro living in America who has not felt briefly and for long periods with anguish sharp and dull in varying degrees or to varying effect, simple, naked and unanswerable hatred: who has not wanted to smash any white face he may encounter in a day, to violate, out of motives of cruellest vengeance, their women, to break the bodies of all white people and bring them low, as low as that dust into which he himself has been and is being trampled? No Negro. Finally, who has not had to make his own precarious adjustment to the 'nigger' who surrounds him and to the 'nigger' in himself?"

Sadly, some white reaction to the racial violence that surfaced in the hot pandemic summer of 2020 superficially focussed on the looting and destruction of property, which by all accounts were not perpetrated by protesters but by lawless elements on the extreme left and right, intent on exploiting the protests under cover of nightfall. The underlining Protest about the 'value gap' was eclipsed.

HONOUR CULTURE

"Dawn will come, and the girls will ask about her, 'Where is she'? And the monster will answer: 'We killed her'. A mark of shame was on our foreheads and we washed it off"- *a female Iraqi perspective on honour crimes.* [190] - Sana al-Khayyat

Honour and shame are parallel labels used to describe either physical conditions or human behaviour which a culture approves or disapproves of. Westerners find it very difficult to appreciate a face-saving or honour culture. The self is a cultural production. In the West, freedom of the individual, the right to self-expression, security, the adventure of love, efficiency and wealth-creation are all prized. Naturally though these values seem to be to those who live in societies of this kind, human individuality is but one way of constructing the self. Other cultures function very differently. Differing roles for men and women, interaction between the individual and family ('I'/ 'we'), honour and shame and the place of hospitality constitute a very different frame of reference.

In the Middle East and central Asia, a major objective is to accumulate honour and avoid anything that could deplete it. Honour can be eroded through shame. Shame brings disgrace down on one's head and dishonours the family. It must be avoided at all costs. To prevent letting the side down, people will preserve appearances. Honour comes from age, from family connections and from hard work and success. In Islamic societies, honour is inseparable from religion. In mechanisms that correspond to older forms of honour in the West, notions of 'sharif' and 'shame' both control and discipline behaviour. *"Honour... provides a nexus between the ideals of a society and their reproduction in the individual through his aspiration to personify them"191*

Honour is a dynamic and relational concept. On the one hand, an individual can think of himself or herself as honourable based on his or her conviction that he or she has embodied those actions and qualities that the group values as 'honourable,' as the marks of a valuable person. This aspect of honour is really 'self-respect.' On the other hand, honour is also the esteem in which a person is held by the person's group that he or she is a valuable member of that group. In this regard, it is about having the respect of others. It was a problematic experience when one's self-respect was not matched by corresponding respect from others, but strategies could be developed to cope with the discrepancy. *"When the powerful and the masses, the philosophers and the Jews, the pagans and the Christians all regarded honour and dishonour as their primary axis of value, each group would fill out the picture of what constituted honourable behaviour or character in terms of its own distinctive sets of beliefs and values, and would evaluate people both inside and outside that group accordingly."192*

Shame, by contrast, signifies being seen as less than valuable because one has behaved in ways that run contrary to the values of the group. Someone who puts personal safety above the city's well-being, fleeing from battle, loses the respect of society. His worth is impugned; he 'loses face'; he is disgraced and viewed as a disgrace. Out of shame as well though, a woman refuses an adulterous invitation; a soldier refuses to flee from battle.

There is no single definition of honour that can be applied to every biblical text and context. How each situation begs the question of what the concept of honour described therein is a complex task. But answering that question has become a biblical industry.[193] Theology has begun to wake up to the role of honour and shame as shaping the thought world in which the Bible was written. Genesis narratives have, for instance, been re-cast as stories of honour and shame. The fall, with Adam and Eve leaving paradise in humiliation, is a narrative of disgrace. Addressing human sinfulness involves taking responsibility for one's actions that lead to shame and a humiliated status. Their status before God as divinely chosen people gives Israel a high honour indeed. The Deuteronomic history in Judges reveals cycles of shame and then renewed honour before God. The Book of Esther demonstrates a theology of being saved from dishonour in contrast to the false honour system demonstrated by Haman. "Thus, shall it be done for the man whom the King delights to honour" (Esther 6v9)[194]. By contrast, in writings such as Hosea, Israel's spiritual promiscuity is symbolised by the shame of a prostitute who experiences reversal (Hosea 3). The honourable line is, however, continued through the line of David, encapsulating Yahweh at work to exalt his people.

The New Testament cultural world was honour-based. The Gospels, particularly Luke, depict Jesus giving honour to people, especially those who merited social ostracism.[195] Jesus' followers were those who pursued honourable actions by his criteria, not those they had been used necessarily. Honourable vs shameful conduct is spelt out particularly in Matthew's gospel.[196] Paul's writings demonstrate awareness that social stigma could accrue or be reversed and that this was very much part of God's plan and purpose to convert the socially marginalised to being an acceptable people.[197]

The new mission to Spain envisaged by Paul as the background to Romans merits a detailed exposition of salvation in which the new covenantal community will live by a different code, paying 'honour to whom honour is due' (Romans 13v7).[198] In Romans 1, Paul uses honour and shame language associated with concepts of masculine and feminine roles when he argues strongly against same-sex relations (1v26- 'God gave them up to degrading passions').[199] Concepts of honour and shame were closely related to power relations between men and women as well as with traditions and even cosmology, as Paul's discussion in 1 Corinthians 11:1–16 demonstrates. Advice was given by New Testament writers regarding what is an honourable behaviour both for young men and older people, according to the context they address (1 Timothy 4:12–5:2; Titus 2:2, 6; 1; Peter 5:1–5). In short, analysing honour-shame has yielded new theological readings of the New Testament.[200]

The anthropologist Julian Pitt Rivers examined how honour and shame is attached to the body.[201] Honour is inherited through blood. The shedding of blood is a stain of honour. Private parts are the seat of shame. They are vulnerable. The right hand is the hand of honour, the left the hand of shame. The head is to be honoured. In court, no one's head should be higher than the ruler's. The head of the ruler is crowned. War is a matter of honour and shame; the battle ground is the field of honour. To the victor go the spoils of war. He can rape the women of the vanquished for the vanquished have no honour to defend. In antiquity slaves were the vanquished. Competition is a means of winning or gaining honour. Titles and trophies are symbols of such honour. In our society the greatest honour tends to be given to athletes and to those who defeat others and win. Someone must know the "agony of defeat" in order for the other to know the honour of victory. In Oedipus Rex, the pollution of the city caused by the incestuous relationship of Oedipus and his mother and the murder of his father requires Oedipus to be killed or banished. He must be expunged from the city.

Cultural honour in the West meant defending your good name. It was worked out differently between genders. For a man it meant a reputation for courage; for a woman it was about chastity.[202] The emblematic figure of an English gentleman combined resolute sense of fair play with class consciousness. The First World War destroyed the highly developed Victorian honour culture in and the idea of the hero. As Wilfred Owen said, men died like cattle. Shame and weakness were re-cast by psychoanalysis as personality problems, a sickness. In tracking the formation of a post-honour society in the West, James Bowman suggests that honour is rooted in the murky reflective instinct that if you get somebody, you must expect them to pay you back.[203]

BEYOND HONOUR CULTURE

To this we will return. It is worth saying that in Western society we have moved considerably beyond honour culture. As explored elsewhere, the kind of society on the contemporary landscape has moved from being shaped by duty, honour and shame (though shame continues to be a driver). A 'sin and guilt' society based on right and wrong has also receded as a driving force. What we have moved into can be characterised as 'voice and choice'.[204] The point is though

154

that certain forms of human action resulting in violence stem from a concept of people having a value and worth which is then violated. We could trace this idea through such phenomenon as torture, rape, gang-based violence, domestic violence or honour culture. Uppermost at the present time is racialised violence.

Racial violence is an everyday occurrence for millions whether through overt acts or micro-aggressions that are smaller scale but no less debilitating. But all violence involves acts of desecration. 'Violentia' is violation. Something (someone) has been breached, the sacred core despoiled. Someone has not just been wronged (which thereby creates obligation and debt). They have been violated, often routinely. Sacred self has been demeaned, trampled on as if of no account.

All sins represent a failure to give honour. The violence of desecration both hardens and highlights that. The question is: Has such notion of extreme dishonour anything to do with atonement as it lies at the heart of Christian faith? For there we see the cross, a place of ravaged shame.

PART TWO – THROUGH A DIFFERENT LENS

Against that background, we now begin to build a lens on the atoning death of Christ and why the experience of violence was central to it. The therapeutic dimensions of this are profound. What does this say to Christian thought and to violence in our time?

i. The value of personhood is a big driver of social life and also of Christian thought. When breached and devalued, it requires redress. It applies at all levels – from the smallest child to God.

ii. Jesus comes as one of us – not above the fray but with us in solidarity and full-on participation.

iii. Violence sets up an intensified transaction, an exchange in which personhood is trashed and devalued and handed to another. Jesus experiences this in full measure.

iv. His violent death is for us – trading places. It is payment for sins that devalue, hence becomes the site of an exchange.

CHAPTER EIGHT
THE JESTER AT THE FARCE: VALUABLE PERSONHOOD

"I was not permitted to see my mother or father or poor sisters and brothers to say goodbye, though going to a strange land and might never see them again. The people who keep slaves think black people are like cattles, without natural affection. But my heart tells me it is far otherwise"
- Mary Prince 1831205

Attention must be paid- even to a salesman'- Arthur Miller, Death of a Salesman. 206

"I will tell you why; so, shall my anticipation prevent your discovery, and your secrecy to the King and Queens: moult no feather. I have of late, (but wherefore I know not) lost all my mirth, forgone all custom of exercises; and indeed, it goes so heavily with my disposition; that this goodly frame the earth, seems to me a sterile promontory; this most excellent canopy the air, look you, this brave o'er hanging firmament, this majestical roof, fretted with golden fire: why, it appeared no other thing to me, than a foul and pestilent congregation of vapours. What a piece of work is man, How noble in reason, how infinite in faculty, In form and moving how express and admirable, In action how like an Angel, In apprehension how like a god, The beauty of the world, The paragon of animals. And yet to me, what is this quintessence of dust? Man delights not me; no, nor Woman neither; though by your smiling you seem to say so."

This scene with its famous speech of Prince Hamlet to Rosencrantz and Guildenstern in Act II, Scene 2 shows Shakespeare at his finest. Though humans may appear to think and act "nobly" they are essentially "dust". Hamlet is in melancholic mood, lamenting to his old friends over the difference between the best that we aspire to be and the reality. It is a divide that depresses him deeply.

Shakespeare was educated into a biblical culture that is becoming a fading memory in contemporary culture. Palm 8 would have been well known to him, especially verse 5: *"You have made [humans] a little lower than the heavenly beings and crowned them with glory and honour."*

So it was for his near contemporary Montaigne who may have influenced him. *"Who have persuaded [man] that this admirable moving of heavens vaults, that the eternal light of these lamps so fiercely rowling over his head, that the horror-moving and continual motion of this infinite vast ocean were established, and continue so many ages for his commodities and service? Is it possible to imagine so ridiculous as this miserable and wretched creature, which is not so much as master of himselfe, exposed and subject to offences of all things, and yet dareth call himself Master and Emperor"*[207].

But then in all the passionately intense self-questioning that Montaigne embarked upon, it emerges that there may be no truths, only moments of clarity, passing for answers. Nature, he says, has very conveniently cast the action of our sight outwards. We are swept on downstream, but to struggle back towards our self against the current is a painful movement; thus does the sea, when driven against itself, it swirls back in confusion. Thus, the commandment given us in ancient times by the god at Delphi was contrary to all expectations: *"Look back into yourself; get to know yourself; hold on to yourself... Can you not see that this world of ours keeps its gaze bent ever inwards and its eyes ever open to contemplate itself? It is always vanity in your case, within and without, but a vanity which is less, the less it extends. Except you alone, O Man, said that God, each creature first studies its own self, and, according to its needs, has limits to his labours and desires. Not one is as empty and needy as you, who embrace the universe: you are the seeker with no knowledge, the judge with no jurisdiction and, when all is done, the jester of the farce."208*

Or we could be instructed by Genesis 1v26 – humankind in the image of God, the 'imago dei'.

Or Psalm 8 –

[3] When I consider your heavens,
   the work of your fingers,
the moon and the stars,
   which you have set in place,
[4] what is mankind that you are mindful of them,
   human beings that you care for them?
[5] You have made them a little lower than the angels
   and crowned them with glory and honour.

THE FIRST STEP: TO SIN IS TO DEVALUE

Our argument here is to use the lens of violence firstly to show how contradictory it is when religion legitimates it also as a way in to understand better the very idea of atonement. The tragedy is that those who espouse a high view of the cross include, for instance, White Supremacists in the US or the Dutch Reformed, Orthodox or Catholic Churches of the past, whose dark history colludes with the perpetrators of violence. If you take the cross seriously, you ought to be on the side of the victims for the simple reason that Jesus was a victim of violence and injustice.

We will be using a sociological lens about violence to help

us understand the deeper meaning of the cross. Violence is a transaction; it sets up an exchange. In a commercial exchange, the currency is money. With violence, the currency is another form of VALUE – the value and worth of people.

Our argument in summary is as follows:

i.   Personhood is valuable – whether this is human or divine. When breached, that sets up a demand for recompense, a form of invoice. This is another way of looking at sinfulness.

ii. Solidarity – Jesus enters the human situation and is qualified to be the representative person; the devalued universal victim but also sin-bearer for the perpetrators of sin.

iii. Trading places – an exchange takes place; the merits of Jesus for human demerit; the devalued person, who is one of us, trading supreme worth in place of the unworthy.

iv. Recompense – not only is there a transfer of status, the price is paid too. This is true to psychological realities where some form of recognition and recompense is often needed.

All this and we haven't had to mention sacrifice or scapegoat! If the above account has merit, Jesus is not some alien other who is then scapegoated in the way that, for example, Rene Girard sets up. Jesus is one of us. The driver of our idea here is a transfer, in what we will label 'symbolic exchange'.

We start with our individual sense of value and worth. We can see this positively – that is, we can articulate the belief that each human soul is unique and possesses enormous, if not infinite value. Jewish and Christian traditions want to say that we are made in God's image (Genesis 1v26). In Islam, humanity is the vice-regent of God, which is fairly similar. However, the theological action really starts, not with an abstract concept but watching what happens when that is breached.

In our different lens through which to view the atoning death of Jesus, the high value of personhood or as some older theologies framed this, 'the infinite value of the soul' means that, when valuable personhood is defaced or trashed in some way, that generates a reaction aimed at upholding our value and worth and seeking to restore it to 'market value', so to speak.

A theological proposition can be advanced here. To sin is to devalue. Disvaluing someone, eroding their worth, is the very essence of sin. While the idea of 'missing the mark' (Greek 'hamartia') is the result of sinfulness, the stance behind it is that of wilful disregard. Wilful disregard is a disregard of someone or something; a refusal to bend the knee and a determination to do what one wishes even if it causes pain or damage, even if it results in dishonouring them or eroding their worth.

Sin itself has gone out of fashion. The language of sin and judgement seems dead in our culture until you remember that moral accountability and recompense for actions is alive and well (as we will see). The word itself is not in cultural vogue, as few recognise, they are sinners. It seems discredited and a relic of Victorian moralism and hypocrisy over double standards.

Violence, as we saw, is a vicious species of devaluing people. It is the point where an act or attitude of writing someone down or writing them off turns nasty. It is Cain's attitude in which a different sacrifice stands for the difference he feels in relation to his brother. Violence can indeed be enacted against property or planets in acts of vandalism. Yet, disconnection experienced by the perpetrator is one of profound separateness from others, from collective property or from nature. Violence is 'violentia', violation or desecration. It sets up a form of symbolic exchange. Something is taken away.

There would probably be widespread agreement about two propositions. The first is this. Human beings have an intrinsic value, a value that must not be defaced. Secondly, human beings have equal status and worth. It is because moral agents have personhood that is of high worth that the problem arises of what happens when that is defaced. An invoice is necessary. Something needs to happen.

This is not to say for a moment that this is what is practiced. The reality of social life is that people are treated and treat each other in ways that contradict this. Nevertheless, the struggle to realise our value and worth is fundamental to what humans try to do and be in the world.

Here is an example. After taking office, the Prime Minister of Malaysia, Mahathir Mohamad, abruptly reversed his country's long-standing pro-UK stance. From then on, Malaysia had a new policy- 'Buy British last'. It was only after he had been invited to a 'peace - meal' at Downing Street by Margaret Thatcher that Mahathir relented. What he had wanted all along was respect. He refused to be treated as a colonial client grateful for the smallest word from anyone with an assumption of superiority.[209] In other words, he sought to be properly valued.

We seem to have an in-built psycho-social need to be worthwhile people engaged in worthwhile projects and therefore active in garnering worth from our world. The impetus to be valued and to feel valuable and the need to feel one is worth something are central to what it means to be human. Organisational or inter-personal approaches that give value to people rather than devalue them tap into an aspect of the human psyche that responds to a sense of worth. People are more likely to flourish in such circumstances. Social processes that give value to people - either through engagement or listening - are those giving a positive environment that cultivates the welfare of staff or customers and communicates, "I am worth listening to!" Understanding how valuing or disvaluing is communicated is a vital insight in many areas of social life.

In contemporary life, value is accorded to individuals and groups in a way that is unrelated to any semblance of inner value or 'value-in-oneself'. What someone is worth is awarded to social participants on the basis of the wage economy (economic value), identity badges (status value such as ownership or appearance) or identity boundaries (social value; being the right sort of person).

Are we psychologically structured so as to require a strong sense of value within which to live and move and have our being and do our best work? Human actions reveal constantly that we seem compelled to live as if we had high value or we wither in its absence. People derive value in a variety of ways. Significance is key to this quest.

Here is a disgruntled sailor when the Imperial German Navy was ordered to sea for one final battle at the close of the First World War? *"I would have fought hard if I had been treated like a human being all these years instead of an animal!"*[210]

Here are some disgruntled staff and workers. Why are they disgruntled and fed up? Often their struggle depends on them not being heard, treated with indifference, or as not having lots to offer. Behind the many problems, clients are working through lie experiences of being devalued. Again and again, statements will surface such as:

I wanted a simple acknowledgement that I had been heard, that I was struggling with a feeling. I wanted to be understood but what I got back all the time was something different so I felt all the time that my needs were not actually being heard."[211]

You don't have to go very far to find reactions to people feeling:

- Being written off or written down as worth less or even worthless
- Being belittled or humiliated
- Being patronised or looked down upon
- Being disrespected or treated as 'rubbish'
- Being treated as being of no account or not being heard,
- The experience of one's worth not being recognised

Reactions to such experiences often take the form of a protest, a response that either shouted or whispered sounds, "I count… I matter... I am worth more than that!" "I won't be spoken to like that!" Experiences generating statements about human devaluation arise through relationships of all kinds but tend to result in these kinds of reactions:

i. The Protest against indifference (the need to be heard and taken seriously)
ii. Indignation and dignity – the anger of a valuable self
iii. The reflex against being put down or belittled– appropriate respect for a valuable self

Being heard or seen (not disregarded), communicates I am worth listening to. William James wrote, *"No more fiendish punishment could be devised, were such a thing physically possible, than that one should be turned loose in society and remain absolutely unnoticed by all the members thereof. If no one turned around when we entered, answered when we spoke, or minded what we did, but if every person we met 'cut us dead' and acted as if we were non-existent things, a kind of rage and impotent despair would before long well up in us, from which the cruellest bodily torture would be a relief"-* [212]

Involvement, dignifying and enlarging are vital approaches towards helping people flourish. They are absolutely critical factors in promoting human flourishing. Whether we are talking about families, political culture, inter-personal life or what goes on in organisations, involving, dignifying and enlarging people will enable them to flourish. By contrast, when humans are not noticed or taken seriously, when we are treated as mere objects and subject to invasive handling, when we are belittled or diminished, such influences threaten to wither us. They collide with our sense of a valuable self which becomes demoralised, acquiesces temporarily or rises up with indignant protest.

The role that value plays as a serious and constitutive driver of society is underlined through its opposite. There would seem to be three reactions to social devaluing which trigger a core challenge.

a. Demoralisation – the effects of social and personal factors which convey absence of any sense that an individual or social group counts, perception that a sense of worth and dignity has gone, and which often throws up desperation and depression. People give up!

b. Resignation – a lowering of value characterised by collusion- going along with the state of things, acting out the scripts handed to you, but which carries potential rather than absence.

c. Protest – a rising up to affirm worth and discovery that you could be what you wanted to be.

For centuries, people have depersonalised or depreciated the Other because of race, class and gender. There has been much progress in all peoples having equal dignity and worth and on the idea that such evils as bullying and racial discrimination (or any other kind) should be outlawed.

Nevertheless, the struggle to realise our value and worth is central to the fight for racial justice. Eddie Glaude in his book *Democracy in Black: how race still enslaves the American soul*, 'argues that the fundamental belief is that white people are valued more than others'[213]

Writers in a former era were much less conscious that the framework within which people operate have been set by society. As Nietzsche trenchantly observes, artists have so often been "*smooth sycophants either of vested interests or of forces newly come to power.*"[214] In '*Thus Spoke Zarathustra*', Nietzsche unmasks the way that 'the good and the just' crucify Jesus because their spirit was imprisoned in their good conscience.' They construe as evil his rejection of their notions of good. Like poisonous flies they sting and 'do so in all innocence'.[215]

Much of our lives is shaped by the value that society places on its participants. Many of the transactions and exchanges that dominate our actions, on closer inspection seem to revolve around the pursuit of a high value for ourselves or our group. By contrast, when we experience disvaluing in various forms, we are hard-wired so as to react. Knowing what helps us to discover our value is to unlock a dynamic principle within human interaction. Put another way, knowing how to release our sense of worth taps into an impetus that is foundational to the way we function.

Human value is a social dynamic. There is an internal driver towards realising our value and worth. This impetus comes up against the endemic reality of inter-personal and social life in the form of experiences that erode our worth and write down our value. This can be translated into words in terms of indifference, indignity and diminishing, which are the prime routes by which devaluation is experienced. The interplay of value and experiences of devaluation, far from just being an aspiration, are descriptive of inter-personal life. The dynamic of value/devaluation plays in personal and organisational life but also in the way subjects are shaped in society.

The classic struggles of the 20th century tended to focus on one form of oppression only - the struggle for emancipation

of women, civil rights, colonialism, disability, homophobia, ageism or class discrimination. Yet, the swirling sands
of social change result in new patterns in inequality. It is
now officially recognised that more and more members of a
growing ethnic middle class have their own homes and good
jobs, whereas some white working class members may be
faced with serial disadvantages.[216] Disadvantage is endemic
to issues of class and poverty, not just race or gender. Behind
the hot collective indignation that will no longer bow down
before forms of domination is a demand for equal value.

The struggle for human rights and for equality comes
down to us having an equal value as people too! Over the
years, over the world, people have learnt to rank other human beings. They ranked them according to whether they
were men or women, rich or poor, strong or weak, black or
white, one of us or from another religious group. In every
society, there were outsiders and insiders. Those who had
money, position and were the right gender, colour or religion
pulled the strings. They had the power. Others were devalued. Devaluation of others has been a large theme in history.
When it goes to an extreme, devaluing others leads to de-humanising them. When we do that, we fail to see them as people like us with feelings and an identity. Difference means
that layers of wealth and importance are formed; it relegates
others to being inferior, less than us. As we have just seen,
we know why we have value and from whence arises the
indignant protest when that is trampled on and discarded.
Both psychological and social necessity, for us to live in our
world, make us desperate to have our value upheld. With it,
we flourish; without it, we wither. Few of us – even mocking atheists or aggressive scientists – will be inwardly silent
in the face of indifference. Few of us will be comfortable
with being diminished, cut down to size, or being meted out
unequal treatment. Few of us will not react in the presence

of indignity. Our value cries out in the night. Human beings have sacred value of awesome dimensions, not just white lives but all lives, black lives and poor lives.

THEOLOGICAL EXCURSION - IN THE DIVINE MIRROR

God is guarantor of human value and worth on account of creation. Just as in human endeavours, the worth of a creator is invested in a worthwhile task. We have high value that comes from God seeing us in a certain light. Probably no verse has attracted more interest than the statement that God created the person according to his image. The literature is vast. One verse about the person has become the centre of attention whereas it is hardly mentioned again in the OT apart from Psalm 8. This is because of the modern interest in what is a person.

"Then God said, 'Let us make humankind in our image, according to our likeness; and let them have dominion over the fish of the sea, and over the birds of the air, and over the cattle, and over all the wild animals of the earth, and over every creeping thing that creeps on the face of the earth. So, God created humankind in his image, in the image of God he created them; male and female he created them." (Genesis 1v26-17)

The main lines of interpretations have been:
i.   Distinguishing image from likeness as indicating natural vs supernatural likeness to God
ii.   The likeness consists of spiritual qualities and capacities
iii. The image of God is seen in the external form
iv.   The imago dei describes the human being as a whole
v.   The person as God's counterpart- whom God can address as 'thou'
vi.   The person as representative of God on earth

Being made in the divine image represents a high value being placed on humanity. It is approximately the same idea as in Islamic thought of human beings as vice-regents of God.

There is also a strong aspect of the human capacity to know God, the foundation of our religious nature. *"If we were not like God, we could not know him."*[217]

There are two elements: image (zelem), reflection or representation, and likeness (demuth). Many older writers thought that the word 'image' referred to the body; by its beauty and erectness being an expression of the divine. The idea of 'likeness' referred to our intellectual and moral nature. Augustine categorised 'image' as the rational element and 'likeness' referred to moral faculties. Scholastic theologians tended to follow this line of interpretation. Luther distinguished between 'image' and 'likeness'. It was moral mirror. The image was lost in the fall and recovered through redemption.[218] Reformed theologians followed Calvin in taking the middle ground between seeing the imago consist in rationality or in moral conformity. Both are included.[219] Reason, conscience and will are bound up with our intellectual and moral nature as is our capacity to know God, the foundation of our spiritual nature. "If we were not like God, we could not know him."[220]

Made in the mirror means that humanity possesses four Cs: Consciousness - Creativity – Conscience – Community.

The religious experience across the globe has witnessed countless examples of creating human (anthropomorphic) images to help devotees feel close to divine reality and that God is close to human beings. Endeavours to give form to that which is formless have been plentiful. Often, the gods were like people, reduced to finite form, allowing humans to glimpse something of the divine, or so they thought. The divine always transcends ordinary experience. It is all the more surprising that the divine can be represented by images – humans depicting his likeness, the image of God.

We are defined in relationship to God. The creation of human beings in the image of God is not saying something has been added to the created person but is explaining what the person is. Their very existence lives in relationship with God. Relationship with God is not something added to human existence. We are not isolated entities. The image of God does not mean that we look at ourselves as if in solitary confinement. We are hard-wired for connection.

Humans are intrinsically related; it is not just in gender differentiation that we are joined at the hip. Personhood is relational. In a mirror, we see our own image. In looking at us, God sees something of himself, some recognition that leaps up, albeit in muted response. The image calls back to the image maker in dialogue. In our horizontal relationships, there is a social refraction of our vertical connection with God. The "imago dei" is about the value and worth of humanity. If God sees his own reflection looking back and calling back, that speaks volumes about how valuable we truly are. The image ought not to be defaced. It is a declaration of the value of personhood, but it is more than that. It is a sharing of the divine worth. Do not touch a painting or rubbish a treasured photo of someone. It represents them. A tramp is as valuable as Michelangelo since God would have it so.

God gives a vote of confidence in something he has made which resembles him in part. Humanity is a microcosm of God, gifted with the capacity to respond. Mad King George could shake hands with an oak tree, but it could not answer back. Humans might commune with nature but not the deep level recognition that comes with being of like mind. It is the recognition through which a parent and child can connect. It is the recognition through which some people can remind us a little bit of God.

1. Devaluation begins with the divine – God is being disrespected by human sin.
2. Devaluation is an affront against the otherness of the other and traduces the sacredness of people along a trajectory and downward gradient.
    i. The put-downs of everyday life between individuals.
    ii. Systems of social life that operate in the collective sphere.
    iii. Violence that defaces and desacralizes people, scraping value from their face.
    iv. Political systems, where life is cheap, which do not hold human life to be sacred.
    v. Extreme politics and ethnic cleansing where people are evil to be eradicated, filth to be expunged or vermin to be exterminated.

DISHONOURING GOD

This descent into violence was depicted in chapter four. The point to note here is that it is precisely because people are valuable that there is a price on it, so to speak. Recompense becomes necessary. The lost value must be restored. This imperative would not be true of the need to restore the value of a house, for example, since market value is a fragile, fluctuating thing. But it is profoundly true of personhood when defaced or desecrated. Does it apply to sin's daring bid to take away from God?

Human devaluation expresses the essence of human sinfulness and all that mars God's creation. This applies towards God and also the other. Both in robbing God of honour as well as affronting the worth of others, to disvalue constitutes what sinfulness means in practice as well as expresses it.

The language of the prodigal, 'against you and you only have I sinned' (Luke 15v21) may seem to be unrelated to my actions against a fellow human being. Yet God as the ultimate source of personal value and supremely deserving of worth has to recognise and guarantee such infringements or failure to acknowledge him. God is involved in this process. In the nexus of human actions that devalue others and deny their worth, he is a major player. This takes place at two levels. Firstly, he is guarantee and source of human value and worth. Secondly, he is not acknowledged. God is devalued by human wilfulness. Christian hymnody and liturgy often speak of merit and de-merit as well as of unworthiness before the God who affirms the value and worth of personal beings. God's honour and value is ultimate. It is attacked by human sinfulness. Sin is an act of dishonouring God, who in himself has a supreme dignity and ultimate 'worth-ship' as cause and ground of the value of personal beings.

The result is idolatry, something or someone at the centre of our lives, the ultimate focus for our living. There is a terrifying possibility. By allowing it to take the place of God, something good becomes a destructive force within us. We can also make something that is evil in itself, such as greed or racial hatred, an idol. One of the deepest motivations for turning something into an idol is the urge to 'get control of life' and give it a focus – of which we are in control. The paradox is that when we devalue ourselves, we end up dishonouring or devaluing God and others.

God is therefore implicated. The work of Christ has traditionally been spoken of as being:
i.   Objective- something done by Jesus towards God that materially changes the situation in terms of how God deals with us; it is not merely subjective, affecting us

internally.

ii. <u>Propitiatory</u> – something that covers sin and renders God gracious to us.

iii. <u>Expiatory</u> – something that wipes out the offence by the discharge of a penalty.

iv. <u>Vicarious or representative</u> - achieving for us and in the name of humanity by doing what we could not do for ourselves.

But does God need placating? Surely yes for the same reason that humans do. If a group of local adolescents trash my garden, they are not trashing me directly, let alone God. Yet, if they compounded the action and failed to acknowledge that this is an issue, they would be definitely walking over me, not just the flower beds. What is needed is recognition as well as reparation. The boys are devaluing me as a moral being worthy of recognition. They are saying in effect: like your garden, you are of no value.

Questions abound. God is beyond all suffering surely. Julian of Norwich observed, God cannot forgive and cannot be offended. How can God suffer loss and dishonour to his glory unless he becomes a victim? How can we be forgiven by God if human victims do not forgive us?

A much repeated assumption of objectors to the idea of a substitutionary atonement is that it would be inconsistent for God to show wrath. The Greek terms 'hilaskomai' (to make propitiation) and 'hilasmos' (a sacrifice of propitiation) have the sense of a sacrifice that turns away the wrath of God. These words were well understood outside the church in reference to pagan Greek religions where their consistent meaning was about making peace with God through sacrifice. The idea of 'expiation' does not quite do this because there is no concept of appeasing God's wrath but only cleansing for sin. "Who required Christ to pay the penalty for our sins?", asks Wayne Grudem in a recent systematic theology. *"It was God the Father whose role was to require that payment."*[221]

In the regime of moral accountability, I have traduced God as well as those around me. Does God therefore demand a blood sacrifice and takes it out on an innocent person? That of course puts things far too emotively and we cannot hear that kind of message without distortion. The cultural meanings we bring to it are too formidable a barrier. The question could be put thus. Does God require compensating, or propitiating (the sacrifice system being a way of expressing this in the culture of the day- we would put things differently)? Surely the answer is yes. We can hear the idea of 'the wrath of God' as God flaring up in anger and being implacably hostile. It may, however, be the biblical way of saying that God is also a personal being. We would have no difficulty to say that people exercise wrath because they are personal agents who can offended. To say that God is not offended by human sinfulness or the things that mar his creation is to state that there is no issue of God's honour or attitude at stake and no question of recognition of divine moral agency. It only makes sense to see God as third party to human-human exchanges if all the time God is present as a moral force upholding the value of moral agents. Sinfulness is an act by which you personally have been wronged. It is a failure to take you seriously. Atonement is owed only to those hurt by actions. But we live in a network of obligations.[222] If there is a God, we have a far greater obligation and duty. The moral worth of people is far lower by comparison. Each human owes atonement to God.

Where this takes us then is to express that humans have the property of a personhood that is valuable. Violence is a desecration, a violation of sacred life. It is not something different to sin but a dimension of it – an extension of the principle. This leads on to the next dimension of our approach here; that Jesus embraces this dynamic flux in which people devalue others and experience it themselves and experienced catastrophic violence.

So often, the church has had an inadequate concept of sin because it did not grasp how sin is sustained and reinforced through the invisible systems that control life. If it had, it would not have condoned such evils as slavery. The haunting persistence of the dark powers is easier to spot in the inter-personal acts and the evil that men (and women) do. Individual sin is more obvious. The church over the centuries has conspicuously failed to grasp systemic and social sin.

Being made in the divine mirror, God identifies with humanity and leaves something of his own being within the Man and the Woman. He sets up humankind as valuable beings; beings who ought not to be trashed. Do not degrade the little clay model of God! It is unacceptable.

CHAPTER NINE
SOLIDARITY: JESUS AS VICTIM OF VIOLENCE

"At the centre of the New Testament lies the narrative of the death and resurrection of Jesus Christ understood as the expression of self-giving love for his followers as well as the self-giving love for the followers to imitate". 223

The story was a mythical portrayal of the last judgment. Assembled on a vast plain before the Great White Throne was a mass of people. It was clear that there was a collision between the living God and a godless life, and they knew it. Some were restive, furtive but others were angry, cursing. "It's all right for Him," cried a surly member of the crowd towards the front, "God doesn't know what it's like being one of us". "Too right," declared the crowd, and murmurs of approval arose from their desperately anxious faces. "Let Him come down here and see what it's like standing in our shoes." And those who could hear in the crowd roared their assent. "Let Him be born a homeless person," shouted a lady a few rows back. In her time, she had been a street kid. "Let Him be a working man," said someone who in his life had ground out the daily round until he was laid in the ground. "Let Him be betrayed by a close friend," said another close by, who could still feel the knife. At that point the words were being spat out with defiant anger. "Let Him be the victim of injustice," "see what he it feels like when you're executed on a trumped-up chance" (shouted a victim of Stalinist purges). "Let Him be humiliated, mocked and sneered at," said another. "Let Him be Jewish," added a holocaust survivor.

Then came the denouement, the searing climax. Just as quickly as voices had risen to fever pitch, the voices died down with a subdued hush that drowned every protest and silenced every indignation. For it was suddenly clear to the vast throng and the clarity was deafening. God had already fulfilled their request.

He was not an anonymous figure, of no fixed abode. Jesus was a Jewish man. He experienced the mindless visitation of pogrom and cruelty that has been perpetrated upon the Jewish man and woman through numerous irrational centuries. These are the people who refuse to be assimilated.

Jesus followed the twentieth century into the anguish of human extremity and pain. He went with us into bereavement and into cancer. He was there with them in the gas chamber while they closed the doors, with every victim of war and injustice and with every mother caring for her disabled child with a heavy heart. No darkness can keep its doors barred against a self-sacrificing love that renders the redemption of the world inevitable. Here is identification at its most intense. The pain of God connects with the children of the Auschwitz generation and a world pursuing the madness of violence and rape of the environment. Despite the post-millennial West giving up on God and wondering if he is relevant, God is no stranger to the complex agony of humanity. Calvary tells us that our condition became his.

The closer we look at the empathy of God, the more we are moved by His degree of solidarity. A cursory glance will not do anything for us. But the more we concentrate on it, the more we become convinced that simple goodness must triumph over evil, that the kind of selfish cruel strife that claimed Jesus as victim is not how we should live our lives. Jesus was the supreme Example of love in the face of suffering and of the power of purity. Jesus was a role model that gently prises the fingers of selfishness from how we have lived. We look at the self-sacrifice of Jesus and we say, here is the solidarity of God with the victims - and we are all victims. The gaunt faces of the tortured, the emaciated faces of the famished, the frightened lonely faces of the refugees - these are his type of people. God is calling us to make a connection with them and become the face of God.

The curtain opened on the twenty-first century to a beautiful world that in some parts resembled a rubbish dump.

The stench of racism, disease, genocide, torture, unemployment, experiments on animals, the way we rape the planet and destroy the ozone layer, the human ride pouring out of war-torn situations disfigure the blue and white plant that hangs mysteriously in space. It is not a pretty sight. But this was the world God came into. The cross was the point where God was immersed not only into human life but in the rubbish tip where dark and messy things are tossed. It was the low point of divine identification with the human condition and Jesus did not shrink back from entering this zone. There was no "keep out" sign that restricted him to the beautiful and noble side of life. Jesus was discarded and dragged outside the city like a bit of rubbish to be got rid of.

There are ways of seeing the cross of Christ. Some stress that Jesus does not so much take the blame for us as standing WITH US amidst our sinfulness. The spirit of this emphasis is participation. It is not that Jesus is there in our place so much as standing in solidarity with the human situation, bearing the kind of things we have to do and transforming them. Jesus takes the worst that violence and grim toxicity can inflict on anyone – and turns it into love. He redeems, not by being the saviour figure from outside but living where we live and taking the violent rubbishing because he identifies with our humanity. Jesus becomes one with the innocent incarcerated in a concentration camp; he becomes one with those faced with hatred and greed and shows us a better way, a way out.

Staunch advocates of substitution (whereby Jesus suffered and died in our place) stress that 'God is FOR US'. Jesus took the place of the sinning man and woman. He died instead of them; bore the punishment on their behalf and in their place so they could go free. Jesus takes the worst but transforms it by being both representative participant and unique scapegoat. In fact, there is less contrast here than many have thought. Some versions of Christianity have tended to stress solidarity rather than substitution; that God is with us in suffering and the banality of evil to enable us to rise above it and turn us to the power of righteous love, the victory that vindicates. Those seeking above all to be faithful to scripture have emphasised that God is for us as a sacrifice for sin.

Both perspectives turn on the idea of solidarity. They trace the incarnation of Jesus to the point where he is fully one with the human condition, including the confrontation with extreme violence. Jesus is not being human only at the cross where he is the scapegoat, accused and brutalised. He comes to his own all the way along the path. From cradle to grave, Jesus was one with their humanity.

In the unrepeatable incarnation, Jesus expresses solidarity with our situation, identifying as human WITH US AND FOR US and then as universal victim. The embrace of embodiment came with all its ambiguity. Jesus was a victim of violence, of injustice. The cross is the meeting point between heaven and earth, the clearing house for recompense and indebtedness. Forget talk of punishing the innocent. Beyond a sacrificial system that is far from our age, right up to date is that a price must always be paid. God's answer- 'tetelestai' (John 19v30) written on receipts in New Testament times is meant to show a bill had been paid in full. Exchange, or 'trading places' (switching positions) is central both to human life and scenes of violence. At the cross, an exchange takes place. At the messy violence that shows the depth of the divine – human encounter, there is somewhere to go.

3

There have been two main routes from which to approach the most influential person in human history. The first is to probe an apparently simple question – how did Jesus become God? How did a first century Jewish teacher come to be regarded as on a par with God?

This route starts with making some very human assumptions about Jesus as a mysterious yet very human figure who possessed such remarkable presence and power and influenced so many that he was elevated beyond his contemporaries and accorded divine status. Somehow, Jesus came to be given an unprecedented identity and position. Christianity is about him. Such was his impact that he came to be seen as revealing God in a unique way: a mirror of God. Jesus was human, it is argued, but his humanity became a very full demonstration of God, not THE definitive and unique one.

The contemporaries of Jesus came by this pathway. For his immediate followers and from staunchly monotheistic soil, Jesus came to regarded as a man yet more than a man. What was it they were encountering that pushed their grasp of God and humanity? Rather than beating their brains trying to figure it out, gradually they responded to it. The teaching of Jesus, his character and especially the power that was at work through him, was beyond anything they had known. It came to a head at Caesarea Philippi from which the Jordan set sail on its southward track, the spot where statues of the gods were placed. In a twilight, murky world, where gods became human and humans became gods by promotion, came the probing question. *'What are the people saying about me? Who do you say that I am?'* Peter gave voice to an instinctive grasp. *"You are the Christ!"* (Mark 8v29).

The other main route has been to approach the question of Jesus not just via another path to the summit, but from the summit itself going downward. This hails the one-off incarnation of our God and Saviour Jesus Christ. Jesus 'from above' is the call to be faithful to the biblical message about descent. God has joined himself to our humanity and has become one of us while remaining fully God.

The word is 'kenosis', the self-emptying of Jesus to be receptive to the will of the Father, the one who made himself nothing. *"He emptied himself"* (Philippians 2v7). The stoop of God in embracing the human situation is the model for Christians to divest themselves of self-interested power and respond with joyful imitation. It is not so much a theory as a call to arms – or a call to be harmless. It is not what the Son gave up but what he gained. It is not the royal status he left but the servant role he embraced in comprehensive self-restraint.

Of what did Christ empty himself? This was a vital question when the debate about whether Jesus was fully divine rent the fourth century church. 'Kenotic theory', a joyless phrase, strips away the divinity from the Word made flesh. The 19th century Lutheran Thomasius suggested that Jesus divested himself of the God-attributes such as omniscience, omnipresence, and omnipotence. Christ weakened himself voluntarily so that He could function as a human being to accomplish something powerful: the work of human redemption. It still assumes the pre-existence of Christ: that he had lived before (though not as a human). Philippians has nothing to say about the God-attributes though. It is about power; the imitation and the limitation, the humility that moved him to seek a far lesser status. To be sure Jesus accepted limitations. Biblical Christianity has urged that he voluntarily accepted self-imposed limits. Its witness has been that Jesus remained fully divine while so doing, thus enabling human redemption could take place. Living in union with God, Jesus gave up none of his divine attributes. He gave up not some part of himself, but status.

Kenosis has fewer friends today. It has become more fashionable now to say that the self-emptying took place in Jesus' own experience while he was alive, or at the cross as he embraced the Father's will. In the days of his flesh, there was then a repeated emptying of himself. Jesus had powers upon which he could have called to deliver himself, but he refused to use them. He had knowledge he could have deployed but refused to use it. Jesus did not know quantum physics.

In attempting to define what is was he had left behind and how he then functioned; thinkers are dealing with something without parallel. In Jesus, we do not encounter someone else, we touch God directly; we touch God personally. Non-Trinitarian groups would deny this and say that Jesus was god with a small 'g', an ambassador of divinity, a representative. They have cut the essential link that makes Jesus an embodiment of God on Earth. But that is not mainstream Christian teaching. The coming of the divine being into the world as a human being cannot be about how much divinity can be shrunk into humanity and still retain either. Neither can it be acceptable to say that we are just as much an incarnation of God as Jesus was; certainly not functioning as a Spirit-anointed servant on the same terms as all who would follow. The incarnation of God in human form was not one of a kind but a one-off, unique event in our world.

Christ embraced our situation in full. But what does that mean for one person to be a representative of humanity, given that humanness is very particular in time and place? Here we have a 1st century Jewish male standing in solidarity with the experience of common humanity from the inside.

Does it matter if it was God in person who came amongst us or whether it was someone else who was sent? According to mainstream Christianity, Jesus was either a living, walking, talking embodiment of God or God sent a third party to be His representative. In Jesus, we are not touching a third party. We are encountering God directly, authentically, not merely His ambassador. This was a totally unique individual in world history who did not just have more of God in him than any other man, but someone who could truly say, *"Anyone who has seen me has seen the Father"*(John 14v9).

How real is your Christ? The humanity of Jesus is only an issue because we want to say divine things about him. Being faithful to the biblical witness requires us to affirm that it was God who became man rather than the man who became God. The question that has dogged Christian thought is how this double reality can be so stated that one part of it does not prevail at the expense of the other.

Probably the very first heresy the church had to confront was "Docetism" - from the Greek word "dokein", "to seem". The church was obliged to combat the false Gnostic teaching that Jesus had only appeared to be human and was God in disguise. This did not constitute identification whereby Jesus affirmed the value and worth of human physicality. The Hebrew letter and other New Testament texts affirmed what was being preached about Jesus, that he had lived before and came to the world, a pre-existent figure on a divine rescue mission for humanity. In Medieval pictures, Jesus is portrayed as an unreal, ghostly figure, to be identified by the halo that surrounded him. It was against these docetic tendencies that Martin Luther made one of his great contributions to the person of Jesus. To understand him properly, we must begin from below; after that, come upwards. Start with the truth of his humanity and work from there to affirm the truth of the deity of Jesus.[224]

This was after all the route by which the disciples began to realise the identity of Jesus. Genuineness in His humanity was never questioned but they were compelled to take in the reality of what they encountered, and which is accessible to us too - a reality that led them to conclude that Jesus was a man but somehow more than a man. But the more that 'the God in Him' came to be understood and Jesus began to be seen as a pre-existent being who had come from heaven, the more doubtful the authenticity of his humanity became. "How could they have it both ways?", they reasoned.

His humanity was real and genuine. Jesus was genuinely God and genuinely human- at the same time. There are powerful reasons for insisting on the total solidarity of Jesus with 'us men and for our salvation'. Jesus is God for us because he is the man for others, the man for all, a representative man. Jesus stood in solidarity with humanity not because he could remotely fill the social position of very many – unless they were a Jewish male under oppressive occupation. Women? Disability?

The empathy of God took Jesus directly and inevitably on a one-way street to Calvary. All along, the cross was where the path of identification was headed. Those who would emphasise the teachings of Jesus and see His significance as a message of love for the world would come to see His death as a tragic and wrong ending to a beautiful story. His death is what happens when someone stands up for what they believe in.

But the gospels speak with a voice that is overwhelming in its loud consistency. The cross was central to why Jesus came. Jesus knew early on that His claims would be rejected and that the bridegroom would be taken away (Mark 2v19 and Mark 3v6). It could not be that a prophet could perish outside Jerusalem. The doctrine of a suffering Messiah was expressly laid out at Caesarea Philippi when Jesus forced the issue - *"who do you say that I am?"* Matthew sees this as a turning point. *"From that time on, Jesus began to explain to His disciples that he must go to Jerusalem and suffer many things...that he must be killed and on the third day, raise to life"* (16v21).

What does the "must" mean? Was it the inevitable outcome to the fatal situation that Jesus was in?

Mark then records Jesus saying that *"the Son of Man did not come to serve but be served and to give His life as a ransom for many"*. At the Last Supper Jesus, knowing that death was inevitable but also indispensable, passed round a cup to express it. *"This is my blood of the covenant which is poured out for many"* (Mark 14v24). It was to be the climax to His ministry. He gave us a meal as memorial.

Luke sees Jesus as a traveller on a journey, destination Jerusalem. *"As the time approached for him to be taken up to heaven, Jesus resolutely set out for Jerusalem"* (9v51). It would be the culmination point to God's plan of salvation that Luke is keen to stress in his opening chapters.

One of the surprising features of much theological analysis of the death of Christ is that it draws heavily and rightly on Paul but neglects the way the gospels present the destiny Jesus knew was imminent. The meaning Jesus brought to the death he knew was awaiting him in Jerusalem is profoundly instructive. Jesus hosted a meal for his followers pregnant with significance. He himself interpreted his own death. At the point he would move towards it in the final lap.

And John portrays Jesus as moving inexorably towards what He called "my hour". (John 2v4 in the literal Greek). *"Now my heart is troubled and what shall I say? 'Father, save me from this hour? No, it was for this very reason I came to this hour... Jesus knew that the hour was come for him to leave this world and go to the Father....'Father, the hour is come'"* (12v27, 13v1, 17v1).

All four gospels have an emphasis on the events of the last week out of all proportion to the life of Jesus. If an editor commissioned a reporter to write an obituary on a figure of some considerable importance, he would be sacked if half the obituary centred on that person's final week as does John, or a third (as does Mark), or even a quarter (as does Matthew and Luke). The cross is central to the gospels and it was where Jesus was moving to. Incarnation makes no sense without atonement. Calvary was the destination of His identification.

In the pathway of identification, there was some very rough territory to go through. *"Going a little farther, he fell with his face to the ground and prayed.' My Father, if it is possible, may this cup be taken from me. Yet not as I will but as you will'"* (Matthew 26v39).

From the Arabic 'Gat Semen', Gethsemane was 'an olive press'. It was where Jesus accepted the cup offered to him and he was to be crushed alive. *"He took Peter and the two sons of Zebedee along with him and he began to be sorrowful and troubled. Then he said to them, 'my soul is overwhelmed with sorrow to the point of death. Stay here and keep watch with me'"* (Matthew 26v37-38).

The place of the press was where the agony of human redemption pressed upon him so strongly, he was being crushed so oil could flow for the world. Already sorrowful, Jesus began to be overwhelmed. Matthew says Jesus was troubled ('ademonein', deeply depressed). And in the depths of heaviness of spirit, Jesus was in a constituency of one that suffering brings. All troubles seem very lonely places. No one else can quite feel and know what we are going through.

Jesus knew at that moment the experiences of three hundred million in our world who suffer from malignant sadness, condemned to dragging dark and heavy days around with them. Jesus knew what it was to be immersed in sorrow so deep that he went under and was almost drowned. He not only tasted sadness and depression of spirit, Jesus ate it to the full and drank the cup dry. He knew what is like when the battery runs dry.

In the Garden at the beginning of things, the Son had been there with the Father and the Spirit as the first humans were tempted and failed. Then instead, three men looked on as

Jesus wrestled against overwhelming pressure and temptation to escape what was to befall him. In the garden, Jesus prevailed over temptation where the first man went down under it. But Jesus fought and won as a man, not just as God. It was far, far more than fear of pain. The sorrows of Jesus were in a different dimension, infinitely more profound and vast, wider and deeper. Jesus was to take on His shoulders the sins of the world. No wonder it was breaking His humanity, the olive crushed in the press.

Jesus became the Representative man, embracing all in order to redeem, persevering in those final hours of identification. He knew the knife of betrayal. *"While they were eating, he said, 'One of you will betray me'. They were very sad and began to say to him one after the other, 'Surely not I Lord. ' ...The one who dips his hands into the bowl with me will betray me...Woe to that man who betrays the Son of Man... Look, the hour is near and the Son of Man is betrayed into the hands of sinners. Rise, let us be going. Here comes my betrayer"* (Matthew 26v21, 23- 24, 45-46).

When John wrote about this, he was reminded of an old Psalm that captures the agony of betrayal in a single verse. Three thousand years have passed, and you can still see the blood pouring from soul-wounds. *"Even my close friend, whom I trusted, he who shared my bread, has lifted up his heel against me"* (Psalm 41v9). How could he do it? It hurt so much more that it was someone close that you had spent time and opened your heart and your table to. If it was an enemy, you would understand it. But it was my friend!

'How could they do this to me?' It is the cry of executive when the knives in the back come from someone you thought you had an alliance with, the cry of a spouse whose partner has had an affair, the cry of parents when their own children turn against them, the cry of those left when someone takes their life in an act of selfish desperation. It was the last cry of Abel before Cain's fratricide closed his eyes for the last time. It was the cry of Jesus when Judas walked out into the night.

Judas betrayed Jesus and Peter disowned Him. Why such a contrast drawn between these two men? Both let Jesus down enormously and failed. Denial - *"I don't know the man"* - sounds a bit like betrayal. But the gospels insist on the different moral quality of their actions. Peter didn't stand with Jesus - Judas stood against Him. Peter couldn't rise to the occasion in a moment of panic and cowardice. Judas actively plotted against Jesus. But Judas was broken by remorse and saw no way back whereas heartbroken Peter was personally re-instated by the very one he had denied.

Jesus was put on trial. It was of course a trumped-up trial on trumped up charges. They falsely accused him and twisted his words. He had never said, *"I am able to destroy this Temple of God and rebuild it in three days"* (Matthew 26v61). Those words kept being thrown back in His face (27v40). It was a miscarriage of justice and Pilate acknowledged it to be so. *"I find no basis for a charge against this man"* (Luke 23v4). Jesus was kicked to and fro like a football between the Sanhedrin, Herod and Pilate before the inevitable ensued.

There came the moment when Jesus stood before the crowd at the judgement seat of Pilate, wearing the crown of thorns and the purple robes. *"Here is the man,"* declared Pilate. *"Ecce homo- Behold the Man!"* (John 19v5). It is a glimpse, but it conjures up unforgettable imagery of the first man strutting around in independence of God in the very place where the thorns came up. Jesus stood in the place of proud man wearing a crown and the imperial purple, enduring the ignominy and the shame. The old Adam humanity was being adopted in full measure but would soon be relegated.

Jesus experienced being mocked and insulted. *"The soldiers twisted together a crown of thorns and put it on his head. They clothed him in a purple robe and went up to him again and again saying' Hail, O King of the Jews!'. And they struck him in the face" (John 19v2-3) ... Falling on their knees, they worshipped him"* (Mark 14v19).

With every step, solidarity got harder going. Throughout history, crowds have almost always been in the wrong; dangerous places where reason and love are easily tossed aside, and ugliness takes over. Jesus knew what it was to have a crowd yelling for your last drop of blood" (Luke 23v18), the nation that He had wept over and sought to rescue from the religion, from sin and from disaster. The world rejected the Son of God and the Prince of Peace and called for a murderer in His place. It got what it wanted. If Cain somehow saw it, he must have smirked. Pilate *"surrendered Jesus to their will"* (Luke 23v25).

Everything was taken from Him. They even bargained for his clothing. *"When the soldiers crucified Jesus, they took His clothes, divided them into four shares, one for each of them, with the undergarment remaining. This garment was seamless, woven in one piece from top to bottom"* (John 19v23). For all those who have been looted or lost everything, Jesus stands in solidarity. But the pathway of identification was still descending, going down and down.

The pain of his ordeal on the cross was intense. So why was the form of His execution one of the most excruciating ever devised? For the nails through the wrists were only the beginning. His body sagged down under its own weight until the urge to snatch a breath forced Him upwards - and the deathly cycle began again. It was six hours of torture. To be nailed on a pole and hung out naked before the sun - this was what they did to Jesus when He identified with humanity. But the physical anguish was only a surface wound.

"At the ninth hour, Jesus cried out in a loud voice, 'Eloi, Eloi, lama sabathani' - my God, my God, why have your forsaken me?" (Mark 14v34).

Jesus drank and drank. Abandoned children, abandoned wives, abandoned social groups, the abandoned man, ambassador of the desolate, tribune of the dispossessed, or of discarded people. 'My God, my God, why have you abandoned me?'

The crown of thorns on his head spoke of a mental and emotional torture that was blinding in its torment. Jesus experienced desolation and felt that even God had forsaken Him. In His anguish, Jesus had a 'why' on his lips. It's the question they all ask. Why? Every nerve of His body screamed it out and His torn flesh demanded an answer. But the unseen agony of His humiliation accentuated the pain and forced a cry unique to him, new and strange, profoundly unsettling. As the sun went dark, a cloud swept over the soul of His humanity. He was alone. Even the Father was out of reach.

Was Jesus aware at that moment of the old humanity in whose shape and likeness he came? As He endured His ordeal, was Jesus mindful of the moment when Adam suddenly experienced a strange new world of guilt, self-consciousness and separation? On that other day, with the other tree, He had become man forsaken by God. Now, to put it right; He was to be a God-forsaken man, nailed to a tree that would become the tree of life.

Jesus was experiencing first-hand the vulnerable nakedness of the derelict sufferer who pours out His soul to God but feels that God is far away. Bearing the sin of a whole world upon Him, Jesus knew that even the Father would turn His back at that moment. Jesus experienced the withdrawal of the face of God. It was the first time He had ever known the absence of God and it drew from deep inside the holy well, His being a cry that was profoundly unsettling. For three hours, the sun stopped shining and the Father ceased smiling. And it had all been envisaged in writing, years before.

He felt their anger like dogs that tore at Him. It had all been foreseen. *"Many bulls surround me... roaring lions tearing their prey... I am poured out like water , and all my bones are out of joint...my strength is dried up like a potsherd, my tongue sticks to the roof of my mouth ... dogs have surrounded me, a band of evil men has encircled me, they have pierced my hands and my feet"* (Psalm 22v12-16).

Calvary was for Jesus an immersion into malice and cruelty. Stripped, Jesus was vulnerable to their violence. He trod the pathway of the vulnerable throughout history, the weak and those that have become a target for bullying and cruelty. Jesus knew that at that point, not from the outside looking on but from the inside looking out. Humiliation was mixed in the cup Jesus was drinking. *"I can count all my bones, people stare at me and gloat over me, they divide my garments among them and cast lots for my clothing"* (Psalm 22v17-18). Stripped of all his possessions, Jesus was left with nothing.

Later, knowing that all was now accomplished and so that the scriptures would be fulfilled, Jesus said 'I am thirsty'... When he had received the drink, Jesus said ' It is finished'. With that, he bowed his head and gave up His Spirit" (John 19v30). It was the culmination of the Christ, victim of violence.

5

Jesus identifies with us in full, thus affirming our human worth, but also taking on himself all the sin and violence and therefore our demerit. By virtue of that solidarity, Jesus stands as representative figure for humanity dying in our place as one of us. *"Jesus knows about human existence from his own experience. He knows what it is to be human. This solidarity is the source of our salvation."*[225]

Should you ask if his human history and identity were relevant to the sacrifice he made, the clear answer from theology seems to be that it was they were. The substitution is of Representative for the represented. Christ is no mere individual. Representation is there in the idea of sacrifice. But as Tom Wright concludes, "representation is important not least because it creates the context for substitution."[226] The idea of representation can imply distance - a rep may be like an MP - and only temporary. These concepts are interwoven with the idea of substitution. Incarnation is the condition of the atonement.

The issue of Christ's identification with humanity comes into sharper focus with theology after Auschwitz. As Richard Rubinstein, the first Jewish thinker to name the Holocaust as a crisis for traditional Jewish theology observed, *'at the time I wrote 'After Auschwitz', one could search through almost everything written by the contemporary establishment without finding the slightest hint that they were living in the same century as Auschwitz"*[227] What would it mean to affirm that Jesus is identifying with female experiences those in the gas chambers, the tortured, the victims of war or at the hands of a lynch mob in the deep South? This may seem to be a question that classic theology sees no need to address. Solidarity is not limited to inter-personal acts for which individuals are responsible. To suffer as one of us must have some sense of taking the place of victim as well as perpetrator, the devalued as well as the devaluer. Otherwise the circle and the cycle are incomplete.

Solidarity meant that, through the violence inflicted on him, Jesus becomes the universal victim. It is as if it is being done to him and Jesus stands for the whole Adam. Taking this idea further, Jesus suffers as the iconic human, the one who spreads the benefit of his redemptive work across the range of his brothers and sisters. The profound identification enables his substitution. In Christian theology, Jesus is the divine–human representative. Christ is one of us.

CHAPTER TEN
TRADING PLACES: AN EXCHANGE OF STATUS

"All our sins and failings, our inadequacies, were somehow dealt with there, so that we- the apostles and all who are called to be 'ministers of reconciliation'- could embody in our own lives the faithfulness of God. At the cross, God made the sinless Messiah to be sin on our behalf."228

The church has always been very successful in divorcing rhetoric from reality. In principle, churches affirm that humans have a high value. But traditionally, this has been a theoretical statement about humanity in general rather than this or that person or social group. The notion that women, other faiths, minorities, Jewish people, those with skin colour other than white, those with disability or the elderly have the same value as white Anglo-Saxon healthy males runs completely counter to experience. The church has a strong message in this area which sadly exposes its own history, but which nevertheless is vital to assert in society. We have a project of emancipation to engage with, that lifts up the heads of all people in self-respect and protest to declare that they are worth more than the script society has handed to them.

The victims of violence encounter power: the power at the heart of the darkness and the dark powers. In its lashing, they come up against the wanton essence of sin; the primordial power that stands over against God. Gratuitous scraping the value off the face of another as a china plate can be marked - this is what sin does in violent, mocking disregard. As the assassin of John Lennon, Mark Chapman, confessed in an interview. 'I thought if I killed him, I would become him, I would acquire his fame'. It is this exchange that Jesus, the highly valued one enters freely. He is trashed through incredible violence. Because of who he is, he sets up a transaction with a transfer of status where he becomes the devalued one. We become righteous AND A transfer of life and divinely given status.

We saw in Chapter Six that violence is a desecration of the sacred, a violation. That bid for respect and the status of another seeks to be served through scraping it from the victim and accorded to the perpetrator. This is the idea of an exchange and it is a thread running through many forms of violence. In sociology it finds resonance with the approach of the French writer Pierre Bourdieu[2].

Bourdieu sought to develop an economy of symbolic exchanges, to delineate the rules and patterns of the cultural and intellectual marketplace. All intellectual and cultural players, he wrote, enter the marketplace with certain forms of capital. They may have academic capital (the right degrees), cultural capital (knowledge of a field or art form, a feel for the proper etiquette), linguistic capital (the ability to use language), political capital (the approved positions or affiliations), or symbolic capital (a famous fellowship or award). People spend their careers trying to convert one form of capital into another. His account of symbolic exchange as a crucial dimension of life was a vital plank of his ideas about the importance of signs. Becoming part of society is a process marked by exchanges and ritual that turn people and the world into material for an uninterrupted, ongoing process of exchange. Everything is part of a cycle of exchanges.

Atonement can be seen as a particular form of transaction and exchange. It combines the notion of devaluing people and indeed devaluing God with the exchange that takes place in relationship trade in many situations and especially in a context of violence. The proposal is that Jesus is a worthy representative figure who stands in our place and who offers himself as sufficient payment for human moral failure and wrong doing. How can this be put to work in the theology of the atonement?

I want to argue for a form of atonement which is not open to the objections raised against some other forms. One way

2   Bourdieu, P. (2002) The Weight of the World: Social Suffering in Contemporary Society Stanford University Press

of approaching this is to see that at the heart of the idea of atonement is exchange. It is because of the value of persons that infringement sets up a deficit. Something happens that can only be discounted at the expense of denial of that being and of their 'rights'. This is of course what makes forgiveness hard work.

In individual life, we may feel used when someone has been milking us for what they can get out of it, as an instrument to meet their needs. We become a 'thing.' In the labour market, life is contractual. We give work in exchange for reward. Nevertheless, in circumstances of exploitation, we can be utterly taken advantage of; reduced to an automaton. There are to be sure very few completely altruistic and mutual relationships. Balance of power marks personal landscapes like shifting sands. But, unless we are consenting adults for a time, most of us would know what that feels like and dislike it. Someone to whom people in his or her world are means to an end we label 'manipulative'. Using people for what you can get out of it means not paying attention to their needs. It means doing what I can to get what I want; valuing someone for their utility to me.

We speak of exchanging pleasantries or greetings or exchanging peace. In a wider sense, however, 'the economy' is a cipher for human transactions. As we are examining, human violence takes place in the marketplace of inter-personal transactions, the space between us that becomes a focus of emotional trade. *"They should go home after this and have trouble sleeping"*- a man on a picket-line talking about a strike – breaker. It seems to be a case of this has cost me, you will pay.[229]

Early societies were static with a fixed hierarchy of social obligations. The means through which later societies were able to unshackle themselves from pre-ordained social orders and become individualistic was money. As Martin

198

shows in his '*Money: the Unauthorised Biography*', money is more than just currency.[230]

To re-iterate then, payment or compensation is needed to recognise what has taken place. Commenting on reports of gas attacks in Syria in August 2013, the French foreign minister declared that, if proven, there would have to be a reaction.[231] In the moral economy, justice entails that the demand for recompense, rooted in recognition, is addressed and indeed addressed correctly.

SACRIFICE AND EXCHANGE

Is the idea of sacrifice the central theme in the idea of salvation? We cannot get away from the reality that sacrifice is the background of much biblical theology and ritual. Neither should we. The Passover lamb clearly had something to do with warding off divine judgement descending heavily on ancient Egypt. To talk of sacrificial animals taking the place of the worshipper and then reproducing that in the context of the cross is not straightforward. It is true that Jesus is seen as the paschal lamb (1 Corinthians 5v7) and his death interpreted within this framework. It is, however, a difficult and contested concept for us today. We understand the donation of an organ, perhaps to save someone from death. The sacrifice of soldiers is readily comprehensible; in some sense they are 'dying for us.'

A story some years ago highlighted a parachute drop involving a woman bound to her instructor. What should have been a tourist highlight turned to tragedy. Their parachute failed to open. At the last minute, the instructor turned his body so as to absorb the blow. He died. This was a sacrifice, a death for another 'in my place'. But sacrificial language implies that there is a sufficient cause that warrants someone offering their life. It does not require a death. As Leviticus makes clear, there were two goats on the Day of Atonement and significantly, the one over whom confession was made was not the one that was slain. (This is not to say that the meanings could not coalesce, only that the one to one equation of sacrifice and sin is not as simple and direct as is often made out). Sacrificial animals bore the sins of the people. But not all the sacrifices were about sin and there were others that expressed consecration. In the theology of the cross, in the Hebrew letter in the New Testament, the sacrifice and the sacrificed are one and the same. Reparation to the offended party is made.

The interesting point about sacrifice for our purposes is that, by definition, sacrifice involves the death of an animal or 'an offering of the fruit of the ground' – witness the different forms of sacrifice with Cain and Abel (Genesis 4v3). In the Old Testament there was the meal or meat offering as well as the burnt offering. It reflected something of value to the one offering it: the worshipper had worked hard for this. No doubt reflecting these two different sacrifices, Cain's did not involve death - so instead he sacrificed Abel! The meaning of Old Testament sacrifice lies with the Hebrew verb 'kipper', usually translated as 'atone' or 'cover'. Ancient Akkadian roots of this word contain the idea of 'wiping away', though in the Hebrew context the concept is more akin to 'ransom price' (koper). Throughout the Bible, atonement procured is much greater in value than the ransom paid.[232]

At heart is the question of how sin is to be done away with. With basic ritual, the removal of sin is accomplished by external actions to perform ritual cleansing. In the ancient sacrificial system in Israel, it is *"the disturbed relationship with the personal covenant God which is to be restored by the removal of sin"*.[233] It is very relevant for our purposes here to note that there was an exchange. Often, worshippers had to eat the sacrifice. They took it in, they internalised the positive benefit of the action to symbolise a transfer of status. The animal has been slain but forgiveness transferred.

Voluntary suffering for others is not necessarily vicarious - for instance, someone toiling in the slums. But the vicarious element is there when someone is drowned in saving another. Bereavement or watching someone die entails suffering on their behalf but not in their place. Representative action is limited by the extent of the fellowship between the parties and this partnership is itself measured by common interests, be it a single class of transaction as in commercial partnerships or power of attorney. The cross makes no sense, unless it is Christ's absolute oneness with God that enables him to act for man, to suffer and to die for humanity. Jesus is not just victimised like all humans by other humans, but rather a human victim suffering the maximum possible victimage to plumb the depths and implications of suffering. In this way, a single suffering becomes a sovereign suffering, capable of representing all suffering and of forgiving on behalf of all victims.

This is what the language of sacrifice and priesthood was affirming. Sacrifice and sacrificed are one.

An understanding of the atonement cannot be separated from notions of guilt and forgiveness. This is why the Old Testament background is important. The sacrificial system is embedded within a moral framework that later came to be highly developed. Sacrifice was of course not just about offering compensation for guilt and wrongdoing, but clearly that concept plays a central role. There was to be sure a differentiation between sins committed unknowingly and sins committed 'with a high hand.' [234] Nevertheless, an offence has been set up - whether intentionally or no. It needs compensating for, otherwise the value of persons, whether on an inter-personal level or on the divine-human dynamic level, is denied rather than affirmed. The guilt was objectively present whether the person failed to realise it or no. If I go over the speed limit, professing ignorance that there were no restrictions on that road will not be an allowable defence.

SYMBOLIC EXCHANGE

Pierre Bourdieu develops a theory of symbolic exchange to show the rules and patterns of the cultural marketplace. His basic thesis is that all social and cultural players enter the marketplace of their society with certain forms of capital. They may have academic capital (the right degrees), cultural capital (knowledge of a field or art form, a feel for the proper etiquette), linguistic capital (the ability to use language), political capital (the approved positions or affiliations), or symbolic capital (a famous fellowship or award). Education is about trying to augment your capital and convert one form of capital into another. Even without educational advantages, exchange is constantly taking place. The economy of symbolic exchange runs right through everyday life as different goods are exchanged with different value. It is central to the Gospels that Jesus' death was a violent one. Outside of some versions of Catholic theology, that fact has not always been given the significance it deserves. In modern terms, would the death of Christ have the same valence, the same charge, if Jesus had taken a suicide pill and martyred himself that way? I think not. There is a feature of violence that it magnifies the payback. As Girard points out, the reason why vengeance is so menacing is that *"only violence can put an end to violence and that is why violence is self-propagating. Everyone wants to strike the last blow"*.[235]

Looking at the atonement as a transfer of value, violence is conceived as an exchange of symbolic value. This applies to the violence of the cross. Anarchists in the 19th century developed what they called 'the theory of the deed', extending the circle of those involved to convert spectators into participants. (There was no neutrality either with the holocaust!). The violent seek to scrape the value off the face of another in order to compensate for their previous devalued identity. In this framing, perhaps the atonement can be seen in terms of God transformation of humanity from shame to honour and value.

Violence often entails a symbolic exchange. The traumatic roots of violence lie in harm visited upon us resulting in an injured psyche that looks for redress. A terrifying reality then confronts us. These strategies to re-value ourselves are transactions at the expense of another. It is a competitive marketplace in which my sense of worth can only be gained if yours is denied. The violent thus engage in a form of monetary calculation in which they assume there is only so much to go round. When it comes to intimate love, land and scarce resources, they may be right. Some sort of exchange mechanism needs to be envisaged by which we are driven to seek compensation somewhere and from someone. Retribution will ensure that my depleted bank account of value is filled again at your expense. The impetus to make up the deficit is then relieved.

But of course, while this may be illuminating, this idea does not do justice to the biblical witness in the earliest Christian preaching that 'Christ died for our sins' (Galatians 1v4). In the kind of public preaching hinted at in the Book of Acts, sacrifice is kept in the background. The concept of sacrifice has different meanings in scripture.

The exchange is a form of market in which there has been a perceived breach of a sense of collective or individual identity. But because of the role that honour and disrespect play in the dynamics of violence, this breach functions as a feeling of devaluation, an insult that needs compensating for. It is not a drive reduction like hunger or sex. It is because of the strong impulse towards value and respect in the human psyche that there is now a deficit. Therefore, I will take it from you. A forcible exchange is set up. The only way I can re-gain value and honour is to scrape it from your face. Something has happened that will only be compensated for through violence.

The symbolic exchange of violence creates an unwilling bond between perpetrator and victim. Against their will, victims are drawn into an exchange, as if they were trading goods. Here the exchange is another type of value, human value that will be scraped off the face of another. The strength of violence is that it creates forcible identities. It is as if an alien force field enveloped the participants, who are re-positioned as someone who has done the violence and those who are on the receiving end. Often with violence, trauma is generated which turns into a daily companion; a rape victim will wear that identity for many years. Those in the middleclass in the West are often on-lookers of violence, watching fictional violence, for example, rather than being participants. Yet we are all involved. Passivity is itself a form of violence since one is taking the stance of a non-intervening voyeur.[236]

Jesus assumes the role and stance of being the representative man. We are in him. He identifies with us in full in his incarnation and extends this to the cross. Jesus pays for our sins by being the victim who is totally devalued and written off. His violent death opens up a circle of those who are affected in a circle of participants in a symbolic exchange. The divine exchange means that we who mar his valuation of us and that of others are involved in trading places. Jesus has taken our place and substituted himself for us. He transfers value to us as it were putting merit and righteousness into our account. This compensates for our unworthiness because his worth is credited to us. On this account, the diving exchange is that of the worthy for the unworthy.

As medieval writers understood, forgiveness is situated within an economy of exchange and obligation.[237] This was not a kind of capitalist economy as Bourdieu and fellow Marxists claimed. *"The [divine] gift was not a commodity refusing to declare itself, because... at no absolutely required time and in consequence not abstractly equivalent to other reciprocities".*[238] Forgiveness inherently involves seeking to repay a debt, an exchange of some sort leading to reconciliation. Yet, as Milbank observes, the circulating economy of forgiveness cannot be reduced to a calculus of self-interest, trading sin for sin, debt for debt.

With his account of the cross as satisfaction that stresses restoration of loving relationship and harmony, Aquinas pointed out that in turn, forgiveness is offered without price to the neighbour. Forgiveness does not obey an ordinary calculable economy since it does not entail a finite price.

Some see human redemption entirely within these terms. This is not God forgiving us, as he has no need to, but humanity forgiving humanity. Divine redemption is not just God forgiving us but his giving us the gift of the capacity for forgiveness. As participators through the membership of the Body of Christ in the divine humanity, we now become capable of the forgiveness of other human beings. The problem with forgiveness lies precisely here. Its challenge is that it seems to betray the value and worth of oneself or of the loved one who has been slighted or even destroyed. To impart forgiveness appears to deny that the perpetrator stands in the exchange of violent actions and words, that he or she will be let off rather than be made to pay in some way. In a raw way, the exchange circle is incomplete.

Yet despite, or perhaps precisely because of its rootedness in violence, the cross educates us to overcome raw or even civilised violence with the raw power of love. *"How then are evil and violence to be overcome? If we are to be saved from their grip, then we must partake of the waters of forgiveness which flow down the slopes of Mt Purgatory."*[239]

Forgiveness is made possible with the acknowledgement that there is a universal victim, namely Jesus. For human redemption ultimately depends on Jesus Christ doing for us what we cannot do for ourselves. To rectify the situation and through the extreme violence Jesus endured as the representative victim, he offers complete forgiveness. 'By what right do you forgive sins?' Jesus was asked before calvary. The biblical witness seems to be that it is by right of conjoined divinity and humanity, by right of victimhood. Jesus stood for 'all victims' able to speak in their name and as one of us. Nevertheless, it was not the agony of death itself that was redemptive but the self-giving love that gave value to the sacrifice. The significance of Jesus is that here is a transfer of value. Stressing that propitiation was the method of reconciling us to the God who loved us, Calvin writes that Christ satisfied for our sins and paid the penalty due by us. *"By that price, the justice of God was satisfied... by paying what others owed, he might acquire righteousness for them."*[240]

To repeat, someone has been devalued, or even trashed. Moreover, we have devalued God. Compensation is needed. Jesus steps forward in solidarity and offers himself as one of us with us in him collectively. The representative of the Adam humanity wearing the crown of thorns enters the place of exchange. The test of any currency is its acceptability. Virtual currency, for instance, or 'bit-coin' can be earned for performing certain on-line tasks. Like money, the cross is a form of exchange.

These ideas can illuminate the letter to the Hebrew Christians where the redemptive act is portrayed in terms of Christ being a High Priest as well as the offering and victim. But it is the Second Letter of Paul to the Corinthians (2 Corinthians 5v21) which brings the main focus of the atonement as an exchange. *"For our sake he made him to be sin who knew no sin, so that in him, we might become the righteousness of God"*

The righteousness of God? The role that plays in the double exchange will wait until the next chapter on justification. But scripture also affirms the righteous life that Jesus represents, the 'just for the unjust' (1 Peter 3v18). It has sometimes been taught that Christ did not need to achieve a life-long record of perfect obedience for us. But Christ did more than just die; he became righteousness before God. This recalls the double-meaning of the notion of sacrifice, as not just the sin-offering but the offering of that which is dedicated to God (the burnt offering especially).

THEOLOGICAL EXCURSION – KATALLASSO (2 CORINTHIANS 5V21)

Justification by faith is a tremendously powerful idea. Long before its rediscovery at the Reformation, it was central to Paul's message in the earliest Christian writing ever' needs in brackets after (Galatians). Our position changes by dint of the identification of Christ with us. Because of who he was and is, there is a new humanity that emerges on the other side of the inclusive cross. His righteousness is credited to our account as it were. As in a ledger, the balance of the books is completely changed. Forgiveness and remission result in a cancellation of the indebtedness (Romans 4v11). There is a positive side of the ledger. The exchange results in positive merit flooding our account. Righteousness is credited to us.

Christ's death was vicarious in that he stood in our place

and represented us. As our representative, he took the penalty we deserve. Standing in corporate solidarity, universal payment is required. Through payback, Christ liberates us from sin, the ultimate root of all disruption, of injustice and oppression. God imputed our sins to Christ- as belonging to Christ. In return comes divine status.

Ancient wisdom recognised this connection. The Greek word *katallasso* meant "to change and "exchange", a compound of *allos*, or 'other'. Something is given in exchange. Yet it came to be applied to people changing from enmity to friendship. Human transactions are a site of relationship trade whereby people move from one state of being to another. In the New Testament it carries the meaning of 'to reconcile,' signifying how humans can be reconciled to God and to each other.[241] It has its roots in the idea of atonement, paying something for an act of wrong-doing. Sometimes, the atoning death of Jesus can be presented in a way that a blood sacrifice was needed to persuade God to be forgiving. But Jesus and the Father are one. Calvary is God Himself standing in full identification with humanity and taking our place. Jesus does not persuade a reluctant Father to forgive. Because of Jesus accomplishing the great work of redeeming humanity, we are now 'IN HIM'. Christ dying FOR us could mean in our favour and not just in our place. But 2 Corinthians 5v21 and other texts point to the death of Christ through substitution. *"If anyone is in Christ there is a new creation"* (2 Corinthians 5v17). It is reconciled humanity, flushed with new power, new orientation, a new perspective and above all, a new relationship. The emphasis on 'reconciliation' highlights Paul's insight that we are profoundly relational, not isolated solitaries. Paul describes the contrast in states and positions. *"For you know the grace of our Lord Jesus Christ, that though he was rich, yet for your sake he became poor, so that you through his poverty might become* rich" (2 Corinthians 8v9).

In Pauline studies, it has been a difficult question as to what is the connection between the reconciliation that goes forth from God and the necessity of the death of Christ. Is the latter the ground of the former? The two ideas are rooted in:

Katallage – arising from social/personal relations

Hilasmos – arising from the sacrificial system.

The exchanged life has always been central to Christian thought. Twentieth century writers noticed the emphasis Paul placed on being 'in Christ', on participation in his life and his standing. The focus for this is solidarity. Jesus took our position that becomes the means by which we can enter his. Justification is often interpreted in terms of God accepting us because he is kind and gracious. The emphasis rather is that a swop takes place. Through faith in Christ righteousness is given to us in place of our filthy rags. It is about position. Being an authentic part of the old humanity by reason of his natural life, Jesus opens up to us the means of being included in the new humanity.

It reprises the honour of God in a highly personal way as it justifies that honour and also imparts it.

2 Corinthians 5v21 with its transfer of subject position (*'for our sake he made him to be sin who knew no sin, so that in him we might become the righteousness of God'*) follows on, however, from a relational understanding of aggrieved parties needing reconciliation. The order of the Greek is, *'Him who knew not sin on our behalf he made sin. That we might become God's righteousness in him.'*

Views differ on how we best understand Paul's thought here. Augustine saw the text as indicating how Christ was made an offering for sin. In his work on Paul's theology, Herman Ridderbos emphasises it as a summary of ideas by which Christ is the only ground for righteousness by faith, expressing the connection between Christ's death and the justifying, acquitting judgement of God.

Riderbos argues that there are two conceptions here which are different but which we cannot separate. The corporate idea is most closely bound up with substitution. Paul in Romans 5v12 onwards grounds a corporate idea in Christ's death for us as entering our mode of existence.[242]

A generation ago, C.K. Barrett, in his commentary on 2 Corinthians, suggested that Paul has not explained yet to his own satisfaction how Christ's crucifixion constitutes a message of reconciliation. It is only as sinless that Christ can bear the sins of others. That the merits of the relatively righteous could be used for the benefit of the sinful was common ground in Judaism. As Barrett notes, Paul develops the thought in terms of an exchange, in terms of relationship trade.

The death of the sacrificial animal is the death of the sinner. *"As the sin was transferred one way, bringing death to the sacrificial animal, so its purity and on-going life were in effect transferred in reverse"*[243] 2 Corinthians 5v21 is the clearest expression of the exchange. A representative view is the same as saying that Jesus died as a sacrifice for the sins of mankind. Incidentally, Dunn questions whether 'substitution' is an adequate word here. It only tells half the story - Jesus taking the place of others. It is not that Jesus dies in the place of others, so they escape (the logic of the word).

Paul does not say that Christ became a sinner, nor does he say that every believer becomes automatically righteous. It is about relationships. Christ became sin, i.e. standing in that relation to God, which is normally the result of sin being estranged. We are acquitted in his court, justified - we stand in that relation to God. This interpretation turns on the meaning of the word 'righteousness'.

The Anchor Bible commentary has a nice point to make. The motif in 2 Corinthians 5v21 is not the sin offering because that would be foreign to the passage. Rather *"Paul is thinking in a more general way of Christ's identification with sinful humanity."*[244] Reconciliation is formulated as a statement about righteousness in 5v21 showing how closely these ideas are linked. Paul is dependent on traditional ideas of atonement with echoes of Isaiah 53.

There is a rich range of metaphors generally to do with the cross and Paul does not hesitate to run them together. The alternative to the sacrificial imagery used by Paul is that of reconciliation and exchange. The image is not that of God having to be entreated but God as the injured party, actively seeking reconciliation, i.e. forgiving hostility towards him. This is surely the immediate background in 2 Corinthians 5 through to v21.

An important text in NT scholarship cast a very different light on Paul's thinking. E. P. Sanders expressed the view that the majority of NT scholars such as Bultmann and Joachim Jeremias, have seriously misunderstood 1st century Judaism and therefore the context of Paul's thought. Judaism was a serious faith in its own right and not some kind of derogation from the OT norm. What Paul was challenging was the goal of religion, that we could become righteous. The 'New Perspective on Paul' argues that the Greek word 'katalasso' in 2 Corinthians 5 (meaning reconciliation) is oriented to what has already taken place. The death of Christ accomplished the reconciliation of the world. Reconciliation is preparatory to receiving life. Paul is saying that God has acted to save the world and therefore the world is in need of saving - not that humans are bound over to sin because they wish to save themselves. Paul moves from solution to plight - not the other way round. It was not a case of believing that we are enslaved, because he himself says he was zealous. Rather it was the revelation of Christ that convinced him. Believe that God raised Jesus from the dead and receive the

Spirit!

Sanders stresses that the concept of righteousness by faith is not the central doctrine for Paul - it is negative: against the idea that keeping the law is vital for salvation. There may be here sets of transfer terms in Paul's thought in this passage. The one might be termed 'participation' (from one sphere to another) and the other to do with the law court or juristic. [245] Sanders argues that Christ dying 'for us' is not the bite; the focus is on being 'with Christ' and 'in Christ'. Righteousness is the goal - not by law but faith. The entire system of the law is worthless for salvation, although it is good. The real righteousness is being saved by Christ and that comes only through faith.

Schweitzer stressed that at the heart of Paul's theology was incorporation into Christ rather than righteousness by faith.[246] The relationship of 'Christ-for-us' and 'we-in-Christ' indeed goes to the heart of the question "how does Christ's death and resurrection have justifying power?"

It is often asserted that the reconciling death of Christ is proclaimed only as divine activity - not as the accomplishment of Christ over against God. Christ dying FOR us could mean in our favour and not just in our place. But 2 Corinthians 5v21 and other texts do point to the substitutionary nature of His death. God turns to the world to offer reconciliation, but Christ also stands in the place of humanity to offer himself up to God to expunge the sin. Christ suffered and died even though he was not a sinner. In other words, he was subject to the consequences of sin. Only in this sense is "he made him to be sin" intelligible. *"Christ entered into the human situation so totally that he accepted the lot of all members of a fallen humanity"*[247]

Tom Wright suggests that 5v21 is not a general statement about the meaning of the cross so much as the basis of Paul's ministry as reconciler. *"All our sins and failings, our inad-*

equacies, were somehow dealt with there, so that we - the apostles and all who are called to be 'ministers of reconciliation'- could embody in our own lives the faithfulness of God" At the cross, God made the sinless Messiah to be sin on our behalf.[248] God is not making Christ in to a sinner but associating him with all sinners and charging him with their sins. [249] In other words, Jesus was regarded as a sinner personally, but He did stand in our place and had to endure the results of sin. God turned this round into a means of reconciling sinful people and transforming us, so we become righteous.

Against this background seeing 2 Corinthians 5v21 as a transfer of value enables us to say:

1. Payment and penalty are mandated to uphold specific acts where value has been breached as well as systemic sin and evil (sin in the singular as an evil entity). Such factors generate unworthiness and shame. They dishonour both God and devalue people.

2. Jesus Christ has inestimable worth, both by virtue of his being God manifest in the flesh but also by living blamelessly and devaluing neither God nor those around him. He is conscious of being 'my son in whom I am well pleased'.

3. The worthy one steps forth, the innocent for the guilty but stands as one of us. His being with us is the basis of his being for us- there could not have been one without the other.

4. Jesus becomes the universal victim, whose death has global and indeed cosmic significance. His worth is transferred to the unrighteous, the unworthy, whose account is flooded with divine possibility and honour. In that exchange, Jesus pays the penalty. Whereas something happened that creates breach, the reparation is an act that reconciles.

Every act of violence is an exchange. It is a particular form of intense transaction.

Not all transactions are like that. In Civil Society there are transactions of civility. People are contractually decent to each other in order to get along and conduct the daily round. Inter-personal relationships are characterised by transactions of friendly mutuality and self-giving love. Violence is different. It is a form of transaction in which it grabs vicious power and tries to control the exchange. Violence is fundamental to the death of Christ not just because of a cross at the heart of it. Jesus enters a transaction and the exchange of value. To sum all this up, there is a transfer of value between Jesus and humanity which affects redemption and reconciliation. In that transaction, the worthiness of the innocent sufferer is credited to the account of the sinful, the unworthy.

CHAPTER ELEVEN
RECOMPENSE FOR PERPETRATORS

PAYMENT IS NEEDED

Bonnie Parker, of "Bonnie and Clyde fame", asked Clyde what it was like to shoot and kill a man. Could he live with it? His response was interesting. *"It's like a big loan, a cloud that hangs over you demanding re-payment."* (The True Story of Bonnie Parker). It always does, because of the value of a life, though no doubt hardened killers find it easier the second time round. The cross involves trading places, so Jesus offers himself within the moral accountability regime as payment for sin. He becomes, to use Barth's famous configuration, the Judge judged in our place.

We come to the final piece of the jigsaw. Paying the price, not just for those who have been sinned against but for those who have sinned: for the perpetrators as well as victims. An action has cost me- I require payment. That could be understood not as a quantity to overcome the deficit but arising in the interaction between us, in an exchange system that characterises violence. Violence is relational. It is not just about what happens to me. Violence is experienced as 'me-in-relation-to-you', not 'me in myself'. It is a deficit of separation that is searching for human connection and reconciliation.

Violence reminds us of what is fundamental to the human condition, that we are hunters as well as hunted. We are all of us perhaps, capable under the right conditions of becoming violent, of acting as devaluers and desecrators of others. Violence as power and domination is men needing to feel powerful, to keep the upper hand at all costs in case their wives should rise up a bit. It is whites controlling the blacks, masters their slaves. It is a bully needing to keep control in case they lose it. It is a woman disrupting a marriage so that she can have a man and then discard him. Look under the surface, behind the need to dominate and control and there often emerges insecurity about being taken over, a threat being acted upon or a reaction against being abused or disrespected. A fundamental meaning of crime for the criminal is to escape control of others and impose control.[250]

It is the essence of sinful actions as with violence that they violate sacredness. This assumes that people have a value and a worth that can be infringed and assaulted. That value is constituted in relation to others. This takes place between people but also occurs in social systems and cultures, for example those that perpetuate white superiority. As we have noted, that is not often understood. Sin is thought to be by individuals. In the minds of most, the default position is that inter-personal actions are better grasped than actions that are constrained by systemic processes. At either individual or higher-order systemic levels, someone is trashed. Their value is walked all over. Clear my name! Some sort of compensation, of recompense is called for by way of response. Letting someone down or hurting someone matters. We become unworthy because value has been eroded.

Every time we sin against each other, we are failing our duty to God. This is a deprivation, an absence of duty and of service though not perhaps an actual offence against God. It is curious that our contemporary mind-set objects to extending New Testament language of law-courts and sacrifice to God's working in favour of emphasising divine human relationship as being one of wounded love. Yet, in the world of relationship trade enforced by law, we are familiar with concepts such as:

a. Libel and slander.
b. Compensation.
c. Justice rather than private revenge.

Think of the latter. In the UK, sentences of Imprisonment for Public Protection (IPPS) were created by the Criminal Justice Act 2003 and started to be used in April 2005. They were designed to protect the public from serious offenders whose crimes did not merit a life sentence. Offenders sentenced to an IPP are set a minimum term (tariff) which they must spend in prison. After they have completed their tariff, they can apply to the Parole Board for release. The Parole Board will release an offender only if it is satisfied that it is no longer necessary for the protection of the public for the offender to be confined.[251] A whole-life order, sometimes called a whole-life tariff, operates in many countries. There are at least 75 prisoners currently serving whole life sentences in England and Wales. These include some of Britain's most notorious criminals, including the "Yorkshire Ripper" Peter Sutcliffe and the serial murderer Rosemary West. As I write these words, the accomplice to the Manchester Arena bomber, Hashem Abedi, was sentenced to at least 55 years for the murders of 55 people for planning the bombing carried out by his brother Salman.[252] This is the longest tariff ever given out by a British Court; equivalent to a whole life payment of debt to society.

Despite a ruling by the European Court of Human Rights (ECHR) stating that whole-life prison tariffs are a breach of a prisoner's human rights, the UK Court of Appeal elected to go against this judgment and decide that such terms could still be handed down to the criminals responsible for the most heinous crimes in our society. The European Court of Human Rights understood that the courts of England and Wales would feel under public pressure to impose whole-life sentences on the most notorious of criminals from time to time; however, it did stress that such sentences would be a violation of the prisoner's human rights. In other words, it is not lawful to throw a person in gaol and lock away the key. The death penalty does not exist in the UK anymore because we have determined that the state does not have the right to take a man's life in order to punish him for a crime – any crime. In many other countries, capital punishment is allowed in recognition of a life for a life.[253]

The inter-personal world is a market, a site of relationship trade as surely as any stall in the markets of town and cities anywhere. Someone does something that has a knock-on effect on others. Maybe it is something relatively small such as obliging them to cancel a night out they were planning. Or it could be a longer-term injury and have a larger impact. Where there is pain, there is cost. If relationships fail or there is tension and strain, there is a cost involved. 'Let me make it up to you', someone may say to an aggrieved party. 'How can I repay you for your kindness?' Within the practice of law, many forms of injury - for example slander - require compensatory recognition. In the prison service, tariffs are imposed to exact reparation.

Examples of the moral and personal value that is breached when an offence is committed arise all the time. Just in the process of writing these paragraphs a conviction was secured against a couple who had caused the most horrendous cruelty imaginable against a four-year-old boy. Vulnerable little Daniel Pelka had suffered beatings, attempted drownings, deliberate starvation and a monstrous regime of neglect. His mother and stepfather, her violent partner, both received a 30-year sentence. To have taken no action against the perpetrators would have been to demonstrate no regard that here was a vulnerable innocent boy who deserved far, far better. It would have been saying that Daniel had no value and his life did not count. The sentence was the highest tariff that could be accorded. Unimaginable and systematic cruelty by an evil stepfather and indifferent, selfish, mother, was made worse and certainly not reduced in any way by the complete absence of remorse. Mrs Justice Cox said that Daniel Pelka had been starved so badly that his condition on his death, weighing just 11kg, was unprecedented; and yet the couple had shown no sign of remorse.[254]

On the news the same day, when four years afterwards the London Metropolitan Police gave an unconditional apology for the death of a bystander at an anti-capitalist protester in 2009, the spokesperson for the family was jubilant. This was the nearest to justice they were likely to get. What was needed all along was recognition, recognition that their loved one was someone of high value. Such recognition was more important to them than financial compensation. It demonstrated that their loved one was someone of high moral status to whom obligation is owed. Deficits here mean that some kind of payment was needed but it was a payment in the moral economy of worth and human value. I am using the economy as a cipher to show that someone atoning for their sins.

The day before, a senior Roman Catholic Bishop had acknowledged a legacy of abuse of children. The Bishop of Aberdeen, Hugh Gilbert, issued an unreserved apology with his unequivocal declaration that allegations surrounding Fort Augustus Abbey in the Highlands had put shame on shamed the church. *"It is a most bitter, shaming and distressing thing that in this former Abbey School a small number of baptised, consecrated and ordained Christian men physically or sexually abused those in their care."* This was in marked contrast to the way that the church had dismissed such claims. For that was saying in effect that the victims do not matter, or matter less than the institution we must protect at all costs.[255] This is the heart of complaints against serious deficiencies in safeguarding by the church. They did not seem to be taking victims of abuse seriously enough.

In social sciences, the question of who does and should exchange what with whom for what reasons and on what terms has been the stuff of analysing society from Plato onwards. The essence of the great social co-ordinating mechanism known as the economic market is that if you exchange this, I will give you something you value more than what I am asking you to sacrifice.[256] As social theorist Georg Simmel pointed out in the context of money, *"exchange takes place not for the sake of an object previously possessed by another person but for one's own feelings about an object".*[257]

The transactional character of human relationships seems inescapable. Some sort of exchange mechanism needs to be envisaged by which we are driven to seek compensation somewhere and from someone. A familiar enough scene is that of a boy or girl, subject to verbal and physical abuse; they lash out subsequently with bottled up anger. Something has been breached in our depths. It is core material, primal wounding. It evokes a primal cry of "I'm worth more than that!" Someone must pay. The same desecration that has been inflicted on us must be visited upon others. Getting back at someone or retribution will ensure that my depleted bank account of value is filled again at your expense. The impetus to make up the deficit is then relieved. The question is whether a valid way of understanding human relationships is theological in nature by reference to the atonement.

Accountability is needed; it is the same moral circle as justice and recompense. Payment becomes due because people have been trashed, people of high value that must be upheld or regimes feel they can get away with it. Failing to recognise people as having high worth and value leads to some sort of payment being required - hence talk of guilt and reparation arising from those deficits.

Infringement then involves payment. It creates a deficit in merit, which is rooted in what is owed. Merit means to bring about something that should in justice be given to someone. *"Merit is an adequacy of recompense or retribution qualifying a gift or a punishment bestowed or inflicted upon the receiver for something he has done with respect to the giver. Thus, God will judge all men according to their merits or demerits."*[258]

221

The usual approach to such deficits though is the idea of 'debt'. ''Forgive us our debt' is a way of articulating the need to cover the aggrieving by the aggrieved. Atonement theology is usually expressed in terms of sacrificial language or that of the slave market and its overtones of redemption. Since everyday human transactions are replete with the metaphor of the circulating economy ('you will pay for that'!), it is instructive to deploy the economy as a cipher for the idea of substitution. Payment must be made. This is inseparable from ideas of judgement. For what judgement means essentially is that this is where the past catches up with you, that we have to face the consequences of our actions.

When Keynes wrote his 'General Theory of Employment, Interest and Money' during the years of the Great Depression, his new architecture of an economy led to him losing former friends at Cambridge University. It is a curious synchronicity that writing about prices resulted in a great personal cost to relationships.[259]

We accept the idea of 'cost', payback or 'getting back' at someone as everyday features of human life. 'It's payback time!' does not only apply to acts of revenge but ordinary relationship transactions where, if someone is crossed and ignored, the perpetrators will know about it! Violence is often reproduced by those who are bereft of any sense of worth through abusive experiences, then try to scrape it off the face of victims as compensation to recover their value or to protect their own value (honour). The tortured landscape of human violence often discloses a significant reality. Where there has been a cost, there must be a payment. These are associated in degree, though demand for payment may or may not be proportionate. Familiar reactions crowd the stage, which may be more easily explained through some form of exchange system and relationship trade to make up the deficit. Losing name or status results in compensation being needed. Comfort eating may well be a human response to this loss. Or the individual may indulge in the blame game- 'I'll make them pay'. Unconsciously, the plan is how to act on it so as to stop feeling this way, so the pain can be relieved. Authority figures such as Police forces are often accused of attracting those who have an inferiority complex and who then need to compensate by throwing their weight around or by reacting unpredictably. This is perhaps a strategy for the recovery of their value.

Saying someone is guilty affirms that they owe something to the person they have wronged. The philosopher Richard Swinburne develops this aspect in his defence of a substitutionary atonement on philosophical grounds. *"By hurting you, I put myself in a moral situation somewhat like the legal situation of a debtor who has failed to repay money borrowed from a bank".260* Swinburne stresses that there is even more to the problem of moral guilt than past failure or present debt. The guilty one has acquired a stain that needs to be removed.[261] Swinburne's account emphasises the need for atonement; that it is impermissible to ignore the offence or go on as if nothing happened. To take an extreme case, if a spouse is murdered, any attitude that tries to say 'the past is the past, let's not nurse a grievance' simply will not do. That attitude trivialises human life, your love for your wife and the importance of right action. And it involves you failing to treat me seriously, to take seriously my attitude towards you expressed in my action.[262]

The world is a marketplace. Rather than being a single market, the global economy is a place of exchange for everything that is bought and sold. A network of myriad interlocking markets in every conceivable product exercises an invisible hand of daily influence in our lives. In countless, contractual exchanges, money changes hands. Money is the medium of exchange for human interactions. There is an exchange system that takes place every time you go to the shops, buy a car or get a paycheck in return for your labour. In using money to make money, the world of signs has been emancipated from the reality of which it speaks but it also dominates it. It is no co-incidence that philosophy was born in Greek Ionia, which was the first monetised state. Money has been fascinating humanity since Aristotle wrote about the arbitrariness of the money sign and its translation into a world of aspiration. Why should *that* piece of metal or paper buy products and influence? The unlimited has defeated limit. In Aristotle's ethical world, that was against the principle of moderation in all things.[263]

The monetary value of the currency enables buying and selling to be separated. It avoids the double-bind of barter; having to find something of equivalent value to trade.[264] The money system of planet Earth rests on trust. These pieces of metal or paper are valuable because a buyer and seller thinks that they are. It is a convention that everyone accepts because experience shows that everyone else will accept it too. As John Stuart Mill argued in his "Principles of Political Economy", money is:

"a machinery for doing quickly and commodiously what would be done, though less quickly and commodiously without it, and like many other kinds of machinery, it only exerts a distinct and independent influence of its own when it gets out of order."[265]

There is a wider exchange system in all human interactions. The system of economic exchange in our material culture is a metaphor for what happens between people in everyday transactions. Seeing human interaction as a kind of market immediately implies some 'goods' that are bought and sold with money. Yet, the idea of an exchange system is a cipher for human transactions. The word 'credit' reflects this, deriving from the idea of 'credo' or 'trust'.

The Austrian philosopher Martin Buber describes "I-Thou" relationships we can have with another, opened via the door of empathy.[266] This contrasts with "I-It" relationships, which stay on the surface. The emotional indifference of an I-It relationship has a very different feel than the connection made with an 'I-Thou' mode. The boundary between them though is fluid. Even in close relationships, we slip into the 'I-It' mode when we are busy. The 'Thou' can become an 'It' to me.

The economic simile is intriguing. "You will pay for this" we say, as if payment of a monetary sum can assuage the debt. A perfectionist could be said to consider that the marginal labour in a project is worth it in order to add the value that will command approval. By contrast, the 'good enough' style does not consider the marginal effort is needed. Those engaging in a 'blame game' do so in order to exact payment if what someone has done does not come up to scratch. A sensitive person carrying out an action that is likely to hurt another may then have to act so as not to create the kind of deficit that arises from having caused an open wound. We might then feel we must make it up to them.

2

Here are two examples. The French poet Paul Valery had a kind of arranged marriage with Jeannie Gobillard. It was, by all accounts, both affectionate and faithful amongst the relationships Valery constructed in his dualistic view of the world. Nevertheless, it left much missing - sexual and emotional intensity, intellectual companionship and a spiritual longing that was never met. These were, in the view of Valery's biographer, significant deficits. Something (s) were felt to be owed that were left unmet.[267] Or the hidden world of the quantum genius Paul Dirac highlights this kind of exchange. Working himself up into an angry state against his father, a disciplinarian bully and principal actor in an unhappy childhood, Dirac's verdict was "I owe him nothing!"[268]

The inter-personal world is a market, a site of relationship trade as surely as any stall in the markets of town and cities anywhere. Someone does something that has a knock-on effect on others. Maybe it is something relatively small such as obliging them to cancel a night out they were planning. Or it could be a longer-term injury and have a larger impact. Where there is pain, there is cost. The person who has been affected may well feel there is 'a price to pay' for this action or even that the perpetrator owes them. If relationships fail or there is tension and strain, there is a cost involved. "Let me make it up to you", someone might say to an aggrieved party. "How can I repay you for your kindness?" "Make Germany pay," was the demand in the British 'khaki' general election of 1918 at the end of the First World War. Within the practice of law, many forms of injury- for example slander- require compensatory recognition.

The link between economic valuing and human value, between the relational sphere and the material realm of things, emerges in the language people use to speak of human actions. Transactions in society often reflect an idea of social responsibility that entails that those who are better off 'owe' something to vulnerable members of society.[269] A deficit arises which needs compensation, even if only an acknowledgement.

Two people meet and interact. In the exchange system of human interaction, a kind of force-field is set up. There is one, there is the other and there is the space between them - the relationship. Sometimes people try to separate the person they relate to from the dynamics between them- 'it's not you, it's the relationship' – as if a dynamic but silent entity exists between them. In developmental psychology, this may have its origins in what the psychoanalyst Winnicott dubbed a 'transitional object'.[270] It is difficult, but not impossible, to separate two people in a pattern of action and reaction from the way they are interacting. People speak about their friendship as a third party. Intimate partners discuss their sex life as if it is had a life of its own and it was a not so silent partner. The power of intimacy itself is so strong as to set up obligations and a sense of easy betrayal if what is owed is not paid. In the laden world of intimacy, we expect to be in a monopoly position rather than a free market. Voices are often heard saying that at the heart of sex and relationships education in schools there should not be an emphasis on 'advanced plumbing' but on the individual, so they feel they are worth something, rather than jumping into bed and selling themselves too cheaply.[271] Through adding a veneer of respectability to sexual titillation, the kind of Playboy philosophy promoted by Hugh Hefner normalised the objectification of women and made it respectable.[272]

Neo-classical economists have studied the way that people feel exploited or engage in exploitation in the non-economic 'good' of human relationships.[273] People fall in and out of love. Exchange patterns shaped traditional marriage involving male providers and female domestic labour.[274] It is worth remembering that, until the First World War, most children in the UK were not getting more than two hours education a day. They were part of the workforce. Children were commodities.

It must be stressed that the economic motif here is thematic. It is a metaphor. In medieval times, people confused this with talk of a 'treasury of merit' that could be supplemented with the merits of the saints and then, foolishly, money transfer. It was this that Luther famously protested against.

3

EXCURSION – A SWEEP FROM HISTORY

Across time and space, the cross of Christ has been a magnet for theological interpretation. The meaning of the cross has been fundamental to Christian belief and a focal point for Christian identity. How we can make sense of the death of Christ has been crucial to what it means to be mainstream and orthodox in belief, where the default position is that Jesus is the Saviour of the world. How the cross forgives human sin was certainly not an invention of the 16th century Reformation. A whole host of early church theologians and fathers probed how the cross can be said to have accomplished human redemption. Then there was Duns Scotus with acceptiliation, Abelard with moral influence and crucially both Anselm and Aquinas with their doctrine of the death of Christ resulting in the satisfaction of God's justice. How the death of Christ two thousand years ago still saves people today and liberates us has been a storm centre for Christian debate.

Plenty reject the view that the cross was a way of assuaging an angry God. Amongst conservative Christians, various versions of substitution continue to rule the day as the focus for the theology of the cross. Put simply, because humans commit sin, God sent Christ as a substitute to suffer and die in our place. Outside of conservative circles, the idea of substitution does not have a good press. In his sketch endeavouring to locate Jesus as first century prophet, the scholar Marcus Borg does not suppose that Jesus deliberately died an atoning death for the sins of the world.[275] Over a hundred years ago, McLaren wrote about substitution and the notion of representation that underlies it. *"It is notorious, however, that such representation can today hardly get a hearing."*[276]

Modern critics abound. *"One must therefore reject those crude accounts of Christian doctrine which... say that that Christ has been justly punished in our place so that he has taken away our guilt and enabled God to forgive us."*[277]

"The doctrine of the atoning death of the Son of God upon the cross has led to many theological errors, among them to theories of substitutionary atonement which outrage the moral sense."[278]

Yet, the root cause of this rejection is, as Niebuhr detected, an inability to believe that life is tragic. Jesus is defeated but is triumphant in that defeat. The Christian faith does not deny the tragic facts of human existence by a single act of victory over tragedy. The atoning death of Christ is a revelation of what life actually is. It also discloses that human life, always in danger of being engulfed by sin, can be redeemed by the transmutation of wrong doing into good. Objection is taken on the one hand to the supposed harshness of the Divine character which can be pleased with such a device as a substitutionary atonement and on the other to the idea that every wrong doing brings its own consequence.

At a service in 2007, the Dean of St Albans, Jeffrey John, caused a stir when he preached that Christ did not die for our sins. He went on to say that the Church's traditional teaching on the crucifixion is "repulsive and insane." Clergy who preach at Easter that Jesus was sent to earth to die in atonement for the sins of mankind are *"making God sound like a psychopath"*. *"In other words, Jesus took the rap and we got forgiven as long as we said we believed in him,"* said John. *"This is repulsive as well as nonsensical... If humans behaved like this, we'd say they were a monster."* A revision of the traditional explanation, which is penal substitution, is fundamentally necessary, urged Jeffrey John. An alternative, and far better explanation, is that Jesus was crucified so he could *"share in the worst of grief and suffering that life can throw at us."*[279] In short, Jesus identifies with us: a description we have noted above.

Both explanations offer some notion of substitution, with Jesus dying in our place. The difference is that, in the latter idea of Jesus sharing in the tragic horror of life, there is no thought of penalty, of punishment. It is not penal. People object to the idea of blood (of Christ or of a sacrifice) in connection with atonement, forgetting that blood is almost always associated with violence.

In the summer of 2013, a popular evangelical hymn, "In Christ alone", sung at the enthronement of the Archbishop of Canterbury only a few months before, was not included in a hymn book to be published by the Presbyterian Church of the United States (PCUSA). It contained the lines *'Till on that cross as Jesus died, the wrath of God was satisfied.'* The compilers regretted losing the hymn with its otherwise powerful witness but said it did not wish *"to perpetuate... the view that the cross is primarily about God's need to assuage God's anger."*[280] That line had also been firmly objected to a former Precentor of Salisbury Cathedral, Canon Jeremy Davies. *"Are we really to believe that the angry God, propitiated by a blameless victim, is the God and Father of our Lord Jesus Christ?"*[281]

4

Scripture does not play on one single string when it comes to how we make sense of the death of Christ. This is now widely accepted. As 1 Corinthians chapters 1 and 2 demonstrate, Paul was aware he had a choice. He could have played down the cross and its significance. He knew the ignominious death of Jesus was both a scandal and an offence. In

Paul's theology of the cross, five motifs stand out:

- worship: sacrifice (1 Corinthians 5:7 and Romans 3v25).
- battleground: triumph over evil (Galatians 1:4; Colossians 2:15).
- the court room: justification (Romans 3:21-4:25; 1Corinthians 1:30).
- the marketplace: redemption (Ephesians 1:7; Colossians 1:14).
- reconciliation and personal relationships: (2 Corinthians 5:18-19; Colossians 1:20-21).

The way that Paul can weave these themes together in a pivotal passage such as Romans 3v21-31 shows how there is an underlying unity here. This passage includes v25, which reams have been written about. Does *hilasterion* mean 'propitiation', 'expiation', or "place of atonement" i.e. 'mercy-seat'? (The whole thrust of the surrounding context and argument from 1v17 onwards is that something takes place through the cross by which God's wrath turns away). Nevertheless, in the end, these are metaphors of meaning. Jesus did not die five times for five different reasons, but once. Each theme is a perspective emphasising the different theological meanings biblical writers bring to the task of making sense of the death of Christ. Massive thinker as he was, Paul and other New Testament writers did not attempt to develop a comprehensive theology of the cross, offering a composite theory of the atonement. That was the task subsequently of church theologians down the ages. Nevertheless, following on from the symbolic meal at the Last Supper, there was a strong and intrinsic link affirming that the cross had something to do with forgiveness of sins.

"The God of our ancestors raised up Jesus, whom you had killed by hanging him on a tree. God exalted him as Leader and Saviour that he might give repentance to Israel

and forgiveness of sins." (Acts 5v30-31)

"He whom God raised up experienced no corruption. Let it be known therefore my brothers that through this man forgiveness of sins is proclaimed to you." (Acts 13v37-38)

"In him we have redemption through his blood, the forgiveness of our trespasses according to the riches of his grace he lavished on us" (Ephesians 1v7)

"In whom we have redemption, the forgiveness of sins" (Colossians 1v14)

The Greek word forgiveness here, "aphesis", involves the notion of sending away or letting go, but the important point is that this offer is strongly connected to the death and resurrection of Jesus. The way this meaning of the cross is embedded within early Christian preaching is reflected in a verse like Galatians 1v4- *"who gave himself for our sins."* This is of a piece with the tradition Paul claims he received at the outset (within a few years of the crucifixion):

"For I handed on to you as of first importance what I in turn had received: that Christ died for our sins in accordance with the scriptures" (1 Corinthians 15v3).

It follows straight in to later statements such as in the Epistle to the Hebrews *("to make a sacrifice of atonement for the sins of the people"*- 2v17), or the first letter of Peter (*"he himself bore our sins in his body on the cross"* – 2v24), the book of Acts, the first letter of John (*"the blood of Jesus his Son cleanses us from all sin"* – 1v7) or the book of Revelation (*"to him who loves us and freed us from our sins by his blood"*- 1v5). In such examples, the Greek word for sin (hamartia) is in the plural. That seems to be important for New Testament writers. One could use the theme of the victory of Christ as Paul does to great effect (such as in Colossians 1v13 & 2v15) or as is deployed in Hebrews 2v14-15 to show the way the cross disarms the powers. The idea of 'sins' most naturally fits into a sacrificial way of understanding the cross rather than wholly as demonstration of God's love (Romans 5v8). Following New Testament era, explanation for how the death of Jesus saves humanity has developed in three main ways, depending on whether the cross was intended for the devil, God or humanity.

Firstly, the idea of Jesus winning an overwhelming victory for us on the battlefield. The idea of the death and resurrection of Christ being an overwhelming victory over dark powers goes back to the New Testament but was developed only afterwards. Origen thought in terms of a miscalculation by the devil, who thereby deceived himself. The notion of the deceit of the devil was present in the writings of Irenaeus and Origen developed by Gregory Nazianzus, who points out that a ransom is usually paid to the captor. In his death Christ paid our ransom, but it was not certainly the Father who had imprisoned us![282] In the way Gregory of Nyssa developed the victory theme, we are set free from slavery to the evil powers because *"the divine nature was concealed under the veil of our human nature so that, as with a greedy fish, the hook of divinity might be swallowed by the bait of flesh"*.[283] Others found the idea of God deceiving the devil morally dubious. Did the devil really have some legitimate rights over man? Though it had fallen out of favour, in the 20th century the battlefield metaphor was re-visited by Gustav Aulen in his 'Christus Victor,' seeing the notion of victory over dark powers as the 'classic' view of the atonement.[284] In the hands of writers such as Marcus Borg, the victory of God is emblematic of how to defeat evil:

"the domination system, understood as something much larger than the Roman governor and the temple aristocracy, is responsible for the death of Jesus... The domination system killed Jesus and thereby disclosed its moral bankruptcy and ultimate defeat."[285]

This was not of course the only theology of the cross in the first few centuries of the church. Stressing human alienation from God before Jesus came, and indeed human sinfulness, Augustine was keen to emphasise how Jesus bridged that gulf and ended our estrangement. His emphasis on sin was to become a very powerful motif in the centuries that followed, attuning Christendom and the emerging Protestantism of the 16th century to the need to become right (righteous) with God.

The second main line of interpretation has been to see the cross as primarily intended to influence humanity- the subjective view as Aulen characterised it. Many would say they are spiritual and see the gospels not the gospel (singular), i.e. the gospel of Jesus, as the highest standard to which people can attain. It is not a message about human salvation per se, except as people respond to it under moral challenge. This is the theory of moral inspiration, associated with Peter Abelard in 12th century France. The basis of the Moral Influence theory was that the cross is a demonstration of the extent of God's love. Because lack of repentance is what needs to be overcome, the cross moves us and wins our hearts far more than punishment can. As a modern translation of one of his hymns says:

Our sins, not thine, thou bearest, Lord; make us thy sorrow feel, Till, through our pity and our shame love answers love's appeal (F Bland Tucker).

Like many writers since, for Abelard the cross was not essential for sins to be forgiven. Jesus pronounces forgiveness before his crucifixion. The purpose of the cross then was not to change anything in God but was designed to draw man to respond to him. The subjective nature of the atonement is what is crucial, what it does in us. Theologians such as Schleiermacher and most liberal writers since have followed this line of interpretation though the Christus Victor theme has returned.

The third approach has been to see the death of Christ in terms of a price to be paid, an objective satisfaction through some kind of substitution intended to take the place of the sinning man or woman. Rather than people bearing the consequence of their own sinfulness, Jesus steps up to the plate and offers himself instead. Very far from being a Reformation invention, this understanding has been associated with the 11th century Archbishop of Canterbury, Anselm. The key idea is that of satisfaction. Honour and justice are satisfied when something is done to make reparation. Yet Irenaeus wrote about it with his doctrine of recapitulation and the idea is there in Ignatius (*Trallians* 2.1 and the *Letter of Barnabas*).[286] The cross was a major theme in Justin Martyr, Eusebius of Caesarea, Hilary of Poitiers, Athanasius, Gregory of Nazianzus, Ambrose, Augustine, Cyril of Alexandria, Gelasius of Cyzicus and Gregory the Great.[287] Athanasius and Augustine are both keen to defend the notion of God as not being contradictory in his love, with God propitiating his own wrath by sending his own Son among us. The teaching was developed by Thomas Aquinas, Luther and Calvin, all of whom were sophisticated commentators and very far from the simplistic 'dumbed-down' version that often substitutes for substitution. Luther and Calvin clearly presented the penal theory, in common with Zwingli and Melanthcon. They certainly did not originate the idea but the notion that there was an intrinsic connection between the death of Christ and the forgiveness of human sin was common currency amongst the Reformers.[288] Calvin, for instance, stressed that there is no contradiction between the grace and mercy of God and the need for the cross, commenting on Romans 3v 24-25 as that here, *"Paul commends the grace of God in that he gave the price of redemption in the death of Christ"*.[289]

These main lines of interpretation are sometimes presented as being a choice of 'A's – Aulen, Abelard or Anselm.
There was of course a fourth 'A', who is much less well
known amongst Protestant Christians. Thomas Aquinas
carefully argued that the death of Christ had two functions.
The cross was intended to make satisfaction. But it was also
intended to merit grace. The first was to deal with what had
happened already; the second corresponds to the inevitability of sinning in the future. Aquinas is quite clear that
*"Christ willed to suffer that he might make satisfaction for
our sins... so that by himself, without any fault of his own
bearing the penalty we owed, he might free us from the sentence of death, in the way that anyone would be freed from a
penalty he owed if another person undertook the penalty for
him"*.[290] As the philosopher Eleanor Stump carefully argues,
Aquinas' account of a satisfaction for sin rests on a different
notion than God being a sort of supreme accountant, a debt
of guilt being registered that must be balanced on the other
side of the ledger by exacting a corresponding amount. God
is rather a parent who is concerned to restore harmony and
hence, as long as the sinner is genuinely willing to make
reparation, it does not matter so much who pays for the damage (as for instance if her son damages a mother's flower
bed).[291]

When commentators present a knee-jerk reaction against
the very idea of a substitutionary atonement, it is invariably an unreflective and simplified version they are reacting against. The crude and unreflective version goes like
this; offence against God results in the need for a penalty
so great and so everlasting that humans could never repay.
God would be unjust not to exact the payment owed but
he is merciful as well as just. So it is arranged that he himself pays the debt by taking human nature on himself and in
Jesus, enduring the punishment which would otherwise be

due. The outcome is that the sins we commit are forgiven and the slate wiped clean.

There are many problems with this simplified version. For instance:

a. *Is this really forgiveness?* If God does in fact extract all the punishment that is required through visiting it on His Son, the debt owed is still paid in full, not forgiven or overlooked.

b. *Is this really justice?* If God's response to human sinfulness is to punish a completely innocent person (i.e. Jesus), how does that serve the cause of justice?

c. *Is this really equal?* If the penalty for sin is everlasting separation from God, how does the awful yet temporary 6-hour horror of the cross cancel that out? The remedy God is merciful enough to provide does not meet the assigned penalty, especially if many humans who do not embrace that remedy through faith in Christ have to end up enduring it anyway.

d. *Is this really effective?* If a prime reason why the cross was necessary was due to our bad record before God, how does a one-off suffering by Jesus remove the tendency we have to commit wrong-doing and continue that record? (I might for instance have incurred penalty points on my licence but wiping the slate clean after four years will not prevent me from incurring subsequent fines or points).

Of these types of objections, it is b) the justice of the atonement that raises most eyebrows. Can guilt really be transferred to someone else who is perfectly innocent? The purpose of sacrifice in general is to restore harmony to the community, to repair the social fabric. Does an angry God really need placating, and can this only be done by demanding blood sacrifice or through extreme violence?

Or, as another British church leader notoriously remarked,

237

"the fact is that the cross isn't a form of cosmic child abuse - a vengeful Father, punishing his Son for an offence he has not even committed. Understandably, both people inside and outside of the Church have found this twisted version of events morally dubious and a huge barrier to faith. Deeper than that, however, is that such a concept stands in total contradiction to the statement that 'God is Love'. If the cross is a personal act of violence perpetrated by God towards humankind but borne by his Son, then it makes a mockery of Jesus' own teaching to love your enemies and to refuse to repay evil with evil."[292]

It is important to grasp how theologies of the cross are shaped by the cultural meanings of the day. In social sciences, human action has long been seen through the grid of interpretivism and not just empiricism. It is taken as read that signs and messages are situated within social relations. This is how meaning is constituted in social life.[293] What is important and interesting about what social participants act out emerges in the meanings they bring to their own actions and the actions of others. It is not enough to know what happens when you cry; why you cry offers in-depth insights into behaviour and motivation. Interpreting human action through considering the meaning of the act takes us beyond the surface facts of any situation so we can drill down into what people are really thinking and feeling. Centuries ahead of his time, the immense intellectual Paul was thoroughly alive to the need to discern how people see the world. In a chapter on hearing and interpretation the voice of God, Paul declares *"there are many voices in the world, and none of them is without signification. If I know not the meaning of the voice, I shall be unto him that speaks as a foreigner"* (1 Corinthians 14v10-11). It is the meaning of the voice that will concern us here.

The challenge of theological interpretation in general or

making sense of the death of Christ in particular is crucially shaped by the meanings we bring to it. As social sciences have long recognised, interpretive models are set up, which become grids for seeing the world. Much depends on how those readings are set up in the first place. The translation of the Christus Victor theory into the liberation theology of South America, as well as in the feminist and black theologies of liberation, demonstrates how far the meanings people bring to the theological task shape the results.[294] Often, what people object to in the penal view is a crude, harsh version of the atonement. In the doctrine, what they see and hear is a vengeful, angry father gratuitously visiting violence on his innocent son and being appeased. Then they complain that this is grossly incompatible with the love of God. Any idea that God, as a personal being, might be aroused into opposition by devaluation of those he loves or that it is possible to dishonour God is rarely considered.

People speak out of their experience. The interpretive grid with which we see the world shapes subsequent thinking (often colouring reactions to particular events or causes).[295] In the first few centuries of the church's life, the complexity of its struggle for existence was reduced to a head on collision between Go[o]d and the [d]evil, between light and darkness. This was a dualistic worldview shaped by the raw experience of insecurity and periodic persecutions. As played out in the book of Revelation, the battle was joined and, though good would triumph ultimately, the forces of evil were powerful and often victorious, at least apparently and temporarily. The church was an alternative to the world. This should not surprise us. A reductionist mind-set is echoed by the conspiracy theorists and cults through the ages, believing that complexity can be easily summarised by simple explanations of what is going on. It is the mind-set of political Islam, wanting to establish the Khalifate to ensure and enshrine the triumph of the sons of light against the sons of darkness.

The Christus Victor motif of atonement was rooted in struggle, in battle, in persecution and in collision. The life of the church was fit for warriors. Once the church did not have to fight for its very existence, we found ourselves in a different time. The Constantinian shift meant that confrontation was not the order of the day anymore. The church could settle down somewhat, although of course the pagan onslaught against Rome presented significant new challenges. Conflict was no longer the dominant experience of the day to day life of the church, No longer perched precariously amidst a life or death cosmic power struggle.

For Abelard things were different. The meaning Abelard brought to the table was that of philosopher and brilliantly clever theologian, a strong believer in logic, in objective epistemology and therefore Aristotle and the new learning sweeping Europe. At the age of 22, Abelard had set up his own school of theology, trouncing opponents with intellectual gifts and not a little pride. God is concerned, Abelard the educator insists, on restoring the sinner to harmony, to achieve a state of mind. Rather than any thought of vicarious satisfaction, the cross is an intrinsic part of God's teaching programme for the world. All that is required is some thoughtful analysis. There was thereafter an intellectual straight line to Faustus Socinus (1539-1604) who taught that Christ's death simply provides us with an example of how we should live.

For Anselm, the interpretive grid was different again. The context of how he saw the world was an honour-based society where honour and loyalty to those above you were crucial to the obedience you owed them. The social experience was the feudal society which was developing in England following the Norman Conquest. Where there was an infringement of that respect and failure to yield obedience, especially when military or agricultural service was required, an offence had been caused. To make suitable reparation, some kind of satisfaction had to be rendered. The social order of the world Anselm knew was about honour and shame and it is the honour of God that needs to be redressed through some kind of satisfaction.

Aquinas sees the death of Christ as overcoming the alienation that comes when we sin. It is not that God withdraws from us; we withdraw from him. The purpose of the atonement is not to inflict suffering on Jesus as a punishment for human sinfulness, but that God accepts it as a way of making reparation. God could have forgiven us without reparation.[296]Moreover, Aquinas endeavours to show that the cross produces not only satisfaction for past sins but salvation from sinful conduct. He develops this under the heading of 'sacrament of salvation'. The idea is that of participation. As with Adam, Christ stands as the head of humanity. All humanity is, potentially, a member of Christ's body. (Believers already are!) Through his death, Jesus merits grace to cure the full range of sin and, as head of the church, he actually infuses this into those who are united with him.

The development of systems of justice and law-based guilt no doubt shaped the way penal substitution was developed subsequently. No longer is guilt determined by arbitrary trials of strength or survival as in the kind that prevailed before the 11th century. Jurisprudence had moved on. Wrongs were to be righted by courts: trial by jury is established. We are in a different world.

"In medieval law codes, the debt of punishment for even serious crimes as killing was literally pecuniary; one paid for the debt by offering monetary compensation. What was important for such purposes as avoiding blood feud was that the debt be paid, who paid it was not crucial. But our intu-

itions about the proper relations of crime and punishment are tutored by a very different picture... a murderer's mother cannot pay his debt of punishment by serving his prison term".[297]

This led to the Governmental theory of the atonement first taught by Hugo Grotius (1583-1645). God did not actually have to require payment for our sins and could have set this requirement aside. But he did not because God must show that when his laws were broken, there had to be a penalty paid.[298]

It does not take away from the scriptural and textual evidence to show that how people have thought about this is shaped by what they bring to the table. As with every field of human thought and action, much depends on the way that our categories are set up and defended (or attacked). That theories of the atonement reflect cultural transformations of the past helps us to see how reactions to those theories are encoded within particular religious and general cultures of the present and forged in encounters between differing worldviews. That then is the context of our discussion. What can the concepts developed in this book add to it?

The notion of 'Christ with us' through His death is acceptable. This is solidarity, this is the identification principle we have been exploring as giving expression to the value of humanity. Enter a discussion about the notion of 'Christ for us', however, and the debate becomes much more problematic. It is beyond the scope of this book to show how a particular theological representation fits in to the way that generation has been taught to see the world. Suffice to say that the contemporary mind-set rubbishes any idea of the death of Christ as a substitution. God is nice to everyone and everything will be fine. Invariably, the cultural transformations that which have taken place within the last 150 or so years mean that any idea of substitutionary atonement is subject to extraordinary caricature. What Jesus thought about the purpose of his own death is clearly a vital part of the picture, but scholarship has gone to great lengths to show that the suffering Servant bearing the sin of many (Isaiah 53) could not possibly have been in the consciousness of the Christ.

More than advocates perhaps realise, these stances and the caricatures they generate are cultural products. Theological ping-pong is played out on the basis of image and metaphor. The way these various interpretations are set up govern how they are responded to. Whatever the propitiatory effect of the death of Jesus, it streams from one place only, the enormity of the love of God. Jesus died only once and from whatever perspective we stand before the cross and contemplate it, all the theories of atonement fit together ultimately. If Biblical metaphors such as worship/sacrifice or slave market arise from the culture of the day, and given the way such cultural meanings are shaped, is there a way of regarding the notion of the cross being 'for us and for our salvation' that makes it more accessible to a contemporary audience?

We are all drawn in as it were to the violence of the cross. The circle of the spectators and those involved went far beyond those clustering round the cross that Friday morning.

4

As I write these words, a story has been running of an elderly man who was on a ventilator. He was in hospital fighting Covid-19. He is clear enough in his grasp of what is going on to notice a younger person in the bed next to him who is also fighting the virus. The younger person, however, does not have a ventilator. There are simply not enough to go round. For this is northern Italy and the lack of urgent medical equipment is having lethal consequences. Without hesitation, the older man, who happens to be a Catholic priest, urges the nurses. They should remove his ventilator and give it to his fellow-sufferer. After a discussion, they comply. His wishes granted; the older man dies shortly after.

Is this an example of substitution; 'it should have been me?' Into the football match, when most needed, a substitute steps into the game to help save it. The older man in the hospital gave his ventilator-enabled place to someone else. He is a substitute in the sense that he stepped up and took the place of another who was suffering in some way. It is the ventilator that was given in his place. The younger man had a chance to live and go free. The Priest literally died in his place. It is a transaction though not a monetary one.

Can we understand the death of Christ as a substitute? Jesus became a fellow-sufferer. He embraced the human situation in its messiness and weary pain and became one of us. Do we experience what it is to be trampled on? So did Jesus. Do we experience mockery and cruel sarcasm? So did Jesus. Do we experience abuse and physical torment? So did Jesus. "He has borne our infirmities and carried our diseases; yet we accounted him stricken, struck down by God, afflicted."

But there is more, as the Servant of God knows. *"He was wounded for our transgressions, crushed for our iniquities; upon him was the punishment that made us whole and by his bruises we are healed. All we like sheep have gone astray; we have all turned to our own way, and the Lord has laid on him the iniquity of us all"* (Isaiah 53v4-6).

The Lord has laid on him the iniquity of us all. It should have been me. The suffering Servant stands in the place of sinners, numbered with the transgressors as he poured out his soul to death and bore the sin of many. This is a vicarious experience. An innocent put himself forward to be a representative of the nation. Travails and hardship fall to the representative man, bruised for others.

Does that mean though that the rest of the nation has a free pass? It could be taken to imply that the suffering Servant of the Lord is experiencing what everyone else is going through so he can speak into that moment from a position of fellow-feeling. Or, that his experiences mean that he becomes the sin-bearer and allows others to get out of jail free.

The way of seeing the cross as a site of substitution is central to the New Testament. It has much to do with that tricky word sin or wrong doing. It sets up the need for recompense as we saw. We owe.

Peter certainly knows his Isaiah. He might well have remembered a dry and dusty desert when in blistering heat, an Ethiopian State official was reading those very words from Isaiah and was pondering, "what they could possibly mean?" *"He himself bore our sins in his body on the cross, so that, free from sins, we might live for righteousness and by his wounds you have been healed"* (1 Peter 2v24).

"Christ also suffered for our sins once for all, the righteous for the unrighteous, in order to bring you to God." (1 Peter 3v18).

"Grace to you from God our Father and the Lord Jesus Christ who gave himself for our sins to set us free from this present evil age". (Galatians 2v20) At the beginning of the first Christian writing stands the idea of Jesus being our substitute; one who sacrificed himself for me.

Sin requires redress because it is an offence against the person. The more serious the offence, the greater the need for recompense. The response to being let off the hook by the self-sacrifice of another in your place will invariably be one of gratitude and joyful release. The substitute goes through something so that someone else does not need to. Through this lens, the death of Christ is in our place; instead of us.

So why is this idea much criticised? One might suppose that the sons and daughters of earth would be highly relieved that here was somewhere to go to expunge guilt and do spiritual cleansing. Yet criticised it has been. Indeed, to question the idea of substitution was a test of how up to date you were. To hold to it still showed how antiquated your thinking was; captive to an old way of looking at the world that seemed to be stuck in the past. At that point we were passed all that. Talk of the blood of Jesus as a lamb slain for us represented the theology of the butcher's shop.

Leader of the opposition seems to be the problem of moral guilt. If the substitution of Jesus dying for the sins of humanity is true, guilt and punishment fall to him rather than human beings. It is not that they have a free 'get-out-of-jail' card, it is that payment does not now need to be made. This is someone coming up to you after the fine due from that parking ticket and offering to pay in your place; except that it is the parking attendant who does this, or even the leader of the local authority.

The penalty notice may be paid by someone else. Punishment could be transferred. Can we transfer guilt though? You still incurred that parking fine. It was your problem and your responsibility. Moral responsibility is a difficult concept when it comes to apportioning to others. Sin and responsibility are a big theme of the Old Testament. Gradually, the emphasis shifted from a family or tribe being blamed for the actions of one member to individual responsibility. 'The soul that sins, it shall die', as Ezekiel has it. Collective guilt remains though. The German people collectively voted for Hitler and brought down on themselves the wrath of Allied armies and airpower. 'We're all in this together'.

The demand for payment is central to everyday transactions when the value of people or their honour has been defaced. We require recompense. The cross is a site of payment in order to compensate for loss of value. Jesus represents God becoming one with us, one of us, one for us. Being one with the human situation at Christmas moves inexorably to its nadir at the first Easter.

CHAPTER TWELVE
THE POWER OF FORGIVENESS

Whose side was God on – the slaveholders or the slaves? Or maybe that is the wrong question. Beyond doubt, the church was central to the triple alliance of capitalism, civilisation and Christianity.

Through the hell of slavery, a great many slaves responded and sang 'negro spirituals' to a God incarnate who took on their burdens and carried them to the cross. Compelled to carry the cross themselves with its oppression and cruelty through being enslaved for financial reward, they could identify with a man broken and carried to the cross who offered 'Amazing Grace' of which they sang.

As we consider the message of the cross, an inescapable reality dominates the skyline. At the heart of Christian faith lies an act of horrific violence. To its detractors, Islam has an enduring problem with violence that stains the landscapes of the world. Other religions, including those that profess peace, have a violent streak. The red stain of Cain has marked Christian history no less. Crimes committed in the name of the Prince of Peace fill the centuries. It is all the more startling to realise that the world was redeemed by violence. In the wake of Auschwitz, some have written about "The pain of God" or "The crucified God". These are evocative phrases. If the challenge of the holocaust has not challenged us profoundly, we have not thought deeply enough. For the pain of God demonstrated at the cross connects radically and powerfully with the world's pain. The longer you look at the cross, the more you are moved and influenced by it. It's an incredibly powerful demonstration, an unforgettable statement that has etched its way into the fabric of our western civilisation: the identification principle in full measure. *"God demonstrates His own love for us in this; while we were still sinners, Christ died for us"* (Romans 5v8). Yet there is more in the cross even than the most powerful statement that can be conceived. Until recent times, much of the

Christian church had little to say about violence. It was a vicious example, amongst many, of flawed and fallen humanity. Violence is vital to a need for atonement and redress because it is about forcible devaluation of humankind, one to the other, whether in word or deed. A theology of violence and power is long overdue. It is easier to talk about sin in general or individual moral failure rather than get grubby and bloody.

When people listen to the violence inside, it becomes clear that much violence is about an exchange, compensating for being trashed or made to feel rubbished by extracting it forcibly from someone else. Those who have a healthy sense of themselves rarely are the bullies. One young lady reported how she needed to re-create the experience of pain through rubbing soap hard into herself to blot out her overwhelming feelings of abuse. *"I'm worthless. If he had just been my stepfather, it might mean I had some value. But I was flesh and blood and he trashed me. He hurt me. So, all I have memories is pain in my body's openings"*. The experience of sexual abuse very often brings about an attitude of self-devaluation. It shatters self-esteem. An abuser is often one who internalises both perpetrator and victim. Then acts it out, maybe having witnessed domestic violence. Shame is a very powerful factor – not "I *made* a mistake" (guilt) but 'I *am* a mistake' (shame). Feeling disadvantaged compared to others in the same society, the violent often develop lifestyles that allow them to become someone. They are trying to get their value back through the kind of people in their world that are highly prized and to whom they are apprenticed (i.e. the concept of mimesis). 'It's payback time!' The proposition here is that violence is often reproduced by those who are bereft of any sense of worth through abusive experiences, then try to scrape it off the face of victims as compensation to recover their value or to protect their own value (honour). The tortured landscape of human violence discloses a significant reality. Where there has been cost, there must be payment!

To its detractors, Islam has an enduring problem with violence that stains the landscapes of the world. Other religions, including those that profess peace, have a violent streak. The red mark of Cain has stained Christian history no less. Crimes committed in the name of the Prince of Peace fill the centuries. It is all the more startling to realise that the world was redeemed by violence.

"Christ suffered leaving you an example so that you should follow in his steps... when he was abused, he did not threaten but he entrusted himself to the one who judges justly" (1 Peter 2v21/23).

This reading of the cross and what took place there is not just one of Jesus being an example. Extreme violence is coming at Jesus, but he is not answering in the same register. He changes the language and responds from a very different place. The river of violence, so to speak, is completely diverted. It is transmuted, converted.

Where does it go? It is converted; converted into love. *"Father forgive them for they know not what they do."* (Luke 23v34). How is it that there is no demand for recompense? Surely lashing out is entirely appropriate: "this hurts!" Encouraging those who face some persecution, 1 Peter 3v18 goes on: *"Christ suffered for sins once for all, the righteous for the unrighteous, in order to bring you to God"*

A God who is concerned about human suffering? That is hardly the image twenty first century people have of God. Persistently, consistently, the pain of the tortured human situation is paraded by those who can relate neither to God or to His church. The problem of suffering they call it. Because it is so perennial and so personal (for it touches us all), the problem of suffering has drawn the attention of the greatest minds in history. Theologians and arm-chair philosophers debate the subject endlessly. Why suffering is allowed into the system is the focus for God-rejection by the crowds. Amidst the responses that can and should be made, there is one response that is distinctively Christian. Leave this out and the good news has not been brought to bear on the problem. The Creator has embraced the very suffering He has allowed into the system. No one can accuse Him of non-involvement. The symbol of Christian faith is the cross, not a celestial deckchair. This is God standing in solidarity with the kind of world we have made for ourselves.

It stands in contrast to other world faiths and their message to the world. Eastern religions have been fatalistic about suffering. Lepers and sick people, the lower castes and the misfortunate are all working out their karma from the last time round. Their previous existence brings a resigned attitude in the present. There is inevitability about it. Why should they be helped? Yet Jesus was indignant

It was taking a long hard look at the cross that moved Isaac Watts to write his immortal hymn - "Love so amazing, so divine, demands my life, my soul my all". Undeniably, the ordeal of the crucifixion has great power to move and stir us. The cross whispers to us that God's love is the greatest force in the universe, greater by far than animosity and violence. God's love can cross the bridge. Self-sacrificing divine love strikes a chord within us as we are moved by what God has done. Jesus made simple goodness, love and humility more powerful than nuclear weapons. A world stained red with violence must grasp that urgently. Yet, there is more.

Jesus followed the twentieth century into the anguish of human extremity and pain. He went with us into bereavement and into cancer. He was there with them in the gas chamber while they closed the doors, with every victim of war and injustice and with every mother caring for her disabled child with a heavy heart. No darkness can keep its doors barred against a self-sacrificing love that renders the redemption of the world. Here is identification at its most intense. The pain of God connects with the children of the genocide generation and a world pursuing the madness of violence and rape of the environment. Enduring Christ love pursues us into the 21st century with its tattered social order, with terrorism and territory in the land of his birth rent asunder in anguish. Despite the post-millennial West giving up on God, God is no stranger to the complex agony of humanity. Calvary tells us that our condition became His, redeeming outside the city though insider to its lore and its core. The identification of Jesus with human distress offers enormous potency for the healing journey pursued by individuals and societies. The psychotherapeutic potential is profound as people can find multiple points of contact –'He is despised and rejected by men; a man of sorrows, and acquainted with grief: and we hid it as it were our faces from him; he was despised, and we esteemed him not. Surely he has borne our griefs, and carried our sorrows: yet we did esteem him stricken, smitten of God, and afflicted." (Isaiah 53v3-4)

We can track the full-time, complete immersion project into the wilderness regions of random cruelty. Jesus drank of the lived experience of everyday. He ate to the full what life is like on ground level. The cross of Christ constitutes maximum exposure to envy, greed, strife and lust that stalk the human heart. The closer we look at the empathy of God, the more we are moved by the degree of His identification. A cursory glance will not do anything for us. The more we concentrate on it, the more we become convinced that the kind of selfish cruel strife that claimed Jesus as victim is not how we should live our lives. Jesus was the supreme exemplar of love in the face of suffering and of the power of goodness: a role model that gently prises open fingers of selfishness. We look at the self-sacrifice of Jesus and we say, here is the solidarity of God with the victims- and we are all victims. The gaunt faces of the tortured, the emaciated faces of the famished, the frightened lonely faces of the refugees - these are his type of people. God is calling us to make a connection and become the face of God. Unfortunately, the situation is more complex. We are also perpetrators.

The victims of violence have experienced the jagged reality that is all around, pervasive in militancy. With searing abrasiveness, they have encountered power: the power that is at the heart of the darkness and the dark powers. In its lashing, they come up against the wanton essence of sin; the primordial power that stands over against God. Gratuitous scraping the value off the face of another as a china plate can be marked- this is what sin does in violent, mocking disregard.

Jesus was a real person going through real things. He was on the receiving end of the most brutal form of violence which can be imagined. This is no accident. The gospels do not portray Jesus as gathering his followers around him and drinking hemlock as did Socrates. Death by crucifixion (after flogging that left him in a weakened condition), was searing, unrelenting and bloody. Did it have to be this way? Yes – for, unless violence could be redeemed, the scope of the cross would be limited. Instead of violent acts of judgement, the cross brings forgiveness back in its place. The sting has completely gone because it has been absorbed. One side of the cross is wanton cruelty, all the more savage for it being sport as well as judicious public execution. After the cross, forgiveness springs.

Would it have worked if Jesus had merely sipped poison and perished? Did it have to be so brutal? Violence converted into forgiveness – this is an important way of understanding the cross of Christ. Forgiveness rather than an eye for an eye is fully and authentically Christian. Jesus took the violence directed at him- and in its place flowed a powerful technology with which to disarm our world.

FORGIVENESS AND THE FIGHT AGAINST FORGETTING

Christianity proposes to civilisation the virtue and power of forgiveness. To forgive is to break free from the cycles of revenge but also honour. This can only happen when love is a gift and a privilege, not a right.

Human violence is an on-going phenomenon that continues to warp individuals, distort relations between people and communities and shape the destiny of nations. The way that humans so often demonstrate a knee-jerk resort to violence as a way of solving problems and meeting needs is so much a part of us that it seems normal; unwelcome and unacceptable, but normal. Arguably, the 21st century will compel us to learn more thoroughly than humanity has learnt hitherto about a new technology for resolving conflict between people and societies than the clenched fist, the gun or the grenade.

The question of non-violence is interesting and highly relevant. Following Gandhi (and before him, Tolstoy and Emerson), non-violence has been seen as a morally superior approach. It was not invented then: the Quakers and Mennonites had their peace testimony, repudiating involvement in the wars of the State and invoking the New Testament- James 4v1 – 'where then do conflicts arise.

Why is forgiveness so hard to do? Does the cross enable people to forgive? Love triumphs!

It was curious. Suddenly, the world was emphasising the need to own up and assume responsibility. Justice and reckoning were on the agenda. Ultimately, it was a spiritual theme.

The interim constitution of the new post-Apartheid South Africa sought to enshrine the principle of "ubuntu", meaning humanity, an inclusive sense of community valuing all of its citizens. A line had to be trod between the political demand of the outgoing Afrikaans leadership for an amnesty from prosecution and the demand of the ANC for a Truth Commission for the new nation to confront its past. The result in July 1995 was the creation of a Truth and Reconciliation Commission.[299] The TRC was vital in helping a nation discover a new politics because it brought out into the public space a myriad voices and traumatic memories suffused with violence. Those voices and memories were being granted the magic moment of recognition. The sense of what happened was not being overlooked anymore. And this is the dilemma facing any victim - whether of crime or of political violence. As a psychologist on the South African Committee on Human Rights Violations remarked, many victims conceived of justice in terms of re-validating oneself and affirming the sense of 'you are right, you were damaged; what happened was wrong'.[300]

Before the TRC in 1997, the former President of South Africa, F W de Klerk, publicly repented for the suffering that apartheid had inflicted on millions of people over nearly five decades. Nelson Mandela apologised for atrocities committed by the African National Congress. Harsh steps taken to preserve white minority rule had included detention without trial, muzzling of the press and military force against protest. The atmosphere was conducive to many of the abuses. *"We have," said de Klerk, "gone on our knees before Almighty God to pray for His forgiveness which, in the final analysis, is more important than anything else".* The National Party had made many mistakes in the past but was then genuinely repentant, he said. Confronting the past, it was intended that the Commission could help South Africans to understand what had happened and move them along the road towards reconciliation.

The rise of collective violence and genocide is the most terrifying legacy of the twentieth century. Memory and representation are especially potent in the Holocaust. The Children's Memorial at Yad Vashem in Jerusalem is a particularly evocative endeavour to re-claim the lives of each individual who had been destroyed. It stands in unspeakable continuity with factories of death such as Auschwitz, where even birds don't sing in chilling resonance with the complete lack of humanity in a place where 1.1 million people were murdered. Germany herself had come to terms with its recent past by repenting for the holocaust and going some way to redressing the greatest crime of history by compensating Israel. Compensation had been offered by industrial giants to its wartime slave workers. The result of acknowledging what had happened was that Germany had been restored to a position of trust in the modern world. In the wake of a few surviving inmates creeping out of the Nazi concentration camps, the Nuremberg Trials confronted the extreme political violence of the Nazi era, establishing the concept of 'crimes against humanity'.[301] The social philosopher Hannah Arendt did much to shift perspective away from seeing the Holocaust in terms of gothic and indescribable evil, stressing that it was all too human and banal.[302] She complained to her friend Karl Jaspers that the Nazi defendants seemed so smug; the horrors of mass genocide exposed the limits of law. No punishment would ever, could ever, suffice.[303] Yet, the Nuremberg trials set a precedent for conceptions of law which included the dignity of the individual, launched an international human rights movement and was the template for subsequent Tribunals in such places as Bosnia and Rwanda.[304]

The point surely is that recognition is crucial, a recognition that something has happened. In the context of an

Inquiry on the war on Iraq, relatives of dead soldiers said, concerning a former Prime Minister, *"we waited all day for him to apologise but he didn't apologise." "What we wanted was acknowledgement."*[305]

As the Polish Foreign Minister observed on the 70th anniversary of the Katyn massacre by Soviet Russia in 1940, *"when you are hurting and others don't recognise your hurt, it hurts all the more."* [306]

"What is so fascinating about the rise in the number of public apologies over the last few years is that although public figures clearly understand their importance, few really know how to do it well."[307] Worried about the political damage of framing a public apology that misfires, politicians and leaders so often miss a dimension of correctly naming wrongs and re-establishing a moral framework. A proper acknowledgement may be a missing stage on the road taken by victims of violence towards a healthier destination marked by recovery. Acknowledging what has happened and taking the swirl of contested emotions seriously is perhaps a simple remedy that is full of transformative possibilities. Its magic power reflects the fact that what is helping to maintain the chains of previous violence is its unacknowledged impact. It is insufficient that 'just anyone' can offer such remedial medicine. He who holds the key must be connected in such a way with the perpetrator – or be the perpetrator in the minds of the injured- that a thread of meaning can be woven between a traumatic event and what is now emerging from this 'significant other'.

The power of acknowledging the pain someone has gone through could lie in the way victims experience a double trauma. Not only did an original event bring a broken world, the injury was magnified by virtue of it being denied and unseen. Pain's invisibility converted it into a sense of self being trampled on. The darkness of devaluation settles over the face of the deep. But proper acknowledgement mandates a fresh seeing, a capacity to re-image the world. A significant other is offering a gaze in a way that emancipates the memory from its unacknowledged aspect that was burdening it. The self is hurting, but it is not now devalued. Amongst those new inner forms of resistance and representation of what has happened is that the self is free to agree that he or she is valuable property. Through the magic vision of recognition, debilitating feelings of humiliation and desecration are drawn off. Even having seen all authority and indeed subsequent relationships through "the lens of extremity,"[308] the self that learns first-hand about the capacity for evil[309] can recover from being severely traumatised by totalitarianism and be re-empowered.

SERIAL APOLOGY

This could explain why the trend towards public apology has occupied more than a passing moment.[310] Confronting a dark past became an obsessive pre-occupation in post-war Germany. Then the habit spread. Some politicians or companies became serial political apologists.

Suddenly the world emphasised the need to own up and assume responsibility. Ex-colonial peoples, tribal victims and minorities everywhere demanded apology for public wrongs.[311] The fear of modern descendants of the perpetrators was that recognition would lead to reparation.[312] In Canada, for instance, the Government apologised for 150,000 indigenous children wrenched from their homes between 1870 and 1996 and sent to schools where many were abused. This may have been motivated by a desire to avert future lawsuits by Indian victims who missed out on earlier compensation to former students of the schools.[313]

Justice and reckoning were on the agenda in the last

years of the 20th century. It was 'a global culture of apology.'[314]Drawn from newspaper accounts of the time, there were significant milestones in the gathering move to make statements which showed atonement and repentance were in the air. Collective guilt was in evidence. Questions were asked and challenges made about this. A statement by a campaigner in scandal which came into the public domain later (that of allegations of abuse that swamped the Catholic Church in the spring of 2010) encapsulates a major question about this. *"We are seeing lots of apologies but not much accountability and justice."*[315]Nevertheless, the world was having a Yom Kippur moment.

September 1997. On the very site of the rail transit camp where most of the 75,000 Jews deported from France were held before being sent to Auschwitz, the French Roman Catholic Church formally apologised for the failure of its bishops to condemn the transportation of Jews.

In early 1998, the Vatican formally apologised to Jews for passivity during the holocaust, "the errors and failures of the sons and daughters of the Church" who did not save Jews from the "horrible genocide" of the Nazi death camps. The Pope said the millennium was an occasion for Catholics to "purify their hearts through repentance of past errors and infidelities and examine themselves on the responsibility for which they, too, bear for the evils of their time". He apologised for Christian treatment of Jews down the centuries.

The Vatican was gearing itself up for a wider recognition of the "past sins of the church" in the year 2000. The Crusades, the Inquisition, the forced conversions- such evils, it was admitted, had contributed to "the disfigurement of the face of the church". A document was being prepared for sins committed in the name of religion. *"Memory and Reconciliation: the Church and the Faults of the Past"* it was called. Would the Pope acknowledge the failure of Pius XII to speak out during the holocaust?

Germany herself had come to terms with its recent past by repenting for the holocaust and going some way to redressing the greatest crime of history by compensating Israel. Compensation had been offered by industrial giants to its wartime slave workers. The result of acknowledging what had happened was that Germany had been restored to a position of trust in the modern world.

March 1998, President Clinton came to Uganda on a visit to Africa. He came close to apologising to Africa for the slave trade."The United States has not always done the right thing by Africa," he said. "European Americans received the fruits of the slave trade, and we were wrong in that".

May 1998. The Japanese Emperor visited Britain. Would this bring full recognition of the cruelty of Japanese soldiers in the Second World War? Survivors wanted the Emperor to make a full apology without reserve, to say, "we are guilty, and we owe". And Japan had never made an adequate apology for its aggression in the 1930's, which had annihilated an entire generation of Chinese. There had never been any question of the Emperor issuing a full apology. So why did veterans and survivors feel that only a full--hearted repentance could resolve the past? Relations with China would be strained until Japan had fully acknowledged guilt. It was the cry for justice.

July 1998. Under brilliant sunshine, the last Tsar of Russia was buried, 80 years after being murdered at Ekaterinburg. With hand on heart, President Yeltsin offered a deep apology on behalf of his nation for the massacre. "By burying the remains of the victims, we want to expiate the sins of our ancestors... We are all guilty," he said. "It is impossible to lie to ourselves by justifying the senseless cruelty on political grounds. Guilty are those who committed this heinous crime and those who have been justifying it for decades- all of us".

"Any attempt to change life through violence is condemned to failure," he said.

August 1998. Switzerland. The settlement and the admission had to be forced out of them. The National Bank had bought gold from the Nazi Reichsbank during the 2nd World War. "The National bank regrets most profoundly that in accepting gold deliveries from the Reichsbank, it may have unwittingly also have acquired gold deriving from victims of concentration camps".

Until recent times, much of the Christian church had little to say about violence. It was a vicious example, amongst many, of flawed and fallen humanity. Yet it is more. Violence is fundamental to the need for atonement and redress because it is about the forcible devaluation of humankind, one to the other, whether in word or deed. A theology of violence is long overdue. It is easier to talk about sin in general or individual moral failure rather than get down grubby and bloody.

The victims of violence have experienced jagged reality that is all around, pervasive in militancy. With searing abrasiveness, they have encountered power: the power that is at the heart of the darkness and the dark powers. In its lashing, they come up against the wanton essence of sin; the primordial power that stands over against God. Gratuitously scraping the value off the face of another as a china plate can be marked- this is what sin does in violent, mocking disregard.

THE WEAKNESS OF GOD

This does not have to mean violence. As the Canadian philosopher Charles Taylor observed, *"Discovering my own identity doesn't mean that I work it out in isolation but that I negotiate it through dialogue with others"*.[316] Jesus look nothing when he is everything. It all seems upside down.

The weakness of God! It is an astounding statement, quite unique to Christianity. Paul explains how the weak God shows up the apparent strength and superiority which whole cultures can flaunt.

"Think of what you were when you were called. Not many of you were wise by human standards; not many were influential; not many were of noble birth. But God chose the foolish things of the world to shame the wise; God chose the weak things of the world to shame the strong. He chose the lowly things of this world and the despised things - and the things that are not- to nullify things that are so that no one may boast before him." (1 Corinthians 1v26-29).

The cross teaches the macho culture where their true strength lies, the cross teaches laddish cultures to admit the weakness within that doesn't dareto emerge. Through the cross, the weakness of God becomes a point of contact with the twentieth century. Here is a Christ whose strength does not repel but whose weakness attracts (providing we recognise our own).

What seemed to be ultimate weakness and an act of shame on God's part had just been used to save the world. It had just happened. What seemed to be the death of a criminal had been converted into a message of salvation and hope. Powerful sophisticated people would rather not be saved by such a message and maybe Paul should have downplayed the cross and coughed at that point. But he refused to. At the cross, a place of shame was a means of glory and weakness a channel of power.

Jesus was indignant in the face of suffering; he fought against injustice and worked to relieve need wherever he could. This is why followers of Christ have been pioneers when it came to building hospitals and schools, not just in India, but everywhere else. Its motivation is not just that people are important, all of them (for we are God's image-bear-ers), but that we serve a Christ who suffered as man. Having entered so deeply into the life of the world that he died for it, Jesus commands his followers not to remain aloof but to engage ourselves with human need and serve the people.

Evangelicals have been good at this- building hospitals, building schools and building coalitions to defeat slavery. But paradoxically, and for historical reasons, evangelicals often down-play a way of looking at the cross that glimpses its profound identification with human weakness. Conversely, more liberal teaching has emphasised God's identification with the poor and the needy but downplay the message of forgiveness and human redemption.

Both ways of looking at the cross are needed. As long as that we miss the way that the cross intersects with suffering humanity, solidarity will not become a working, operating principle that allows us to make connection with a hurting world.

For the ordeal of the crucifixion has great power to move and stir us. The cross whispers to us that God's love is the greatest force in the universe, greater by far than hate and animosity. God's love can cross the bridge between God and man and overcome the gap between man and man. Self-sacrificing divine love will strike a chord within us as we are moved by it and touched by what God has done. Jesus made simple goodness, love and humility more powerful than nuclear weapons. A world stained red with violence must grasp that urgently.

3

Talk of violence becomes part of the lived experience of communities, of nations and ethnic groups. Incidents of collective violence arise initially out of common occurrences such as a drunken brawl, the theft of an idol in India, the rape of a girl, or such occurrences as terrorism. Some stay localized; others fit into broader frameworks of meaning supplied by dominant beliefs such as religion.[317]

Symbols and stories of a contested past abound. As the hundred year's war in the Middle East amply demonstrates, continuing talk of violence contributes to its persistence rather than its reduction. Experiencing and re-experiencing the past is a matter of collective memory. Retaliation and the desire for extending the conflict depend upon a continually re-lived past which merges with the present and constrains the future. The cycle of hatred draws on and is fuelled by the dangerous combination of myth and history. It is as if the past, with all its saga of actions and counteractions, is before the participants to evoke a crowd psychology, a collective memory. Rehearsing the past with a prejudicial perspective becomes more and more reinforced with successive acts of violence or perceived injustice. The mechanism by which an interpretation becomes fixed in collective memory is complex. Somehow, violence and memories of violence become grafted on to successive generations and embedded in the thinking. Cultures of violence are substantiated by the memory of who is good out there and who is bad in a way that conflates myth and history. What would it take to interrupt the collective memory of violence which not only repeats the reality but reproduces it? The story of what happened is repeated. The message acted out in the next generation is held in its collective memory. Mythmaking invariably takes place in the slippage between remembered and recorded fact. But are there alternative futures which can be imagined so a story ends differently? There is a political fashion for easy apologies but arguably, forgiveness is something else.[318] It is not achieved unilaterally but comes out of dialogue which involves reciprocal communication.

There is a hard law... that when a deep injury is done to us, we never recover until we forgive- Alan Paton [319]

Memory and the representation of the past force themselves to centre stage when the subjects of reconciliation and forgiveness arise. Another route towards the re-valuing lies in the self disburdening itself of its load, facing the violence and coming to an attitude towards its perpetrator that which can best be described by using the term 'forgiveness'. This began to be on the agenda for recovery from violence at a time when the prevailing talk in the logical of moral discourse was that of the 'hooray'- 'boo!' theory of ethical emotivism. In the USA, research grants began flowing in the 1980's to investigate the role of forgiveness in repairing psychic damage.[320] A leading researcher was Dr Robert Enright, professor of educational psychology at University of Wisconsin-Madison and president of the International Forgiveness Institute.[321] In an utilitarian perspective stressing the psychological benefits of forgiveness (as distinct from a de-ontological focus on the duty of forgiveness), Enright proposed a four-stage model of forgiveness as process.[322]

- An uncovering phase, where the individual becomes aware of the emotional pain that resulted from a deep, unjust injury.
- A decision Phase, where the individual now realizes that to continue to focus on the injury and the injurer may cause more unnecessary suffering.
- A work Phase, to begin the active work of forgiving the injurer which may include new ways of thinking about the injurer, to see the injurer as a member of the human community.
- An outcome or Deepening Phase, where the emotional relief and newfound meaning may lead to increased compassion for self and others.

This is a potential route towards the re-humanising of the world for the victims of violence. Clearly forgiveness is contested. *"Don't talk to me about closure. It's the most overworked phrase in the English language. I don't want bloody closure. I want justice."* [323] And this is the problem of forgiveness. It seems to be an approach that compounds the desecration and is therefore a betrayal. Anecdotally, the major objection to the very idea of forgiveness is that it lets the offender off the hook. For this is not someone out there that the polite label 'offender' can be affixed to; this is someone who has trashed someone or something that is dear. There is a cost involved, a deep pain.

Forgiveness brings with it a new resource for human connectedness and the valuing of self and others after violence has occurred. It means that victims are no longer carrying anger and bitterness around with them. A Palestinian human rights lawyer observed that it is the assertion of one's dignity to have the means an ability to forgive and observed, *"if there is to be peace here, there has to be forgiveness...We have to forgive the Israelis for what they did to us."* [324]

Forgiveness is a healthy accompaniment of truth-telling. Guatemala had its own gruesome saga of the disappeared. In "La Violencia" from 1978 to 1985, more than 200,000 were murdered or never seen again. 200,000 children were orphaned. As part of the recovery process, the Roman Catholic Church initiated the "Recovery of Memory Project"- [325] the REMHI, which compiled 52,467 testimonies of human-rights violations. *"Discovering the truth is painful, but it is without doubt a healthy and liberating action,"* as Bishop Juan Gerardi observed.

As the literature on violence suggests, the unwelcome possibilities of further devaluation have to be reckoned with by anyone who urges forgiveness on its victims. Yet, as Martin Luther King perceptively commented, forgiveness is not ignoring what has been done or putting a false label on an evil act. It means that the evil act is no longer a barrier to relationship. *"Forgiveness is a catalyst creating the atmosphere necessary for a fresh start and a new beginning."*[326]

So, violence inspired by religion is acutely contradictory. New ways of living co-operatively WITH the Earth must be found. New ways of living co-operatively ON the Earth must be found.

BIBLIOGRAPHY

1   BBC Newsnight, 4th August 2020, www.bbc.co.uk

2   Witness speaking on BBC2 Newsnight, 15th January 2020

3   New York Times, October 29[th]1995

4   Bailie, G. (1995) *Violence Unveiled- Humanity at the Crossroads.* New York, Crossroads Publishing Co

5   Junger, E. (1928), *Der Kampf als inneres Erlebnis.* Mittler & Sohn; Auflage: 3. Auflage (1928)

6   Pinker, S. (2012), *The Better Angels of our Nature.* London: Penguin

7   Gerwath, R. (2016), *The Vanquished: why the First World War failed to end 1917-1923.* London: Penguin Random House

8   Keynes, J. M. (2017), *The Economic Consequences of the Peace.* London: Freeland Press

9   Winston Churchill. Speech. Hansard Official Report, House of Commons, 8/7/1920; col. 1707.

10   Personal reflections by the author in September 2017 on Kazansky railway station en route to Ulyanovsk, Lenin's hometown. *Moskva-Kazanskaya* is one of nine railway terminals in Moscow.

11   Rosie Boycott, The Times, 29th March 2006

12   "People Are Dying Alone Because of Donald's Failure to Lead", Interview with Mary Trump. Der Spiegel International, 31st July 2020

13   'At Home in One's Past – Nostalgia as a Political and Cultural Force. Report Launch 5th June 2018' https://www.demos.co.uk/event/at-home-in-ones-past/

14   Crooke, A. (2009) *Resistance: The Essence of the Islamist Revolution.* London: Pluto Press

15   Axworthy, M. (2008) *Empire of the Mind: A History of Iran.* London: Hurst

16   www.bbc.co.uk/radio4/WorldTonight.   10th   June 2009

17   Ziauddin Sadar, London New Statesman, June 2008

18   Quoted in Dupont, C. (2013) *Mississippi Praying: Southern White Evangelicals and the Civil Rights Movement* ,1945-1975, p116

19   Marsh, C. (1997) *God's long summer.* Princeton, N.J: Princeton University Press

20   The Cross and Black Liberation'. Sunday Worship Radio 4 8th August 2020 www.bbc/radio4

21   Zimbardo, P. (2007) *The Lucifer Effect: How good people turn evil.* Rider

22   Ahmed Mushfiq Mobarak Yale University & Alejandra Ramos The Effects of Migration on Intimate Part-

ner Violence: Evidence for Exposure Reduction Theory in Bangladesh (2019) Trinity College Dublin

23   'Russian women' http://masterrussian.com/russian-culture/russian_women.htm accessed July 2018

24   Ruttenberg, N. (2008), *Dostoyevsky's Democracy*. Princeton University Press.

25   Figes, O. (1996), *A People's Tragedy: The Russian Revolution 1891-1924*. London: Pimlico p96

26   Reese, R. (2008) *The Soviet Military Experience*. London: Routledge.

27   Felshtinsky, Y. And Pribylovsky, V. (2008) *The Age of Assassins: The rise and rise of Vladimir Putin*. London: Gibson Square

28   Indigenous Peoples and Violence https://www.indian-affairs.org/indigenous-peoples-and-violence.html accessed January 2020

29   Indigenous Peoples and Violence https://www.indian-affairs.org/indigenous-peoples-and-violence.html accessed January 2020

30   Ending Violence Against Native Women Indian Law Resource Centre. https://indianlaw.org/issue/ending-violence-against-native-women accessed January 2020

31   Mental Health, Substance Abuse, and Domestic Violence in American Indian and Alaska Native Communities. Child Welfare Information Gateway. *https://www.childwelfare.gov/topics/systemwide/diverse-populations/american-indian/mentalhealth/* accessed January 2020

32   Editorial in the *Raleigh News and Observer,* 1930, cited at the opening of America's first memorial to lynching victims.

33   J. Alex Mull, Tales of Old Burke (Morganton: News Herald Press, 1975), 93-95 ref H. Clay Ferree, "The Day the Mob Took Over," Crime and Criminals Vertical File, Burke County Public Library, Morganton, NC, quoted in unpublished thesis THE WORLD OF BROADUS MILLER: HOMICIDE, LYNCHING, AND OUTLAWRY IN

EARLY TWENTIETH CENTURY NORTH AND SOUTH CAROLINA by KEVIN WAYNE YOUNG submitted to the University of Georgia 2016.

34   Claudia Gould (2009) *Jesus in America, and Other Stories from the Field* Logan, UT: Utah State University Press p50

35   Lefkowitz (1997*) Our Guys: The Glen Ridge Rape and the Secret Life of the Perfect Suburb (Men and Masculinity)* Berkeley, CA.: University of California Press

36   Drawn from a special report 'From our home correspondent' BBC Radio 4 www.bbc.co.uk/Radio4 16th February 2020

37   https://www.ilivehere.co.uk/northfield-birmingham-2.html 16 February 2020

38   https://www.ilivehere.co.uk/northfield-birmingham-2.html 16 February 2020

39   Abused children 'lack protection at home' Church Times 7th February 2020 https://www.churchtimes.co.uk/ar-

ticles/2020/7-february/news/uk/abused-children-lack-protection-at-home

40   Myrdal, A. (1977). The extreme right in Scandinavia. In T. Modood (Ed.), *Politics of multiculturalism in the new Europe* (chap. 7). London: Zed Books

41   London Independent. 10th June 2008

42   Layla Saad's '*Me and White Supremacy: How to Recognise Your Privilege, Combat Racism and Change the World*' (Quercus 2020)

43   Biko, S. (1986) *I Write What I Like*. San Francisco: Harper & Row

44   Keenan, B. (1992) *An Evil Cradling*. London ppxii-xiii

45   Volf. M. (1996) *Exclusion and Embrace*. Abingdon: Nashville. P54

46   Volf. M. (1996) *Exclusion and Embrace*. Abingdon: Nashville. P57

47   London Daily Mail, August 21[st]2007

48   Browne, K. D., & Herbert, M. (1997). *Preventing family violence*. Chichester: Wiley. p57

49   Frances Lawrence, Interview, Today Programme, BBC Radio 4 August 21[st]2007

50   Von Rad, G. (1972) *Genesis* London: SCM Press p105

51   Girard, R. (2001) *I See Satan Fall Like Lightning* Orbis Books

52   Cain and Abel: The First Fight (More Midrash) https://jayasherlevine.com/cain-and-abel-more-midrash/

53   Shakespeare, T. (2013) *Disability Rights and Wrongs Revisited.* London: Routledge

54   www.rethink.org March 2010

55   Martindale, B. (1998) On Dying; death and eternal life. *Psychoanalytic Psychotherapy.* 12:259-70

56   Written when he was 49! Freud, S. (1905) *On Psychotherapy.* Standard ed vol 7 London: Hogarth Press

57   Cain and Abel: According to Levinas March 26, 2009 by Rabbi Michael Leo Samuel https://www.rabbimichaelsamuel.com/tag/levinas-on-cain-and-abel /

58   "Where Is Abel Your Brother?" Levinas' Response to a Psychological Reading of the Story of Cain and Abel

Mezgebu Feleke and Johan De Tavernier https://core.ac.uk/display/34636816

59   Joachim Duyndam (2008) *Contagion Journal of Violence Mimesis and Culture* 15(1) · January 2008

60   Levinas, E. (1985). *Ethics and infinity: conversations with Philippe Nemo* (F. Cohen, Trans.). Pittsburgh: Duquesne University Press p98-100

61   Bauman, Z. (1993). *Postmodern ethics.* Oxford: Blackwell p79

62   De Zulueta, F. (1993). *From pain to violence - traumatic roots of destructiveness*. London: Whurr Publishers. p135

63   Wiesel, *Dialogues 1, "One Generation After"* from Roth, J.K. & Berenbaum, M. eds (1989), *Holocaust. Religious and Philosophical Implications*. NY, Paragon House pxiii

64   Fondana, B *Exodus*. Yad Vashem website accessed June 2020

65   Pastor Andrew Trocme, August 10[th]1942

66   Kaufmann, T. (2017) *Luther's Jews* Oxford: OUP

67   Brodiez-Dolino. A. (2013) *Emmaus and the Abbe Pierre: an alternative model of enterprise, charity and society*. Science Po: Les Presses.

68   *Sharing Catholic Social Teaching: Challenges and Directions* (No. 5-281) and other social teaching documents, 2005, United States Conference of Catholic Bishops. Washington, D.C.

69   Yeomans, R. (2013) *Visions of Annihilation: the Utasha Regime and the Cultural Politics of Fascism*. University of Pittsburgh Press.

70   Crimes in the Jasenovac Camp. Croatian State Commission for Establishing Crimes of Occupying Forces and their Assistants, Baja Luka, 2000.

71   Berryman, P. (1984) *The Religious Roots of Rebellion: Christians in the Central American Revolutions*. London: SCM Press

72   Yallop, D. (2007) *The Power and the Glory*. London: Constable. p368

73   Calderisi, R. (2013) *Earthly Mission: The Catholic Church and World Development*. Yale University Press

74   Bauman, Z. (1989). *Modernity and the holocaust*. Cambridge: Polity Press.

75   Dawidowicz, L. (1989) *Thinking about the Six Million: Facts, Figures, Perspectives. In Holocaust: Religious and Philosophical Implications*, Roth, J.K and Berenbaum, M (Eds), Paragon House, NY

76   Elly Hileswi's diary, Yad Vashem.

77   Berenbaum, M. (2001) The Impact of the Holocaust on Contemporary Ethics in Banki and Pawlikowski, J ibid Ch 10 page 241

78   Hoss, R. (1992). Death Dealers: The memoirs of the SS Kommandant of Auschwitz (S Paskulky, ED.) Buffalo, NY:Prometheus.

79   Ortmeyer, B. (1996) *Eyewitnesses Speak out against Denial: testimonials by 100 Surviving Jewish Students of their school days in Frankfurt/Main Germany during the Nazi era*. Bonn: Whele Verlag p80

80   Rogers, C. (1951) *Client-Centred Therapy: Its Current Practice, Implications & Theory*. Houghton Mifflin

81   Time Magazine- March 2nd2009

82   *1914-1918: The Great War*. Collapse- the end of the war. BBC TV documentary

83   www.bbc.co.uk/radio4 Today Programme 21st April 2010

84   Kant, I. (1991) *The Metaphysics of Morals.* Mary Gregor Cambridge p255

85   Hearings before Treasury Select Committee. By Paul Moore 10th Feb 2009 reported on Newsnight, BBC2.

86   Einarsen, S., Hoel, H. Zapf, D., & Cooper, C.L. *Bullying and Emotional Abuse in the Workplace.* p396

87   HowToHaveABullyFreeWorkplace.com   March 2009

88   Adorno, T. Et al. (2019) *The Authoritarian Personality.* London: Verso

89   Levi, P. *"If this is a Man"*

90   Biko, S. (1986) *I Write What I Like.* San Francisco: Harper & Row

91   Smith, M.M. (2006) *How Race is Made: Slavery, Segregation, and the Senses.* Chapel Hill, NC: University of North Carolina Press,

92   McIntosh, P. (1988) Working Paper 189. "White Privilege and Male Privilege: A Personal Account of Coming To See Correspondences through Work in Women's Studies" Wellesley College Centre for Research on Women, Wellesley: MA.

93   Quoted in an article in the UK Daily Mail, July 26[th]2008 about the Italian crackdown on Roma.

94   Ruvimbo Bungwe, from *Credit to the Nation,* The Refugee Council 2002, quoted in the Times Educational Supplement 20/9/2002

95   Stephenson, P. (2002) *Billy,* London: Harper Collins p44

96   The author vividly recalls talking with an elderly Jewish lady who was amongst the last refugees to come over on the last Kinder transport train out of Germany before the border closed at the end of August 1939. Frieda had witnessed Kristallnacht and seen a Rabbi burnt to death with his synagogue, holding the Torah above his head as he did so. She never forgot the dreadful night. She escaped though her grandmother later perished in Auschwitz.

97   Guardian Newspaper UK, 18th November 2008

98   Gilligan, J. (2001). *Preventing violence.* London: Thames and Hudson.Ch 2. See also Blau, P.M. (1964). *Exchange and power in social life.* New York: Wiley.

99   May, R. (1976). *Power and innocence: a search for the sources of violence.* London: Fontana.p44

100   Smith, J. (2019) *Home Grown: how domestic violence turns men into terrorists.* London: River run press

101   Pawlikowski, J (2001) *The Holocaust: Its Challenges for Understanding Human Responsibility,* in Banki, J & Pawlikowski, J. ibid Ch 11 p264

102   https://www.washingtonpost.com/nation/2020/05/28/minneapolis-protests-george-floyd-death/ 28th May 2020

103   https://english.alaraby.co.uk/english/in-depth/2020/1/28/how-many-people-have-died-in-syria-since-2011

104   Church Times 17th January 2020

105   https://www.pbs.org/auschwitz/40-45/liberation/ accessed January 2020

106   Ilibigazia, I. (2006) *Left to Tell: One woman's story of surviving the Rwandan holocaust*. London: Hay House p79

107   Fest, J. (2002) *Hitler*. London, Penguin. p212

108   *Slavery*, Engerman et al ibid page 6

109   Vaughan, A.T (1995) "The Origins Debate: Slavery and Racism in Seventeenth Century Virginia" from *Roots of American Racism: Essays on the Colonial Experience*. New York. Oxford University Press p171

110   Berenbaum, M. (2001) *The Impact of the Holocaust on Contemporary Ethics in Ethics in the Shadow of the Holocaust: Christian and Jewish Perspectives* Eds Banki, J. & Pawlikowski, J. Chicago, Sheed and Ward Ch 10 page 24

111   Hemming, J. (2008) *Tree of Rivers: The story of the Amazon*. London: Thames and Hudson

112   Taussig, M. (2004) *Culture of Terror, Space of Death*. From Scheper-Hughes, N. & Bourgois, P. eds. *Violence in War and Peace. Malden, MA*. Blackwell Publishing p46

113   Amery, J (1989) *Torture*, from In Holocaust: Reli-

gious and Philosophical Implications, Roth, J.K and Beren-baum, M (Eds), Paragon House, NY ibid page 171

114   https://www.thenational.ae/opinion/comment/has-the-world-learnt-anything-from-the-horrors-of-srebrenica-25-years-on 10th July 2020 Has the world learnt anything from the horrors of Srebrenica 25 years on? Janine di Giovanni

115   Stern, J. (2020) *My War Criminal: Personal Encounters with an Architect of Genocide*, New York: Ecco

116   Cowley, C. (2013) *Moral Responsibility*, London: Routledge

117   https://www.thenational.ae/opinion/comment/has-the-world-learnt-anything-from-the-horrors-of-srebrenica-25-years-on 10th July 2020 Has the world learnt anything from the horrors of Srebrenica 25 years on? Janine di Giovanni

118   RJ Wallace (1998) *Responsibility and the Moral Sentiments*, Cambridge, M.A.: Harvard University Press

119   Williams, B. (2002) Shame and Necessity Berkeley, C.A.: University of California Press

120   *SERBIAN ORTHODOX; Church of Milosevic's Rise Now Sends Mixed Message,* by Blaine Harden With Carlotta Gall July 4, 1999, New York Times

121   Mirko Djordjevic (2001) *The Crusade of Serbian Church*, Belgrade 2001.

122   Fanon, F. (1963) *The Wretched of the Earth*. Tr Constance Farrinton. New York: Weidenfeld p42-3

123   Cunningham. P. (2009) *Tiannanmen Moon: Inside the Chinese Student Uprising of 1989.* London: Rowman and Littlefield.

124   As reported on BBC 2 Newsnight. 3rd June 2009

125   Time Magazine. April 27th2009.

126   Amnesty Magazine. Issue 151 September/October 2008, www.amnesty.org.uk

127   Guidi, C. & Chuntao, W. (2006) *Will the boat sink the Water? The Life of China's peasants.* Tr Zhu Hong. Public Affairs press

128   Shao Chuan Leng & Palmer, N.D. (1961) *Sun Yat –Sen and Communism.* London. p157

129   Mankell, H. (2009) *The Man from Beijing.* New York: Knopf

130   Hutton, W. (2006) *China and the West in the twenty-first century.* London: Abacus

131   Zhisiui, Li, (1994) *The Private Life of Chairman Mao: the Memoir of Mao's Personal Physician.* Tr Tai Hung-Chao, London p122

132   Byron, J. & Pack, R. (1992) *The Claws of the Dragon.* See also Becker, J. (1996) *Hungry Ghosts: China's Secret Famine.* London p33

133   Zhenua, Zhai. (1992) *Red Flower of China: An Autobiography.* New York. p95

134   Chang,J. (1991) *Wild Swans: Three Daughters of*

China. London pp436-8

135   Chang,J. (1991) *Wild Swans: Three Daughters of China*. London p658-9

136   Hutchinson, J. (1996) *Champions of Charity: War and the Rise of the Red Cross*. Boulder & Oxford: Westview

137   www.bbc.co.uk/radio4pm 15th February 2010

138   The Economist May 16th2009

139   Solzhenitsyn, A (1974), *The Gulag Archipelago*, London, Collins & Harvill Press, p93

140   Bailie, G. (1995) *Violence Unveiled- Humanity at the Crossroads*. New York, Crossroads Publishing Co

141   Scheper-Hughes, N. & Bourgois, P. eds (2004) *Violence in war and peace*. Blackwell Publishing. Malden. MA p1-2.

142   Merchant of Venice Act 3 scene 1

143   Bailey, R. (1977). *Violence and aggression*. New York: Time-Life Books. p31

144   Changon, N. (1968). *Yanamamo: the fierce people*. New York: Holt, Rinehart & Winston.

145   Darwin, C. (1872). *Expression of the Emotions in Man and Animals*. London: Murray.

146   Lorenz, K. (1966). *On Aggression*. London: Methuen

147   Freud, S. (1927). *Beyond the Pleasure Principle.* Chicago: Chicago Press.

148   Storr, A. (1992) *Human Aggression.* Harmondsworth: Penguin Books p37 and p126

149   Collins, R. (2008) *Violence: A micro-sociological theory.* Princeton: Princeton University Press

150   Peters, M., McMahon, R., & Quinsey, P. (Eds.). (1992). Aggression & violence throughout the life span. In *21st Banff International Conference on Behavioural Science.* London: Sage. p 10

151   Wilson, E. (1975). *Socio-biology: the new synthesis.* Cambridge, MA: Harvard University Press

152   Prior, M. (1989). The Australian Temperament Project. In F. Kohnstamm (Ed.), *Temperament in childhood* (pp. 537-558). Chichester UK: Wiley. Prior, M. (1990). Resilience and coping - the role of individual temperament. In E. Frydenberg (Ed.), *Learning to cope - developing as a person in complex societies* (chap.3). Oxford: Open University Press. Reiss, A.J., & Roth, J.A. (Eds.) (1993). *The development of an individual potential for violence in understanding & preventing violence.* Washington, DC: National Academy Press p357. Goldsmith, H. (1987). Roundtable: what is temperament - four approaches. *Child Development,* (58) pp. 505-529

153   Mednick, S.A., & Christiansen, K.O. (Eds.) (1977). *A preliminary study of criminality amongst twins.* New York: Gardner Press. Prentky, R. (1985). Neurochemistry and neuroendocrinology of sexual aggression. In D.P. Farrington & J. Gunn (Eds.), *Aggression and dangerousness*

(chap. 1). New York: John Wiley & Sons p8. Cardoret, R. Et al (1995) Genetic-Environmental Interaction in the Genesis of Aggressivity and Conduct Disorders. *Archives of General Psychiatry* 52 pp916-24. Loeber, R., & Stouthamer-Loeber, M. (1986). Family factors as correlates and predictors of juvenile conduct problems and delinquency. In N. Morris & M. Tonry, (Eds.), *Crime and justice: an annual review of research: Vol. 7* (pp. 29-149). Chicago: Chicago Press. Zahn-Waxler, C. (1994). Altruism, aggression and social interactions in young children with manic depressive parents, *Child Development*, (55), pp112-122. Bowlby, J. (1975). *Separation, anxiety and anger*. Harmondsworth: Pelican. p2 Bowlby, J (1999). Forty-four juvenile thieves. London: Routledge. Rutter, M. (1985). Family & school influences on behavioural development. In P. Barnes (Ed.), *Personal, social & emotional development of children* (chap. 1). Milton Keynes: Open University. Belsky, J. (1988). The "effects" of day care reconsidered. *Early Child Research Quarterly*, 3, 235-272.

154   Brownmiller, S. (1975). *Against our will: men, women & rape*. Harmondsworth: Penguin p15. Archer, J. (1994). *Male violence*. London: Routledge p5 Davis, M. (1993). *Women and violence: a global crisis*. London: Zed Books. Enloe, C. (2000). *Bananas, beaches and bases*. Berkeley: University of California Press p195 Farrington, D. (1994). The causes and prevention of offending, with special reference to violence. In J. Shepherd (Ed.), *Coping with violence: a practical handbook for health-care workers* (chap. 5). Oxford: Oxford University Press. p180. Giddens, A. (1993). *Sociology* (2nd ed.). Cambridge: Polity Press. Hanmer, J., & Saunders, S. (1993). *Women, violence and crime prevention: a West Yorkshire study*. Aldershot: Avebury Press. p3. Kelly, L. (1988). *Surviving sexual vio-*

lence. Cambridge: Polity Press. p27 Stanton, A. & Gage, E. (1889). *History of women's suffrage*. Rochester, NY: Mann. p79. Wiltsher, A. (1985). *Most dangerous women; feminine peace campaigners of the great war.* London: Pandora. p99

155   Audit Commission *Misspent Youth:* 1996 Bandura, A. (1973). *A social learning analysis.* Englewood Cliffs, NJ: Prentice-Hall. Bandura, A. (1977). *Social learning theory.* Englewood Cliffs, NJ: Prentice-Hall. Reiss & Ross Eds, 1993 p357 Coie, J.D., & Underwood, M. (1991). Programmatic interventions with aggressive children in the school setting.   In D.J. Pepler & K.H. Rubin (Eds.), *The development and treatment of childhood aggression* (chap. 5). Hillsdale, NJ: Lawrence Erlbaum Associates. p389-410. Dinitz, S. (1982). *Careers of the violent: dangerous offender project in Columbus, Ohio.* Lexington, MA: Lexington Books. p216-219Office for Standards in Education. (2002). *Sex and relationships education.* London: Her Majesty's Stationery Office. Sutherland, E. (1949). *Principles of criminology.* Chicago: Lippincott.

156   Bonger, E. (1916). *Criminality and economic conditions.* London: Heinemann. p402-5 Australian National Committee on Violence, 1990 p96). Farrington, D. (1994). The causes and prevention of offending, with special reference to violence. In J. Shepherd (Ed.), *Coping with violence: a practical handbook for health-care workers* (chap. 5). Oxford: Oxford University Press. Ch9 James, O. (1995). *Juvenile violence in a winner - loser culture.* London: Free Association Books. Murray, C. (1990). *The emerging British underclass.* London: Institute of Economic Affairs. Bettelheim, 1952) Glueck, S., & Glueck, E. (1950). *Unravelling juvenile delinquency.* Cambridge, MA: Harvard University Press. Minuchin, D. (1966). *Families of the slums.* New

York: Basic Books. Farrington, D.P. (1987). Early precursors of frequent offenders. In J.Q. Wilson & G.C. Loury (Eds.), *From children to citizens*: Vol. 3. *Families, schools and delinquency prevention* (chap. 3). New York: Springer. p27-51 Edgar, D. (Ed.). (1989). *Child poverty*. Sydney: Allen and Unwin. Child Poverty p56 Utting, D. (Ed.). (1993). *Crime and the family: improving child-rearing and preventing delinquency*. London: Family Policy Studies Centre p19

157   Anthias. F. and Yuval-Davis, N. (1992) *Racialised Boundaries: Race, Nation, Gender, Colour and Class and the Anti-racist struggle*. London: Routledge. Jenkins, R. (1996). *Social identity*. London: Routledge. Harre. R. (1986). *The Social Construction of Emotions*. Oxford: Blackwell. Madden, F., & Lion, H. (Eds.). (1976). *Rage, hate, assault and other forms of violence*. New York: SP Books. p146). Merton, R. (1957). *Social theory and social structure* (rev. ed.). Glencoe: Free Press. Modood, T. (1997) 'Culture and Identity'. In Modood, T. et al (eds) *Ethnic Minorities in Britain*. London: Policy Studies Institute p295-6. Oppenheimer, F. (1914). *The state*. Indianapolis: Gitterman. Parsons, T. (1954). *Revised analytic approach to social stratification - essays in sociological theory*. Glencoe, ILL: Free Press. Rex, J. (1983). *Race relations in sociological theory* (2nd ed.). London: Routledge. Rutherford, J. (1990). *Identity: community, culture, difference*. London: Lawrence & Wishart.

158   American Psychological Association Commission. (1993). *Violence and youth: psychology's response: Vol. 1. Summary Report*. Washington DC: Author. Australian National Committee on Violence. (1990). *Violence- directions for Australia*. Canberra: Australian Institute of Criminology. p86). Clinard, M. (1978). *Cities with little crime: the case*

of Switzerland. Cambridge: Cambridge University Press. Fagan, J. (1990). Intoxication and Aggression. In M. Tonry & J. Wilson (Eds.). *Drugs and crime* (chap. 10). Chicago: University of Chicago Press. The UK Home Office. (2005, April 20). Statistics in violent crime 2004

159   Buckingham, D. (1993). *Children talking television*. Lewis: Falmer Press. Gulbenkian Foundation Commission Report. (1995). *Children and violence*. London: Calouste Gulbenkian. p72 Blackburn, R. (1993). *The psychology of criminal conduct: theory, research and practice*. Chichester: Wiley. Hampton, J. (Ed.). (1996). *Preventing violence in America*. Thousand Oaks, CA: Sage. Bugental, D. (1985)

160   Billington, J.H. (1980). *Fire in the minds of men*. London: Maurice Temple Smith. Giddens, A. (1993). *Sociology* (2nd ed.). Cambridge: Polity Press p357. Kaldor, M. (1999). *New and old wars*. Cambridge: Polity Press. Lyon, D. (2000). *Jesus in Disneyland*. Oxford: Blackwells p105. Marshall, S.L.A. (1947). *Men against fire*. New York: Marrow. Richer, D. (Ed.). (1972). *The challenge of violence*. Tadworth: Ardua Press. p36

161   Clarke, R & Cornish, D (2001) *Rational Choice*, in Paternoster, R & Bachman, R, *Explaining Criminals and Crime*, Los Angeles, Roxbury

162   Vold, G et al (2002), *Theoretical Criminology*, New York and Oxford, Oxford University Press p205

163   Meltzer, B (1967), *Mead Social Psychology*, in Manis, J & Meltzer, B eds, *Symbolic Interaction*, Boston, Allyn and Bacon, p9-13

164   Foucault, M (1979) *Discipline and Punish*, New

York, Vintage

165   Adler, P et al eds (1998), Ethnography at the Edge: Crime, Deviance, and Field Research,

166   Katz, J (1988), *Seductions of Crime: Moral and Sensual Attractions in Doing Evil*, New York, Basic

167   Ferrell, J (1997) *Criminological Verstehen: Inside the Immediacy of Crime*

168   Newspaper accounts of the time on May 9th2008

169   Tittle, C (1995) *Control Balance: Towards a General Theory of Deviance*, Boulder

170   Palmer, S. (2006) *Toxic childhood*. London: Orion Books

171   Cooley, G. (1962). *Social organisation*. New York: Schocken Press. Pulkinnen, L. (1982). Self-control and continuity from childhood to late adolescence. In P.B. Baltes & O.G. Brim (Eds.), *Life-span development and behaviour: Vol 4*. (chap. 7). New York: New York Academic Press.

172   Girard, R. (2001). *I saw Satan fall like lightning*. Maryknoll, NY: Orbis Books. p11

173   Huesmann, L, R., & Eron, L.D. (1986). *Television and the aggressive child: a cross-national comparison*. Hillsdale, NJ: Lawrence Erlbaum.

174   Bandura, A. (1973). *A social learning analysis*. Englewood Cliffs, NJ: Prentice-Hall.

175   De Zulueta, F. (1993). *From pain to violence - trau-*

matic roots of destructiveness. London: Whurr Publishers. p135

176   Chambers 20th *Century Dictionary,* 1977

177   Lawrence, B.B. & Karim, A. Eds. (2008) *On Violence: A Reader.* Duke University Press

178   www.bbc.co.uk/radio4 Today March 15th 2010

179   Das, V., & Kleinman, A. (Eds.). (2000). *Violence and subjectivity.* Berkeley: University of California Press.

180   Eshelby, K. (2008) 'If a woman says no, we use force'. *Church Times,* 15th August 2008

181   Bourke, J. (2007) *Rape: A history from 1860 to the present.* London: Virago.

182   Amery, J (1989) *Torture,* from In Holocaust: Religious and Philosophical Implications, Roth, J.K and Berenbaum, M (Eds), Paragon House, NY ibid page 171

183   May, R. (1976). *Power and innocence: a search for the sources of violence.* London: Fontana.p44

184   Author's client notes- name withheld and used with permission

185   As reported in the London Daily Mail, August 25th2007

186   Gilligan, J. (2001). *Preventing violence.* London: Thames and Hudson.Ch 2. See also Blau, P.M. (1964). *Exchange and power in social life.* New York: Wiley.

187   Glaude, E. (2017) *Democracy in Black: How Race Still Enslaves the American Soul.* Broadway

188   Glaude, E. (2020) *Begin Again: James Baldwin's America and Its Urgent Lessons for Our Own.* New York: Crown Publishing Group

189   Baldwin, J. (2001) Another Country New York: Penguin Classic

190   Sana al-Khayyat (1990) *Honour and Shame: Women in Modern Iraq.* London: Saqi Books p35

191   Pit-Rivers, J. (1977) *The Fate of Shechem or the Politics of Sex: Essays in the Anthropology of the Mediterranean.* Cambridge: Cambridge University Press p1

192   David A. de Silva: *Honour, Patronage, Kinship and Purity: Unlocking New Testament Culture*, Downers Grove, Ill.: Inter-Varsity Press p.25

193   Danker, F.W. (1982) *Benefactor: Epigraphic Study of a Graeco-Roman and New Testament Semantic Field.* St. Louis: Clayton

194   Lanaik, T. (1998) *Shame and Honour in Esther.* SBLDS 165 Atlanta, G.A.: Scholars pp7-17

195   Malina, Bruce J., and Jerome H. Neyrey (1991) "Honor and Shame in Luke Acts: Pivotal Values of the Mediterranean World." *In The Social World of Luke–Acts.* Ed. J. H. Neyrey. Pages 25–65. Peabody, Mass.: Hendrickson. See also Green, J. (1995) *The Theology of the Gospel of Luke*, Cambridge: CUP, pp76-101

196   Neyrey, J.H. (1998) *Honour and Shame in Matthew.*

Loiusville, KY.: Westminster John Knox Press pp164-211

197   DeSilva, D.A. (2000) *Honour, Patronage, Kinship and Purity*. Downers Grove, Ill.

198   Price, S. R. F. (1984) *Rituals and Power: The Roman Imperial Cult in Asia Minor*. Cambridge: Cambridge University Press.

199   Brunt, P. A. (1990) *Roman Imperial Themes*. Oxford: Clarendon

200   Georges, J. (2010) 'From shame to honour': a Theological Reading of Romans for Honour-Shame contexts, in *Missiology: An International Review*. 38:3, pp.295-307

201   "Honour" in International Encyclopedia of the Social Science vol 6 David L. Sills Editor McMillan 1968 pp. 503-510

202   Bowman, J. (2006) *Honour; a History*. New York: Encounter Books

203   Bowman, J. (2006) *Honour; a History*. New York: Encounter Books

204   Steed, C. D. (2018) *We count, we matter: voice, choice and the death of distance*. London: Routledge

205   Ferguson, M. ed (1993) *The History of Mary Prince, a West Indian Slave, Related by Herself*. Ann Arbor: University of Michigan Press, 1993 p60-3

206   Miller, A. (2000) *Death of a Salesman*. Harmondsworth: Penguin Plays

207   Olivier, T. (1980). "Shakespeare and Montaigne: A Tendency of Thought". *Theoria*. 54: 43–59.

208   Quoted in Jane Kramer 'ME, MYSELF, AND I: *What made Michel de Montaigne the first modern man'* The New Yorker 31st August 2009 https://www.newyorker.com/magazine/2009/09/07/me-myself-and-i

209   Wain. B. (2010) *Malaysian Maverick: Mahathir Mohamad in turbulent times*. Basingstoke: Palgrave Macmillan

210   *1914-1918: The Great War*. Collapse- the end of the war. BBC TV documentary

211   Moore, J. (1995) Person- Central Psychotherapy. From Walker, M. (ed) *Peta: a Feminist's Problem with Men*. Buckingham: Open University p15

212   James, W. (1890) *The Principles of Psychology*. Boston

213   Glaude, E. (2016) *Democracy in Black: how race still enslaves the American soul*. New York: Crown 2016).

214   Nietzsche, F. (1956) *The Genealogy of Morals*. Garden City: Doubleday P236

215   Nietzsche, F. (1969) *Thus Spoke Zarathustra*. P204 and 269

216   www.guardian.co.uk 14th January 2010. Reporting a speech by the then Labour Communities Secretary John Denham

217   Hodge, C. (1872) *Systematic Theology*. Vol 11 Ed-

inburgh: Nelson p97

218   Luther Sermons on Genesis

219   Calvin Institutes Bk 1 Ch XV p3

220   Hodge, C. (1872) *Systematic Theology*, Vol 11 Edinburgh: Nelson p97

221   Grudem, W. (1994) Systematic Theology Nottingham: IVP p577

222   Swinburne, R. (2009) 'The Christian Scheme of Salvation' in Rea, M (ed) *Oxford Readings in Philosophical Theology*. Oxford: OUP p295

223   Volf. M. (1996), *Exclusion and Embrace*. Abingdon: Nashville. P30

224   Luther Works WA10/12.297.5

225   Den Heyer, C.J. (1998), *Jesus and the Doctrine of the Atonement*. SCM Press p115

226   Wright, N.T. (2004) 'Redemption from a New Perspective? Towards a Multi-layered Pauline Theology of the Cross.' In Davis, S.T., Kendall, D. And O'Collins, G. (Eds) *Redemption*. Oxford: OUP p69-100

227   Rubinstein, R. quoted in Rosemary Radford Ruether (1999) *The Twentieth Century: A Theological Overview*. G Baum (ed). Maryknoll, NY: Orbis Books p77

228   Wright, T. (2003) *Paul for everyone: 2 Corinthians*. London: SPCK p66

229   "Life without work" – BBC2 29th October 2010

230   Martin, F. (2013) *Money: The Unauthorised Biography*. London: Bodley Head

231   www.bbc.co.uk/radio4worldatone   22nd   August 2013

232   Morris, L. (1955) *The Apostolic Preaching of the Cross*, Grand Rapids: Eerdmans p162/167

233   Eichrodt, W. (1967) *Theology of the Old Testament*, vol 2 p444 London: SCM Press

234   Numbers 15v28-31

235   Girard, R. (1977) *Violence and the Sacred*. Baltimore: John Hopkins University Press. P26

236   Milbank, J. (2003) *Ontology and Pardon*. London: Routledge ch 3

237   Bossy, J. (1985) *Christianity in the West 1400-1700*. Oxford: OUP

238   Milbank, J. (1995) 'Can a Gift be Given? Prolegomena to a Future Trinitarian Metaphysics', *Modern Theology* 2, no 1 (January 1995): 119-61

239   Milbank, J. (2003) *Ontology and Pardon*. London: Routledge ch 3

240   Calvin's Institutes. Book 11. Ch xvii

241   Brown, C. Ed (1986) *Dictionary of New Testament Theology*. Vol 3 Grand Rapids Mi.: Zondervan p166

242   Ridderbos, H. (1977) *Paul: An outline of his theology*. London: SPCK p168

243   Dunn, J.D.G. (1998) *The Theology of Paul the Apostle*. Grand Rapids, MI: Eerdmans p222

244   Furnish, V. P. (1985) *II Corinthians. Anchor Bible*. NY: Doubleday p340

245   Sanders, E.P. (1977) *Paul and Palestinian Judaism*. London: SCM Press p497

246   Schweitzer, A. (1956) *Paul and his interpreters*. London: W Montgomery

247   Murphy-O' Connor, J. (1991) *The Theology of the Second Letter to the Corinthians*. Cambridge: CUP p62

248   Wright, T. (2003) *Paul for everyone: 2 Corinthians*. London: SPCK p66

249   Aletti, J.N. (2004) 'God made Christ to be sin: reflections on a Pauline paradox.' In Davis, S.T., Kendall, D. And O'Collins, G. (Eds) *Redemption*. Oxford: OUP p101-120

250   Tittle, C (1995) *Control Balance: Towards a General Theory of Deviance,* Boulder

251   https://www.justice.gov.uk/downloads/legislation/bills-acts/legal-aid-sentencing/ipp-factsheet.pdf

252   BBC News 20th August 2020

253   Are Whole-life Prison Tariffs against Human Rights? 02/03/2014   https://www.legalsecretaryjournal.com/whole-

life-prison-tariffs

254   http://www.independent.co.uk 5th August 2013

255   http://www.heraldscotland.com accessed 5th August 2013

256   Bredemeier, H. (1978) 'Exchange Theory' in T. Bottomore & Nisbet, R. *A History of Sociological Analysis.* London: Heinemann ch11

257   Simmel, G. (1971) *On Individuality and Social Forms.* Ed D. N. Levine. Chicago: University of Chicago Press p44

258   Torrance, J.B. (1981) 'The vicarious humanity of Christ' in T.F. Torrance (ed) *The Incarnation: Ecumenical Studies in the Nicene-Constantinopolitan Creed A.D. 381.* Edinburgh: Handsel Press p169

259   Skiddelsky, R. (2003) *John Maynard Keynes: 1883-1946. Economist, Philosopher, Statesman.* London: Pan Books p550

260   Swinburne, R. (2009) 'The Christian Scheme of Salvation' in Rea, M (ed) *Oxford Readings in Philosophical Theology.* Oxford: OUP p295

261   Anselm argued this in Cur Deus Homo 1.19

262   Neblett, W. (1974) 'The Ethics of Guilt', *Journal of Philosophy* 71: pp652-63

263   Aristotle. Nichomachean Ethics.

264   Patinkon, D. (1965) *Money, Interest and Prices; An*

Integration of Monetary and Value Theory. 2nd ed.

265   Mill, J. S. (1909) *Principles of Political Economy.* W.J. Ashley ed. p488

266   Buber, M. (1937) *I and Thou.* Trans Walter Kaufman. New York: Simon & Schuster

267   Jarrety, M. (2008) *Paul Valery.* Paris: Fayard

268   Farmello, G. (2009) *The Strangest Man.* London: Faber

269   Etzioni, A. (1990) *Towards a New Economics.* New York: The Free Press. p83.

270   Winnicott, D. (1971) *Playing and Reality.* London: Tavistock

271   For example, the unanimous reactions of the panel on Question Time, BBC 1, March 26th2009.

272   Watts, S. (2009) *Mr Playboy: Hugh Hefner and the American Dream.* London: Wiley

273   Walster, E., Walster, G.W, & Berscheid, E. (1978) *Equity: Theory and Research.* Rockleigh, N.J.: Allyn & Bacon

274   Becker, G. (1981) *A Treatise on the Family.* Cambridge: Harvard University Press.

275   Borg, M. (1994) *Jesus in Contemporary Scholarship.* Valley Forge: PA

276   McLaren, W. (1912) *Our Growing Creed: The*

Evangelical Faith as Developed and re-affirmed by current thought. Edinburgh: T. & T. Clark p156

277   Ward, K. (1970) *Ethics and Christianity.* London: George Allen & Unwin p240

278   Niebuhr, R. (1979) *'On Myth and its place in the Christian Religion'.* In Tinsley, E.J. (ed) Modern Theology. London: Epworth Press p259

279   www.bbcradio4/ archives April 2007

280   Church Times 9th August 2013

281   Church Times, Features 24th September 2010

282   Or 45.2 from The Work of Christ. Select writings from Gregory Nazianzus, in H. Bettenson (1970) ed. Later Christian Fathers. Oxford: OUP p112

283   Or cat. 21-24 from The Work of Christ. Select writings from Gregory of Nyssa in H. Bettenson (1970) ed. Later Christian Fathers. Oxford: OUP p142

284   Gustav Aulén (transl. by A. G. Herber SSM) *Christus Victor: An Historical Study of the Three Main Types of the Idea of Atonement* (London: SPCK, 1931; New York: Macmillan, 1969)

285   Borg. M (2003) *The Heart of Christianity. Rediscovering a Life of Faith* San Francisco: Harper. p. 95

286   Ignatius. Letter to Barnabas 5.1f., quoting Isaiah 53; *Barnabas* 7 (on the scapegoat) 8 (on the sacrificial heifer).

287   Ovey, M. Jeffrey, S. and Sach. A (2007) *Pierced for Our Transgressions: Rediscovering the Glory of Penal Substitution* (IVP, 2007)

288   MacDonald, H.D. (1992) 'Models of the atonement in Reformed Theology' in Donald K. McKim (ed), *Major Themes in the Reformed Tradition*. Grand Rapids: Eerdmans pp117-31.

289   Calvin's Institutes. Book 11. Ch xvii

290   Summa Theologica 111, q 46, a, 1. See also Summa contra Gentiles 1V, ch 55.

291   Stump, E. (2009) 'Atonement according to Aquinas' in Rea, M (ed) *Oxford Readings in Philosophical Theology*. Oxford: OUP p275

292   Chalke, S. (2003) *The Lost Message of Jesus*, Zondervan p182

293   Hodge, R. & Kress, G. (1988) *Social Semiotics*. Cambridge: Polity Press

294   Denny Weaver, J (2007). *The Nonviolent Atonement: Human Violence, Discipleship and God*. Grand Rapids: Eerdmans

295   For example, someone very concerned about the environment might adhere to that cause as a 'lobby' and then interpret any actions or events, such as 'fracking' in the light of that grid.

296   Summa Theologica 3 q 46 a 1-4.

297   Quinn, P. (1989) 'Aquinas on Atonement' in R.

Feenstra and C. Plantinga (eds)*Trinity, Incarnation and Atonement*. University of Notra Dame Press pp171-2

298   Summa Theologica 111, q8, a.5-8

299   The National Unity and Reconciliation Act, Act no 34 1995. Republic of South Africa, Government Gazette, vol 361, Cape Town July 26[th]1995

300   Minow, M. (1998) *Between Vengeance and Forgiveness: Facing History after Genocide and Mass Violence.* Boston: Beacon Press. p60

301   Rosenberg, T. (1995) *The Haunted Land: Facing Europe's Ghosts after Communism.* New York: Vintage p350

302   Arendt, H. (1963) *Eichmann in Jerusalem: A Report on the Banality of Evil.* New York: Penguin Books

303   Arendt, H. (1992) *Hannah Arendt- Karl Jaspers Correspondence, 1926-1969.* Arendt to Karl Jaspers, 17th August 1946, ed. L. Kohler, & H. Saner New York: Harcourt Brace p51

304   Steiner, H. J. & Alston, P. eds. (1996) International Human Rights in Context; Law, Politics, Morals. Oxford: Clarendon Press

305   www.bbc.co.uk/radio4 a family member commenting on the evidence by Tony Blair, 29th January 2010

306   www.bbc.co.uk/radio4 Today Programme, April 9th2010

307   Goolpacy, P. (2005) www.Perfectpoliticalapology.com

308   Herman, J. (1992) *Trauma and Recovery*. New York: Basic Books p92

309   Herman, J. (1992) *Trauma and Recovery*. New York: Basic Books p93 & 157

310   Slansky, P. *My Bad: 25 Years of Public Apologies and the Appalling Behaviour That Inspired Them*

311   *Torpey, J. (2006) Making whole that which has been smashed: On reparation politics.* Harvard University Press

312   De Grieff, P. ed. (2006) *The Handbook of Reparation Politics*. Oxford University Press

313   The Economist June 14th2008

314   Nicolaus Mills, an American commentator. The Economist October 4th2008

315   www.bbc.co.uk/radio4. PM 22nd April 2010

316   Taylor, C (1992) *Multiculturalism and the Politics of Recognition*. Princeton, Princeton University Press p34

317   Brass, P. (1997). *Theft of an idol: text and context in the representation of collective violence.* New Jersey: Princeton University Press

318   Griswold, C. (2007) *Forgiveness: A philosophical explanation*. Cambridge: Cambridge University Press

319   Source unknown

320   For instance, Journal of Family Therapy vol 20 no 1, Journal of Psychology and Christianity vol 10 no 2 and vol 11

no 2, Journal of Moral Education vol 21

321   Enright, R. (2001) *Forgiveness Is a Choice: A Step-By-Step Process for Resolving Anger and Restoring Hope.* American Psychological Association Lifetools

322   www.forgiveness-institute.org 2002. See also Enright, R. And North, J. eds (1998) *Exploring Forgiveness.*

323   Author's client notes- name withheld and used with permission.

324   Source unknown

325   Tombs, D. & Liechty, J. (2008) *Explorations in Reconciliation: New Directions in theology.* Ashgate

326   Martin Luther King, Strength to Love.

Index

9   Foreword

12   Rationale

14   Development

20   Setting the scene - On the day the soldiers came

    20   2

    24   The mountain spoke

    25   4

31   Chapter One
2020 Vision

    35   Excursion – the way we were

    35   Relativity rules

    38   Drawing a new map

    38   The Evil twin

    40   Wilson's travails

    40   Infamy in Amritsar

    41   Doctor Democracy

    43   Faces of Cain

    44   Stop the traffic!

    45   War on women

    48   On Kazansky railway station[10]

51   Chapter Two
Understanding the transmission

    52   The key of identity

57   Christian history has a problem too

61   Russia

63   North America

65   It's the system

66   Boys will be boys

68   Not so tall stories from the front-line

72   Chapter Three
Understanding the separateness

73   War on the skin

76   2

78   3

82   3

84   4

87   **Chapter Four**
The longest hatred and the descent into darkness
"Who are you?
A number.
Your name?
Gone. Blown away. Into the sky. Look up there.
The sky is black, black with names"

94   2

97   3

100   Level 1 - Denigration (a kinder world)

103   Level 2 - De-personalisation

106   Level 3 – Desecration

109   Level 4 - De-humanisation

111   Level 5 – Demonisation

113   Why the slide?

117   Chapter Five
**Between rhetoric and reality: denial and human
responsibility**
118   The roots of refusal
121   History is complicated
125   The sanctity of life? – who actually
believes it...

129   Chapter Six
The many faces of Cain: A question of definition

140   Chapter Seven
A question of desecration– violence as violation
142   "This is not all of me!"
145   Violence as a bid for significance
148   Racial violence as disvalue
150   Honour culture
154   Beyond honour culture
156   Part Two – through a different lens

157   Chapter Eight
The Jester at the Farce: valuable personhood
159   The first step: to sin is to devalue
168   Theological excursion - in the divine mirror
171   Dishonouring God

176   Chapter Nine
Solidarity: Jesus as victim of violence
177   1
178   2

180   3

187   4

192   5

195   Chapter Ten

Trading places: an exchange of status

199   Sacrifice and exchange

202   Symbolic exchange

207   Theological excursion – katallasso

(2 Corinthians 5v21)

215   Chapter Eleven

Recompense for perpetrators

216   Payment is needed

225   2

228   3 Excursion – a sweep from history

230   4

243   4

248   Chapter Twelve

The power of forgiveness

255   Forgiveness and the fight against forgetting

259   Serial apology

262   The weakness of God

264   3

269   Bibliography